PUBLIC OPINION IN POSTCOMMUNIST RUSSIA

Public Opinion in Postcommunist Russia

Matthew Wyman
Lecturer in Politics
Keele University

First published in Great Britain 1997 by
MACMILLAN PRESS LTD
Houndmills, Basingstoke, Hampshire RG21 6XS and London
Companies and representatives throughout the world

A catalogue record for this book is available from the British Library.

ISBN-13: 978-0-333-64419-5 (hardcover)
ISBN-13: 978-0-333-64420-1 (paperback)

First published in the United States of America 1997 by
ST. MARTIN'S PRESS, INC.,
Scholarly and Reference Division,
175 Fifth Avenue, New York, N.Y. 10010

ISBN 0-312-15943-9

Library of Congress Cataloging-in-Publication Data
Wyman, Matthew.
Public opinion in postcommunist Russia / Matthew Wyman.
p. cm.
"Published in association with Centre for Russian and East European Studies, University of Birmingham."
Includes bibliographical references (p.   ) and index.
ISBN 0-312-15943-9 (cloth)
1. Public opinion—Russia (Federation)   2. Post-communism—Russia (Federation)—Public opinion.   3. Russia (Federation)—Politics and government—1991—Public opinion.   4. Russia (Federation)—Economic conditions—1991—Public opinion.   I. University of Birmingham. Centre for Russian and East European Studies.   II. Title.
HN530.2.Z9P886 1996
303.3'8'0947—dc20   96-4376
                                                                    CIP

© Matthew Wyman 1997

All rights reserved. No reproduction, copy or transmission of this publication may be made without written permission.

No paragraph of this publication may be reproduced, copied or transmitted save with written permission or in accordance with the provisions of the Copyright, Designs and Patents Act 1988, or under the terms of any licence permitting limited copying issued by the Copyright Licensing Agency, 90 Tottenham Court Road, London W1P 9HE.

Any person who does any unauthorised act in relation to this publication may be liable to criminal prosecution and civil claims for damages.

The author(s) has asserted his/her/their rights to be identified as the author(s) of this work in accordance with the Copyright, Designs and Patents Act 1988.

This book is printed on paper suitable for recycling and made from fully managed and sustained forest sources. Logging, pulping and manufacturing processes are expected to conform to the environmental regulations of the country of origin.

10 9 8 7 6 5 4 3 2 1
06 05 04 03 02 01 00 99 98 97

To Liz

Contents

List of Tables		viii
List of Figures		x
Preface		xiii
1	The Development of Russian Public Opinion	1
2	The Mood of the Nation	20
3	Public Opinion and Soviet Political Institutions	53
4	Public Opinion and Postcommunist Political Institutions	89
5	Continuity and Change in Russian Political Culture	120
6	Russians and Non-Russians on the Collapse of the USSR	149
7	Attitudes to the Market Economy	174
8	One Nation?	213
9	Public Opinion and Post-Soviet Politics	230
Notes		239
Bibliography		253
Index		266

Tables

1.1	Response effects in 1992	10
2.1	Self-assessment of living standards, 1981–87	25
2.2	Self-assessment of living standards, 1989–90	26
2.3	Views about change in the early 1980s	31
2.4	Perceptions of recent change	34
2.5	Greatest problems for respondent's family, 1988–90	40
2.6	Greatest fears, 1989–94	48
2.7	Spare time activities, 1990 and 1994	49
2.8	Greatest pleasures, 1990	51
3.1	Views about causes of Soviet social problems, 1988–89	55
3.2	Attitudes to the Communist Party, February 1990	61
3.3	Attitudes to Soviet history, 1990	63
3.4	Trust in organs of social control, 1989–92	67
3.5	Trust in organs of social control, 1991	71
3.6	Positive appraisals of state institutions by republic, May 1990	74
3.7	Views about leaders, May 1990	75
3.8	Trust in national and republican authorities, May 1991	75
3.9	Perceptions of local government, 1989	77
3.10	Trust in the mass media, 1989–91	79
3.11	Trust in the media, 1991	80
5.1	External efficacy, 1991	129
5.2	Views about the socially deviant, 1989	136
5.3	Views about minority rights, 1989	137
5.4	Views about minority rights, 1991	137
5.5	Views about freedom of speech, December 1989	139
5.6	Views about order versus democracy, June 1993	139
5.7	Rights consciousness	140
5.8	Attitudes to multi-party politics	143
5.9	Interpersonal trust	147
6.1	Views about the future of the Soviet Union, 1989	153
6.2	Desirable forms of federation, 1989	154
6.3	Views about centre–periphery relations, 1990	156
6.4	Views about the desirable distribution of power, Russia, September 1990	157
6.5	Attitudes to secession, 1990	160

6.6	Russian views about secession, 1991	162
6.7	How Russians envisage the future organisation of the country, 1991	167
6.8	Acceptability of secession, 1991	169
6.9	Attitudes to return of Russian irredenta, 1991	169
6.10	Attitudes to secessionist movements, 1992	170
7.1	Costs and benefits of economic transition, 1990–91	184
7.2	Advantages and disadvantages of co-operatives	187
7.3	Meaning of unemployment	200
7.4	Views about the new rich, 1993	206
7.5	Conceptions of poverty, 1991	209

List of Figures

2.1	People's own assessment of their recent moods, March 1993 to July 1994	22
2.2	Quality of life, 1991–93	24
2.3	Living standards, 1993–94	28
2.4	Russian possessions, 1991	30
2.5	Views about recent change, 1988–90	32
2.6	Changes in recent period, 1991–93	37
2.7	Views about recent changes, 1992–93	38
2.8	Greatest social problems, 1991–94	41
2.9	Political priorities, April 1994	43
2.10	Personal expectations, 1989–94	46
2.11	Personal expectations, 1992–93	46
3.1	Views about political institutions, Summer 1989	57
3.2	Trust in political institutions, Summer 1989	58
3.3	Trust in the CPSU, 1989–92	63
3.4	Trust in state institutions, 1989–92	65
3.5	Trust in USSR and republican Supreme Soviets, 1989–91	73
3.6	Trust in local government, 1989–92	77
3.7	Trust in 'religious organisations of Christians, Moslems, etc.', 1989–91	83
3.8	Views about religious revival, 1989	83
3.9	Views about leaders, 1989–91	85
4.1	Attitudes to socialism and democracy, 1992–93	90
4.2	Positive attitudes to 'the communist political cause' by age and monthly income, January 1993	91
4.3	Ratings of Boris Yeltsin and Mikhail Gorbachev on a 10-point scale	93
4.4	Yeltsin's supporters, June 1991	95
4.5	Relative trust in institutions, June 1993	96
4.6	Relative trust in institutions, September 1994	97
4.7	Trust in the Russian Government, 1992–93	99
4.8	Attitudes to the Russian Government, 1994	99
4.9	Assessments of Russian Government policies, 1992	100
4.10	Trust in the Russian Congress of People's Deputies, 1993	103

List of Figures

4.11	Social composition of parliamentary supporters, May 1993	105
4.12	Newspaper readership, 1992–93	108
4.13	Trust in the mass media, 1991–94	109
4.14	Trust in the armed forces, 1992–93	111
4.15	Trust in the state security services, 1990–94	113
4.16	Trust in the police and courts, 1990–94	113
4.17	Trust in the Orthodox Church, 1990–94	115
4.18	Attitudes to the revival of Orthodoxy, 1993	115
4.19	Trust in trade unions, 1990–94	118
4.20	Views about trade unions in the communist period	118
4.21	Views about postcommunist trade unions	118
5.1	Political interest, 1990–93	125
5.2	Political participation, 1989–92	127
5.3	Support for autocratic leadership 1991–94	132
5.4	Russian views about various nationalities, May 1991	134
5.5	Russian views about ethnic minorities, October 1993	135
5.6	Party identification, 1994	145
6.1	Views about secession by Union republics, 1990	158
6.2	Support for use of force in Lithuania, Leningrad, 1989–91	161
6.3	Russian views about secession, 1991	163
6.4	Percentage regretting the break-up of the USSR, Moscow, 1992	167
6.5	Views about self-determination, December 1992	170
7.1	Support for transition to a market economy, 1990–93	176
7.2	Views about transition to the market, December 1990	179
7.3	Support for transition to a market economy, March 1993	180
7.4	Views about prospects for economic improvement	182
7.5	Attitudes to co-operatives, 1989–90	186
7.6	Attitudes to private ownership, 1989–91	189
7.7	Attitudes to private ownership	190
7.8	Attitudes to foreign ownership	191
7.9	Attitudes to private ownership, 1991–93	192
7.10	Attitudes to private property, January 1993	194
7.11	Desirability of privatisation, 1993–94	195
7.12	Views about effects of privatisation	196
7.13	Attitudes to unemployment, 1988–93	201
7.14	Attitudes to the new rich by demographic group and voting behaviour	207
7.15	Conceptions of poverty, 1992–94	210

List of Figures

8.1	Political interest by age and gender	215
8.2	Views about the Communist Party by age	215
8.3	Political interest by age and education	217
8.4	Attitudes to inequality by age and gender	217
8.5	Support for private property by age and gender	218
8.6	Attitudes to democracy by age and gender	219
8.7	Support for private property by age, income and education	220
8.8	Hostility to democracy by education and age	221
8.9	Views about the market by employment sector	222
8.10	Desirable economic and political systems by occupation	223
8.11	Desirable economic system by rurality	225
8.12	Attitudes to the imposition of dictatorship by rurality	226
8.13	Political and economic views by religiosity	227

Preface

In December 1993:

- Almost half of Russians owned their own home.
- One in every five adults had a private car.
- Over half said that they belonged to the Russian Orthodox Church or other Christian churches, but only a quarter ever attended religious services.
- Just one in every eight Russians still believed in communist ideals, but nearly six in ten admitted that they once had.
- 50 per cent thought that unemployment was unacceptable in any circumstances.

This information comes from public opinion polls. There is no other way we could find it out. No single person could travel around a country so vast and diverse – 10 000 kilometres from West to East (roughly the distance between London and Peking) – and hope to make sense of its people, describe their lives and report honestly their views and aspirations.

Before 1988, such information hardly existed. The communist system had little room for opinion polls, since their findings threatened to undermine the myth of mass popular support for that system, and Soviet sociologists had little experience of the statistical techniques needed to carry out polling. But the period since Mikhail Gorbachev launched his campaign of *perestroika* to reform Russia and the Soviet Union has seen an explosion of interest in public opinion, and the development in Russia of an industry dedicated to finding out what Russians really think.

Strangely, though, this information is hardly available to the English-language reader. Western scholars have collaborated with Russian pollsters to produce the occasional monograph based on a snapshot of opinion at one particular time. But these works scarcely do justice to the mood of the Russian people during a time when so much has changed. This book aims to fill the gap. How have Russians responded to the collapse of their empire? What, if anything, do they regret about the collapse of communism? What do they think of their new postcommunist leaders? Who favours the introduction of capitalism, and who is against? How, if at all, do older people, who spent the majority of their lives living under communist rule differ in their attitudes from the younger, postcommunist, generation? How have attitudes shifted over time? These and other fascinating details of Russian attitudes and values will be its theme.

Acknowledgements

Thanks are due to the ESRC, for its financial support during the period October 1990 to September 1992 when the bulk of the research upon which the thesis is based was undertaken, under Award Number 800832.

The book has developed out of a doctoral thesis written at the Centre for Russian and East European Studies at Birmingham University. I would like to thank everyone at CREES for making my time in Birmingham both enjoyable and rewarding. Particular thanks should go to Professor Julian Cooper, for his considered criticism and encouragement of the work as it progressed, Professor Ron Amann, and Professor Michael Kaser for pointing me in the direction of Russian studies and then in the direction of Birmingham in the first place.

The thesis was being completed while I worked as research assistant on Glasgow University's project on 'Public Opinion and Democratic Consolidation in Russia and Eastern Europe' under the directorship of Professor Bill Miller, Professor Stephen White and Dr Paul Heywood. All three of them deserve immense thanks.

Finally, I would like to acknowledge the contribution of the examiners of the thesis, Dr Judy Batt of Birmingham and Dr Richard Sakwa of the University of Kent at Canterbury. Their many helpful suggestions have helped make this a better book.

1 The Development of Russian Public Opinion

THE NATURE OF PUBLIC OPINION

Because we most often encounter public opinion in the form of polls, it is easy to forget that polls and public opinion are by no means the same thing. Public opinion can take many forms. When thousands of Muscovites demonstrated outside the Russian Parliament, the White House, against the attempted *coup d'état* by communist hardliners in August 1991, this was a particularly intense form of public opinion. But equally, conversations in the street or on the bus, letters to newspapers, wearing a badge or putting up posters during election campaigns, all of these are more mundane forms of the same phenomenon.

Furthermore, public opinion is not a fixed object. The great theorists of public opinion, people like Thomas Jefferson, the French statesman and author Alexis de Tocqueville and the historian Lord Bryce had in mind something which was amorphous, constantly fluctuating, sometimes contradictory.

Some opinions are more likely to change than others. One shorthand way public opinion specialists have of describing this is the distinction between 'attitudes' and 'opinions', on the one hand, and 'values' and 'beliefs' on the other. The poll ratings of politicians are a particularly good example of transitory 'attitudes'. How else could Mikhail Gorbachev have been trusted by eight in ten of the population at the end of 1988, but just one in ten by mid-1991? Values are much less likely to change, however, and are much more central parts of individual identity. 'I believe in God' or 'I have always been a communist' are examples of values of this kind. However, even the most seemingly immutable beliefs do sometimes change, in great tectonic shifts. One of the themes of this book, the collapse of the communist value system, is such a shift.

Public opinion also involves varying levels of intensity. People often have particularly strong views on a few issues, vague feelings about others, and have simply never thought about some matters of public concern. This situation too is not static. Issues which were previously ignored can become the major political issue virtually overnight. Mikhail

Gorbachev was taken aback in the period when he first launched his plans to reform the Soviet political system by the speed with which the issue of official privileges moved to the centre of public concern, and he never fully recovered from the setback, as rival Boris Yeltsin constantly criticised the Soviet leader's fondness for good living.

Countless examples of contradictory opinion exist. Many Russians, for example, were strongly against the creation of a competitive market economy, in favour of forbidding unemployment and returning to a centrally planned economy, and yet voted for Russia's Choice, the party of right-wing free marketeers, in the December 1993 parliamentary elections.[1]

There are many reasons why we might appear to hold contradictory opinions. It may be a lack of understanding – that we are simply unaware of the contradiction. It is simply not worth the effort to think every thought through to its logical conclusion, to make all our views consistent, even if this were possible. But there are other explanations of contradictory opinions which are just as convincing. Many times when we give an opinion in public it might be different to what we really think. Tocqueville was writing about this when he said 'Dreading isolation more than error, they professed to share the sentiments of the majority.'[2] It is often easier to respond with a cliché from newspapers or the television than it is to give one's own view, especially if this view is unusual or unpopular. Furthermore, it may be that we really do sometimes have more than one opinion about a particular issue. We might be in a state of agonising uncertainty about, say, whether there should be capital punishment for the most serious crimes, expressing one view at one time, another later the same day. We might have a range of views, which we use in different contexts. Russians under communist rule, for example, might have been willing to condemn communism in private, while outwardly conforming.[3]

If polls and public opinion are not the same thing, is it really acceptable to use poll results as a substitute? The justification lies in the fact that nobody has come up with a quicker or cheaper way of making generalisations about the opinions of large groups of people based on information from just a few. Furthermore, it is useful that the public should have some means of obtaining independent information about its collective positions. However, using the methodology has implications. Reassuringly 'scientific' poll numbers may lead us to treat public opinion as fixed, static and measurable when it is in reality amorphous, fluid, illogical and constantly shifting. The sophisticated analyst must seek to avoid such pitfalls.[4]

PUBLIC OPINION IN SOCIALIST SYSTEMS

The socialist system had no room for public opinion. The Communist Party, claiming as it did to embody the will of the working class, knew the truth. What need then to find out what the people thought? Indeed to do so would have threatened the whole ideological basis of the regime, since it would have undermined the myth that the people were lined up in monolithic unity behind their rulers. Nadezhda Mandelstam described the situation in her memoirs, *Hope Against Hope*:[5]

> In his letter to Stalin, Bukharin added a postscript saying he had been visited by Pasternak, who was upset by the arrest of Mandelstam. The purpose of this postscript was clear: it was Bukharin's way of indicating to Stalin what the effect of M.'s arrest had been on public opinion. It was always necessary to personify 'public opinion' in this way. You were allowed to talk of one particular individual being upset, but it was unthinkable to mention the existence of dissatisfaction among a whole section of the community – say the intelligentsia or 'literary circles.' No group has the right to its own opinion about some event or other.

Even in the easier political climate of the post-Stalin period, where the regime's policies were more oriented towards public demands, the political leadership was reluctant to allow opinion research in the Soviet Union, and prevented the dissemination of the little research that did take place.

There is thus very little systematic information about Soviet public attitudes under the old regime. What we do know comes from three main sources. The first of these was the limited amount of survey research that was permitted by the regime after the mid-1960s. This was mostly about attitudes to work, and aimed at finding ways of increasing labour productivity. Studies were never representative samples of the population as a whole, since regional authorities were reluctant to permit any bad news at all about their areas to be publicised. Some of the data, such as the project at Taganrog, did have political implications, in the sense that they revealed a degree of mass dissatisfaction, but such results remained classified. In the case of Taganrog, the researchers subsequently lost their jobs as the regime punished the bearers of bad tidings.[6]

The second main source of information about popular attitudes was surveys of Soviet émigrés carried out by Western social scientists. These took place in two waves: shortly after the Second World War, and again during the 1970s, the times corresponding to the peaks of emigration from the Soviet Union. Analyses of both data sources, the Harvard Project and the Soviet Interview Project, drew broadly similar conclusions. These were that there was a considerable degree of congruence between many social values and the values of the regime. This helped to explain the relative stability of the system.[7]

With the benefit of hindsight, these conclusions seem odd. They – in particular the SIP study – were premised on the view that there actually was a public opinion in the Soviet Union, or in other communist countries, at least in normal times. The third major source of our understanding – impressionistically from émigré and dissident literature, and from some theoretical work – would question this. Influenced by various conceptions of totalitarianism, such approaches denied that it was possible to speak about a public opinion, since popular attitudes simply did not matter politically. This is not to deny that private views existed. The approach therefore concentrated on such private attitudes. One aspect was the consideration of what led people to actually identify with the regime. Seminal here was Czeslaw Milosz's *The Captive Mind*, in which he sought 'to create afresh the stages by which the mind gives way to compulsion from without.'[8] He looked at the attraction to intellectuals of a system of ideas which sought to explain everything and which offered them a clear sense of purpose and meaning to their lives. Others speculated in terms of the appeal of communism to the masses, in terms of its simplicity, use of violence, or similarity with religious beliefs.[9]

What then of those who did not share the regime's values? After the use of mass terror as a means of social control had ended, a few individuals were prepared to speak out. Many argue that it is precisely this dissident movement that marked the emergence of a 'civil society in embryo' and an alternative public opinion in the Soviet Union.[10] However, this was as yet quite unsophisticated, tending often to an automatic reversal of everything the regime said. This was very much a world of moral imperatives rather than the practical politics of solving problems and building support.

However, for most people the way of dealing with powerlessness was the retreat into private life, avoiding the political. Everyone, in order to get on, would mouth the official Newspeak in public, but in reality, most were simply de-politicised.[11] The defining features of private opinions, then, were a combination of ignorance and fear. For this reason, public opinion as an independent social institution that affects the political process – the sense in which the term was discussed above – simply did not exist.

This was the situation in the Soviet Union when Mikhail Gorbachev came to power. It had been the situation in all of communist Eastern Europe except at abnormal times – 1956, 1968, Poland in the 1980s. For the reformer faced with the need to reinvigorate the stagnant economy, and to overcome the inertia of the party–state apparatus, it was a worrying situation. The policy of *glasnost* was aimed to introduce the system to criticism and to allow the expression of alternative points of view, within ever-widening limits. Therefore, the ideological and physical constraints that had prevented the study of public attitudes were gradually removed. Sociologists were for the first time, from about 1988, allowed to engage in systematic survey research on popular attitudes.

THE DEVELOPMENT OF RUSSIAN PUBLIC OPINION

Survey research in the Soviet Union before the Gorbachev era had been limited and heavily politicised. It was dominated by a sociological establishment appointed in the 1970s by a regime anxious not to hear about the population's 'negative attitudes'. The major institutions that carried out quantitative work – in particular the Institute of Sociological Research of the USSR Academy of Sciences, and the Academy of Social Sciences, subordinate to the Communist Party Central Committee – were deeply conservative ones. Although some interesting research was conducted, all surveys were unrepresentative of the population as a whole, and restricted to non-controversial themes. The quality of data analysis was unsophisticated, results were not widely publicised, and, if controversial, they were not published at all. Furthermore, all questionnaire-based research suffered from the problem of self-censorship. Scholars were reluctant to ask anything that might achieve politically awkward results, and respondents were unwilling to admit to views that were not in accord with the official line.

This was a state of affairs that persisted for the first three years of the Gorbachev period. Research remained restricted to matters such as the population's standard of living, newspaper readership, problems at work and other relatively anodyne themes.

Reform in this area was clearly an important part of the whole reform project in the Soviet Union. Public support was an important potential resource for attempts to overcome the inertia of the party–state apparatus. Furthermore, the study of likely responses to particular changes under consideration was desirable to the more reform-minded sections of the leadership. Thus 1987 saw a debate about the state of the Soviet sociological profession, initiated by an article entitled *'Perestroika* and Sociology' in *Pravda* that February by the prominent sociologist Tatyana Zaslavskaya.[12] By March 1988 the situation had changed enough for it to be possible to create the All-Union Centre for Public Opinion Research (VTsIOM), attached to *Goskomtrud* (the State Labour Committee), and the All-Union Trade Union Council (VTsSPS). The new institute was headed by Zaslavskaya herself and brought together several of the most important reform-minded sociologists in the country, scholars such as Yuri Levada and Boris Grushin.

Initially the new institute operated cautiously. Its full name, the All-Union Centre for Public Opinion Research on Social and Economic Issues, avoided reference to politics since this was deemed too likely to offend Kremlin hardliners.[13] Its early studies, in 1988, were on relatively non-controversial issues such as the proposal for workforces to elect managers at state enterprises. But rapidly – paralleling and contributing to the process of *glasnost* itself – the areas of investigation broadened. By the end of that year it was asking about where blame lay for the country's difficulties, and about public feelings on the new co-operatives, and by the end of 1989 the popularity of individual politicians and the leading role of the Communist Party were acceptable topics for study.[14]

All this had a substantial effect on other institutions: through 1989, for example, the Institute of Sociology – as the Academy of Science's Institute of Sociological Research had been renamed – published poll data showing that Soviet citizens were both highly critical of the slow pace of change and sceptical about the effectiveness of some of the most important reforms.[15] The liberal press – newspapers such as *Moskovskie novosti* and *Komsomolskaya pravda* – began regularly to publish polls showing support for more change. Contacts between Soviet and Western survey organisations and scholars helped boost the professionalisation and improve the technological basis for Soviet survey research. By 1991 no issue was in principle off-limits for study. Surveys were published showing, for example, that many thought Gorbachev to be guilty of hypocrisy and of indifference to human suffering.[16] Party institutes such as the Academy of Social Sciences, meanwhile, battled against the tide by continuing to publish data showing support for socialism, support for banning jokes about Lenin and backing for the leading role of the Communist Party.[17]

The continuing popularity of opinion polls in Russia and the growing possibilities after the collapse of the Soviet Union for the creation of private businesses independent of the academic establishment has

The Development of Russian Public Opinion 7

led over the period 1991-4 to a profusion of survey organisations. The most professional of these see themselves as being a vital part of the process of social transformation that is taking place in Russia.[18] However Russian survey data remain of variable quality, and they are often used rather uncritically by analysts. A brief review of several aspects of Russian survey research – its political context, questionnaire design and sampling procedures, the organisation of surveys and their dissemination – in the light of Western practices is therefore useful.[19]

Political Aspects

In the early stages in the development of independent survey research political interference remained an important issue. Self-censorship was evident, with pollsters reluctant to ask, for example, about Gorbachev's personal popularity, trust in the Communist Party or the desire for a multi-party system. The party–state apparatus retained its traditional sanctions for stepping out of line. In a notorious incident, Gorbachev threatened to dismiss the editor of the reform-oriented journal *Argumenty i fakty*, Vladislav Starkov, for publishing politically inconvenient survey data.[20]

Such heavy-handed interference and censorship has become rather less common in the recent period however, although there are still localised cases: for example the authorities in the Siberian republic of Buryatiya refused researchers permission to conduct a survey at the end of 1991 on the grounds that it represented Moscow's interference in the affairs of a sovereign state![21] However, no topic is in principle off-limits for research. This is not to say that self-censorship by researchers has ended, of course. There are findings that pollsters might be reluctant to release: data on the extent of intolerance towards ethnic minorities and intolerance of social deviance (discussed in Chapter 5) would be an example, since there is a danger that publishing this information might further encourage prejudice. This is an ethical problem for survey research in general, not a problem confined to Russia.

Another objection relates to the question of whether respondents tell the truth when being interviewed (in pollsters' jargon, are there 'response effects'?). Soviet citizens lived for many decades under a system where to speak out of line was to put oneself and one's family at risk: risk to life itself under Stalin, to liberty, property and prospects under his successors. Many have suggested that there may be a legacy of this intimidation factor, which leads respondents to answer according to what they think the authorities want to hear, or even to refuse to be questioned at all. Thus Willerton and Sigelman:[22]

Even though respondents were promised anonymity, poll-takers commented that in some cases people seemed to answer *po-gazetam* – based on what they surmised from the official press – rather than from the heart. One interviewer was quoted in the *New York Times* as saying 'Sometimes you ask "Do you support..." and they say yes before you even finish the sentence. They know from the official slogans that if the question says "support" the answer is supposed to be "yes".'

Such a state of affairs is familiar to the well-informed survey analyst, and not a problem unique to Russia. It appears to be true almost everywhere that people prefer to agree with questions than disagree (pollsters term this 'positivity bias'). One team of researchers, for example, found that for surveys in the United Kingdom, people were more likely to agree with a statement than disagree with the comparable negative statement by anything from 6 to 19 per cent.[23] This appears to reflect a desire to express in public attitudes that identify the respondent with the values of society in general.[24] The conclusion for survey research is that clichéd or unbalanced questions should be avoided.

Beyond such effects, there is no evidence specific to Russia that respondents do indeed engage in self-censorship. Impressionistically, it seems bizarre to claim that questions were not answered honestly when as early as March 1989, before the challenges to its authority that summer, the Communist Party was only rating 40 per cent trust, according to VTsIOM.[25] This is backed up by the views of Russian pollsters themselves. Hedrick Smith quotes the remarks of two VTsIOM researchers, Lev Gudkov and Aleksandr Golov, in 1989. 'Through the decades, people have never been asked *anything*. All of a sudden their opinion is being counted – someone is seeking their answers. They feel this is a sign of trust towards them, a demonstration of their worth.' 'People are saying things like "I have lived for eighty years and no one has ever wondered about my opinion. For the first time in my life I have experienced that moment."'[26]

Furthermore, response rates in Russia and much of the rest of the former Soviet Union remain rather high by Western standards. Many Western survey organisations consider a 30 per cent refusal rate in surveys conducted through face to face interviews to be normal, and 50 per cent is certainly not unusual for telephone surveys. However, response rates of 90 per cent were commonplace in the Soviet Union in 1989–90. For example, the New Soviet Citizen survey conducted by researchers from the University of Iowa in conjunction with the

Academy of Sciences Institute of Sociology achieved response rates of 89–90 per cent in Russia, Ukraine and Lithuania.[27] As of 1993, targets of 80 per cent responses are standard for the more reputable Russian pollsters.

Direct evidence exists that many Russians have favourable attitudes to being asked to take part in surveys. VTsIOM began in 1990 to record respondents' attitudes to the questionnaire being conducted. An article entitled 'How to help the interviewer', based on the experience of researchers from their Central Black Earth Department in Voronezh, revealed that attitudes were overwhelmingly positive, although, typically, somewhat less so in cities than rural areas, and dependent on the subject matter of the survey.[28] The writers gave some individual responses too:

> one respondent replied . . . 'It is my duty!'. Another announced with satisfaction that at last the government wanted to know even her opinion. And these weren't isolated cases. Generally people were satisfied (although it is true that sometimes too much time was taken). They were prepared to co-operate and even to give their telephone number and a time when they were likely to be in. But there were also those who considered the job to be unnecessary, as nothing was changing in their lives. A negative attitude is found most often among ignorant people [sic], although if it is explained that in order to successfully administer the country it is necessary to know the opinion of all citizens, their attitudes change rapidly, and they not only complete the questionnaire, but even agree to further co-operation.

It is sometimes argued that Russians have become more reluctant to be surveyed since 1992, not through fear of political reprisals, but through rising indifference to politics, or through fear of rising crime. Clearly response rates have fallen, but not by much. The prominent sociologist Boris Grushin has published research based on asking interviewers in a number of surveys conducted by his organisation, Vox Populi, in 1992 to record the first reactions of people when asked to take part in an interview. Table 1.1 illustrates the data.

As can clearly be seen, while a degree of mistrust or a lack of interest affected small parts of the samples in these investigations, for the overwhelming majority this was not the case. The patterns were consistent for each investigation.

There are, then, no compelling reasons to mistrust the honesty of responses to Soviet or post-Soviet surveys, at least to any greater degree than is the case with all survey evidence. Indeed if anything the

Table 1.1 Response effects in 1992

	Moscow 1 Jan. (%)	Russia 1 Jan.–Feb. (%)	Russia 2 Feb. (%)	Russia 3 Apr. (%)	Moscow 2 Apr. (%)	Russia 4 Jun.–Jul. (%)
First reaction of respondents to request to be interviewed						
Anxiety, caution	10	17	15	16	11	14
Indifference	17	12	14	12	14	12
Trust	36	35	32	31	35	36
Interest	33	34	37	34	31	37
Overall appraisal of how the visit went						
Easily	80	85	83	86	81	86
Tensely	9	12	15	12	9	12
Not understanding question as cause of tension						
	1	3	6	4	2	2

Source: *Nezavisimaya gazeta*, 28 October 1992, p. 3.

honesty of response might be greater in Russia, owing partly to the novelty value of polls, and partly to the fact that the issues being studied are often central ones for people's lives. In more stable democracies, political issues can often seem marginal to everyday concerns, but in Russia questions of the course of economic reform or who rules are only too important.

The Organisation of Russian Survey Research

A much more problematic area for polling organisations is in the sheer technical difficulty of organising polls in Russia and the rest of the former Soviet Union. Grushin provides an illustrative extract from a diary of problematic incidents kept by Vox Populi:

> February 1992 – in the city of Tuimazy (Bashkortostan) a drunk respondent holds an interviewer by force for three hours, demanding proof that he is not from the KGB.
> February 1992 – Many non-Russian respondents in Komi (Syktavar) refuse to speak to the interviewer in Russian, insisting that the interview be in their native language ...
> March 1992 – At Kazan station in Moscow, a violent assault on a courier carrying field information from Kemerevo. The injuries received as a result put the courier in hospital for three weeks and the information is irretrievably lost ...

The Development of Russian Public Opinion

June 1992 – A group of interviewers in Kazan (Tatarstan) refuse to take part in field work because they hadn't been paid since February (not VP's fault, but because local banks had no money) . . .

Grushin concludes the diary by commenting that 'the conduct of scientific investigations within the former USSR is not so much difficult as impossible', before going on to make a case that it is worth believing them anyway.[29] Difficulties can be summarised more technically as those of human capital, the technical basis for survey research, communications infrastructure and language and culture-related issues.

Human capital simply relates to the lack of trained sociologists and trained interviewers in Russia due to the neglect of the discipline of sociology before 1989. This has implications for the conceptual and technical standards of questionnaires, for the practice of field work, and for analysis of data received. The absence of experienced interviewers, for example, meant that many of the earlier polls had to rely on untrained students to do the work in some parts of the country. In this context Michael Swafford is no doubt correct to draw our attention to the national institution of *khaltura*, which is creating the impression that sloppy work has in fact been done efficiently.[30]

A further problem relates to educated interviewers surveying less well-educated respondents. In societies where there is a relatively large gap between the intelligentsia and the masses the temptation to lecture respondents on the meaning of questions is common. However, there is no doubt that there has been an effort to improve matters, with resources made available for study abroad and efforts at interviewer training by the more reputable survey organisations, and, particularly importantly, much learning by doing. Clearly the interviewer standards reached by say American election studies with budgets running into millions of dollars and the cumulative experience of 60 years of survey research to draw upon, are unattainable, but it is not a completely neglected area.

The technical basis for survey research is also an area of concern. This relates to the lack of office technology such as fax machines and photocopiers, and to appropriate information technology such as personal computers and appropriate software. Even where this is adequate, statistical analysis of data tends to be rudimentary, rarely going beyond frequencies and cross-tabulations. The wider availability of technology in the postcommunist period helps matters, but its cost is often prohibitive.

Still more important are issues relating to the communications infrastructure. Anyone with experience of the Russian telephone and postal systems will appreciate how unreliable these can be. This rules out representative telephone or postal questionnaires. It also creates major difficulties in transmitting questionnaires and other information from one part of the country to another. Commonly pollsters have to rely on informal couriers to carry questionnaires from remote areas. The impossibility of checks by phone or post makes verification of surveys dependent on personal visits, and impossible in some cases. Shortages and cost of fuel and spare parts make it very difficult to include some parts of the country in samples. As Swafford again points out this inevitably leads to a trade-off between costs and accuracy.

Language- and culture-based problems do not simply relate to the difficulty of translating Western concepts to Russian conditions (dealt with on pp. 12–15 below). They also concern difficulties relating to the non-Russian sections of the population. What language should interviews be conducted in? It is hardly feasible to have dozens of different versions of the same questionnaire for every survey to satisfy the more significant Russian minorities. It is apparently not uncommon for interviewers familiar with one or other minority language to carry out free translation during the interview.[31] Also, cultural differences often change the meaning of questions within the country, although this is more a problem for post-survey analysis rather than one undermining the project of survey research itself.

Problems of Question Construction

Good question construction is a problem universal to those who conduct surveys. Opinion poll sceptics have only too many easy targets in poorly worded questions. Garry Trudeau, creator of the *Doonesbury* cartoon strip once parodied a poll commissioned by the American tobacco industry to justify opposing restrictions on smoking in public. The question: Do you favour Gestapo-style police tactics to prevent smoking in public?[32] Since the issues are so familiar, it is merely necessary to review them in the Russian context.

1. Questions are Frequently Loaded
That is, they put the argument in favour of or against a particular issue without the opposing view. Possibly the most notorious example of this was not an opinion poll question at all, but rather the question that Mikhail Gorbachev put to national referendum in 1991 on the preservation or otherwise of the Soviet Union: 'Do you consider it

necessary to preserve the Union of Soviet Socialist Republics as a renewed federation of equal sovereign republics in which human rights and freedoms for all nationalities will be fully guaranteed?' Pollsters too have committed sins of the 'Are you in favour of motherhood and apple pie and against incest and satanism?' variety too. One example of many would be in VTsIOM's 1989 study of strikes, which asked 'Does the possibility exist that strikes in our country will cause economic catastrophe?' The results, incidentally, were yes, 50 per cent; no, 27 per cent; can't say, 23 per cent.[33] This at a time when the coal miners' strikes in the Donbas, Kuzbas and Vorkuta regions were an important and worrying issue for the country. The linking of the emotive term 'catastrophe' with strikes no doubt prejudiced the outcome. There are many other examples, often reflecting the political commitments of the researchers. As a general point, good questions should be balanced, designed to put both sides of arguments where possible, although there are circumstances where one might wish not to do this, such as when one thinks that an overwhelming number will choose one position.

2. Questions are Often Vague or Ambiguous
The question about strikes again illustrates the point. The key phrase is, 'Does the possibility exist...?' Clearly there was a logical possibility that strikes in the Soviet Union would cause economic catastrophe, whether or not this was the respondent's view. 'Beware the literal-minded respondent' was apparently one of George Gallup's key pieces of advice to the survey researcher. He used to cite the case of the Canadian poll which asked people to give their 'length of residence'. One farmer was said to have proudly replied 'Twenty-six feet and six inches.'[34]

3. Questions Create Opinions that do not Exist
This problem can be overstated, but is worth consideration. Few want to admit to interviewers their ignorance on a particular issue, so, it is argued, they often simply reply to questions at random. The important article by Philip Converse, based on data from University of Michigan panel studies of the American electorate proposed that, for America in the early 1960s at least, responses gained to many questions only made sense if they had indeed been random.[35]

This is a particular problem when one wants to look at abstract values rather than attitudes to specific issues, although it can affect the latter too. An example might be the attempt to look at the freedom versus equality dilemma by the cross-national survey carried out for the American Times–Mirror organisation in May 1991. Their measure was the following: 'What's more important in Russian society: that everyone be free to pursue their life's goals without interference from the state, or that the state play an active role in society so as to guarantee equality?' While this is a distinction that political theorists might want to make, it is clearly not a problem that has occurred to most people.

However, the obverse is the failure of questions to get at attitudes that exist only vaguely or that only exist after some prompting. Such attitudes can clearly become important. Indeed it is precisely this kind of stimulation that occurs during election campaigns. It is simply necessary to bear the criticisms in mind when interpreting survey data. A high level of 'don't know' responses will often indicate questions that are difficult to understand.

4. Same Phenomenon, Different Meanings
Although not the context in which it is mentioned, Michael Swafford's example about asking about attendance at religious services is appropriate. This question is in general a much better indicator of religiosity than asking whether people believe in God. But as he points out, in many Muslim communities, women are not allowed to attend religious services.[36]

Again, though, this is a general problem for survey research, rather than a particular one for Russia. The important point is simply to be aware of the possibility.

5. Questions Ask for Dual Responses
A glaring example of this was the question designed by the European Commission for their Central and Eastern Eurobarometer surveys to measure support for the market economy. It reads: 'Are you personally in favour of a market economy, that is, one which is largely free from state control?'[37] Which do they want to know about: the market economy or the market economy largely free from state control? Some unfortunate consequences of this sloppiness are discussed in Chapter 7.

6. Questions are Excessively Open-Ended
Clearly there is a place for open-ended questioning, but the problem with not pre-coding answers is that surveys do not discover the attitudes of some people, and often end up making arbitrary assumptions about what should be classified with what. The question 'What is the

The Development of Russian Public Opinion

main cause of our country's problems?', commonly used in VTsIOM's early end-of-year surveys is a good example.[38] Because people could give any answer they chose, information about how many people thought each possible cause was important was unobtainable from the results. This problem could have been avoided by more careful consideration of what the question was seeking to measure. Early post-1988 studies were particularly prone to this kind of fault, although most questions are now much more unambiguous, closed and therefore interpretable.

Summing up problems with questionnaire design, a group of VTsIOM researchers in 1990 complained thus:[39]

> In relatively stable and developed societies where the study of public opinion is long-standing and systematic, its aims are concentrated on the whole on investigations of marketing and election studies. These spheres of interest were alien to a system of chronic shortages and – up to the very recent period and the multi-candidate elections of Spring 1989 – were completely useless to us... the splendidly organised and technically equipped system of opinion surveys in the West, which is adjusted to the slightest fluctuation in political and consumer sympathies of the mass, is not suitable for analysis of a situation of social fractures and shocks and a crisis of social institutions and values.

Those familiar with the problems of Western survey research will certainly be touched by the faith that is put in their existing measures, but the overall point is well taken. Soviet and post-Soviet researchers do in many ways face a unique situation. It is greatly to their credit that scales and measures which are now commonly used by several of the polling companies are in general balanced, unbiased, and avoid many of the pitfalls of question design, while measuring new problems in illuminating ways.

Sampling

Credible sampling is one of the most central aspects of serious survey research, as well as one of the most abused. It has certainly been a major problem for Soviet and post-Soviet poll research. At the early stages any attempt to construct a sample that was reasonably representative of the population at large was simply impossible: VTsIOM's first poll was only of three cities, since the infrastructure of trained personnel was simply absent. Considerable contortions were often got into by researchers in order to justify blatantly unrepresentative samples:

a common one was to claim that it did not matter that the sample over-represented highly educated people since these were society's opinion formers, and the rest of the population would soon follow behind.[40] The comment itself shows ignorance of the most rudimentary techniques for weighting samples.

The situation was understandable when efforts were directed at building up survey organisations from nothing. But to what extent do unrepresentative samples remain a problem? One of the difficulties in judging this is that in reporting polls, many organisations give no details of how selections were made, or how raw data were weighted, tending simply to assert that their sample is in fact representative. There are grounds for scepticism here, particularly in the case of smaller survey organisations. The following are some of the more important problems relating to sampling.

1. A Tendency Overly to Restrict the Sample
Commonly, surveys are of just one city (usually Moscow or St Petersburg), of urban areas only, of just European Russia or, when they claim to be national, restricted to the more easily accessible South and West. Such samples cannot be taken as representative of Russia as a whole. We know, for example from election returns, that the views of rural and urban areas are very different, and a distorted sample gives a misleading picture. This criticism is just as true of the New Soviet Citizen survey and the *Eurobarometer* studies, conducted on behalf of Western organisations, as it is of many domestically inspired studies.

However, the costs involved in reaching more remote areas are prohibitive. Pollsters in the United Kingdom commonly eliminate more remote areas of, for example, the Scottish highlands from their sampling frames for cost reasons, and it would be unreasonable to expect more of Russian organisations than we do of our own. But if samples are not of the whole country, they should not be written up as if they were.

2. Samples Too Small for Any Degree of Accuracy
This is not so much the case with the size of overall samples – invariably over 1000. It is more important when investigating sub-groups within the whole sample. The normal rule of thumb for survey researchers is that samples of 50 to 100 are necessary before one is willing to talk with any confidence about individual groups. But one often finds analysis based on much smaller numbers than this.

However, it is increasingly the case that the larger survey organisations in all Russian surveys are using considerably larger samples than was previously the case even in surveys of the entire USSR. Thus, for example, VTsIOM's 'monitoring' surveys of the whole adult population as of 1994 frequently sample 4000, while Vox Populi commonly interview around 2000. The advantage of these over previous attempts is that it makes it possible to talk with some confidence about small but interesting groups such as workers in a particular industrial sector, or some of the larger ethnic minorities.

3. The Absence of Reliable Statistics
This makes it difficult to ensure that samples – appropriately weighted – do conform to the social and demographic characteristics of the country as a whole. Glasnost clearly made a considerable difference to the availability of census data, with detailed information by *oblast* now available for some demographic characteristics.[41] *Goskomstat*, the State Statistics Committee, does now update its figures annually. However, factors such as rapid change in income levels and standards of living, in the industrial and employment structure of the country, and massive population movements caused by ethnic tensions and economic difficulties certainly complicate the researcher's task.[42]

4. Excessively Small Numbers of Primary Sampling Units
Often polls only sample 10 or 20 different population points, sometimes claiming that these are 'representative', if they give any information about their sampling procedures at all. Clearly, taking what are believed to be typical sampling points eliminates some interesting variation in the data.[43] However, again, the better pollsters will more commonly use 80 or 100, randomly selected, and this should be expected of professional research.

5. The Absence of Appropriate Data to Construct Samples
This is a familiar problem for survey research, but an important one. In urban areas, files of address bureaux or electoral registers, and in rural areas collective farm membership records provide some information, but it is generally agreed that these are rarely accurate. Unlike British electoral registers, Russian ones are continually updated, but there are various disincentives for registration, such as that electoral registers have been the basis for enlistment for compulsory military service for young men. One source 'guesstimates' that in some cities registers may be inaccurate by as much as 10 to 15 per cent.[44] Again, though, this is a problem common to survey research everywhere, and

it is largely a question of learning from experience which method of generating a sample is most appropriate for the area in question. Random walk procedures, for example, are often used effectively.

6. Verification

Shortages of telephones (it is estimated that as of 1985 only 23 per cent of urban and 7 per cent of rural inhabitants possessed them) and the inadequacies of the postal service greatly complicate the task of verification that interviews actually took place.[45] Personal calls by interview supervisors are for this reason the most common method, but this is costly of time and effort.

There are then particular complications with sampling in the Russian context. The more reputable organisations do publish information as to how the sample is selected, but this is rarely as complete as one would wish.[46] However, there are reasons to believe that the procedures have improved greatly in the past few years.

Publication of Survey Data

Again, problems here are familiar ones. Opinion polls published in the mass media rarely give details of the method by which the survey was conducted, a crucial failing given the uselessness of telephone surveys in Russia. Sample sizes are often omitted, and the expected margins of error based on a given sample size are still rarer. Sometimes the sampling universe is not mentioned, so that polls of Moscow are passed off as polls of the entire country. Breakdowns by social, demographic or opinion group are often partial, and the number in each category is rarely given. The press often gives details of polls without saying what the question was that achieved the particular result. Thus, for example, all polls that measure the popularity of leaders are treated in the same way. For example, notorious polls in mid-1992 which showed Vice President Aleksandr Rutskoi 'ahead' of Boris Yeltsin were in fact based on positive and negative appraisals of the two as individuals.[47] However, they were reported as voting intentions, while every poll on the lines of 'If there were an election tomorrow ...' was showing Yeltsin as the more popular. The whole exercise is given a spurious scientificity by reporting numbers to one decimal place – meaningless given the margins of error of polls. Such media distortions are understandable: polls are intensely political, legitimating or de-legitimating individuals and views. But it is the professional responsibility of those who conduct them to insist on standards for their presentation.

THE USEFULNESS OF RUSSIAN SURVEY RESEARCH

The polling industry in Russia has had a bad press. Pollsters are said to have 'failed' to predict the result at every important election since the industry developed.[48] This is a travesty, and based on sociological illiteracy. Polls conducted several weeks before the election date are criticised for not predicting how people would actually act on the day. Critics would do well to note that post-election polls conducted by those organisations with high standards of professional competence do not show any such error.[49]

This is not to argue that all survey research in Russia is conducted to high standards. The sophisticated analyst should be aware of what constitutes an unprofessional poll, and avoid it. Problems in the area exist. However, many are problems universal for survey research, and it is easy to fall into the trap of overstating flaws in Russian methods while understating the actual practical distortions that occur in the conduct of surveys everywhere. Those who run the major Russian survey organisations now are highly professional and aware of the problems, and there is no reason to suppose that the visible improvement of standards over the period 1988–93 is a trend that will be reversed. Political interference is at present not an issue, and the popularity of polls in Russia has created a reasonable financial basis on which a survey industry can operate. Most importantly, survey research provides an insight into attitudes which would otherwise remain uninvestigated.

2 The Mood of the Nation

Before 1985, the lives of most ordinary Russians were at least predictable. Living standards were not high, the economy had stagnated and queues for basic goods were the rule, not the exception. However, prices of essentials were low and stable and there was a high degree of job security. The country faced important social problems – poverty, homelessness, alcoholism and the like – but the all-pervasive culture of secrecy meant that many Russians were simply unaware of the seriousness of the situation they faced.

The changes brought about by Mikhail Gorbachev shattered the calm. Attempts to transform the moribund economy and shake up the increasingly corrupt political system through the policy of *perestroika* ('restructuring') affected many aspects of Russian life. So how did the feelings of Russians about their living standards change in the Gorbachev years? What improved in their lives, and what were the new difficulties? Did the changes affect the way that Russians spent their spare time, and did it alter their aspirations for the future? And how did the introduction of economic 'shock therapy' in Russia in January 1992 change the national mood?

THE MOOD OF THE NATION

The language of Soviet socialism – the language of 'newspeak' and 'doublethink' – insisted on images of a contented population. 'Life has become happier and more joyous' was the official line at the time of the Great Terror under Stalin, when life for many was anything but happy and joyous, and the prospects for those who told the truth were, to say the least, uncertain. Bad news was supressed as a matter of course.

Sociological research in the pre-*perestroika* period was often part of this official conspiracy to present a distorted picture. Respondents were asked how satisfied they were, and were expected to affirm their positive commitment. As Václav Havel and others have written, forcing people to tell lies in public in this way was a vital component of the regime's system of social control.[1]

A typical example of this is research conducted by the Institute of

Sociology of the USSR Academy of Sciences in 1981. The published findings of this suggested that at that time, over half (52 per cent) of Russians questioned said that overall their life seemed good, and just 2 per cent that it seemed poor. The remainder felt it to be satisfactory. The Institute repeated the question in 1987, and found that matters had scarcely changed: 48 per cent said that their life was good overall, the same number that it was satisfactory, and again just 1 in 50 that it was poor.[2] While this research is not based on a representative sample of Russians – indeed no information on how the sample was chosen is given – the results illustrate that as late as 1987, virtually nobody was prepared publically to admit that they were dissatisfied.

Once the campaign of *glasnost* (openness) began to remove the necessity for lying in public, however, the picture of a joyful and contented population gradually faded away. Public opinion research contributed to the change. People no longer felt compelled to hide their true feelings, and so polls began to show that unhappiness was on the increase. Thus by December 1989, VTsIOM, in a survey of the whole Soviet Union asked people 'In life anything can happen – good things and bad things. But overall are you happy?' 7 per cent said that they were completely happy and 39 per cent mostly happy, 12 per cent not very happy and 3 per cent not at all happy. The remainder either said that happiness is not what is important, or that they could not really say. It would be an exaggeration to say that there was a large rise in discontent though: only 15 per cent of the sample were not very or not at all happy.[3]

By 1992, following the launch of economic 'shock therapy', there appears to have been such a rise. That March, VTsIOM found that 64 per cent in the Russian Federation, 65 per cent in Ukraine and 44 per cent in Kazakhstan were dissatisfied with the life they were leading.[4] Similarly, the organisation, Vox Populi, in May put the question, 'Overall, how satisfying is your life?', and found that while 4 per cent said that it was excellent and 23 per cent said it was good, 56 per cent said that it was only so-so, and 15 per cent that it was bad or very bad.[5] Of course, the apparent rise may just reflect the different measure: it is likely that some people are reasonable happy, but at the same time dissatisfied with the life they are leading.

Since early 1993 VTsIOM's regular 'Sociological Monitoring' surveys have used still another measure, one which asks respondents to assess their overall mood. Figure 2.1 shows the trends.

The data present a more stable picture of moods in postcommunist Russia than one might imagine. While the number of 'happy Russians'

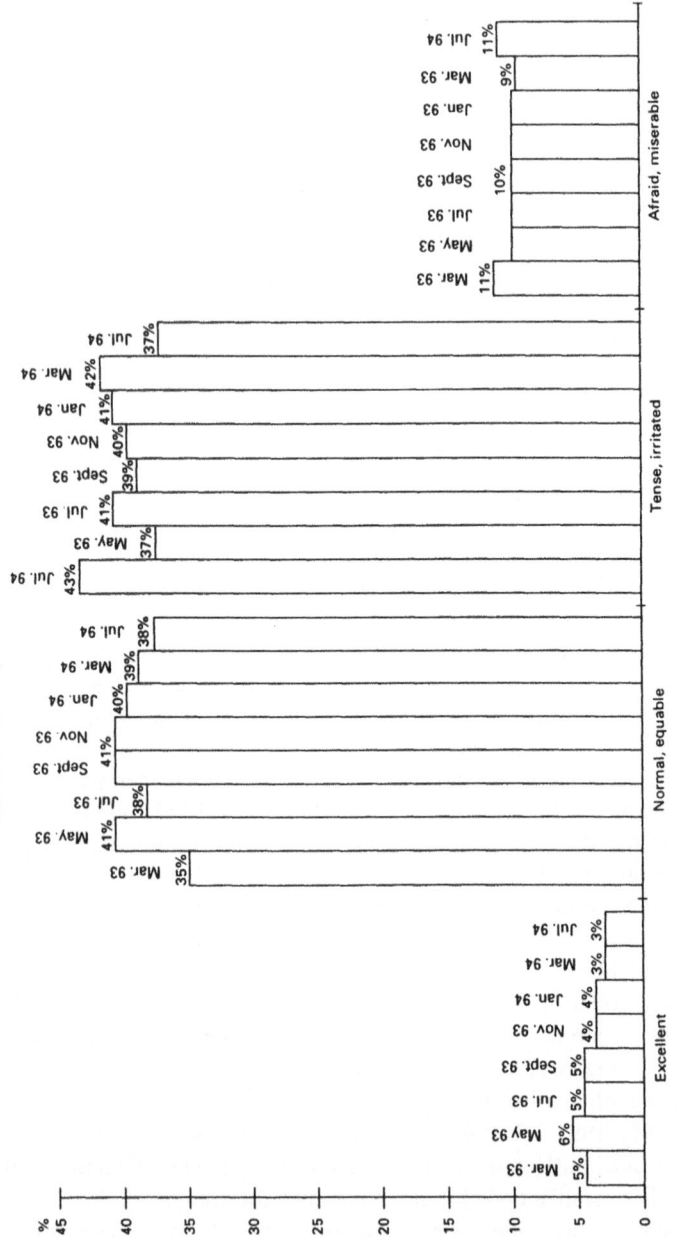

Figure 2.1 People's own assessment of their recent moods, March 1993 to July 1994

Source: Ekonomicheskie i sotsial'nye peremeny: monitoring obshchestvennogo mneniya, 3 (1994), p. 34.

who said that they were in an excellent mood remained a tiny 1 in 20, the number of unhappy people who replied that they were either afraid or miserable at the time was also constant at around 1 in 10. The remainder of the population remained approximately evenly divided between those who were in a 'normal' state of mind and those who felt tense. Russian newspapers were filled with gloom, but the Russian people scarcely reflected this.

Which groups were most likely to be happy? As of early 1993, significantly more men than women (56 per cent to 38 per cent) and young people than old (in a ratio of seven to four) were found to be in a good frame of mind.[6] In 1994, the young, especially students, inhabitants of Siberia and the Far East, those with less than secondary education, workers in the private sector and those with higher incomes were significantly more likely to be in an excellent or at least 'normal' mood.[7]

Overall, then, poll data suggest that recent changes have somewhat increased the degree of unhappiness and social tension. This is as a result of increasing awareness of the state of the country, but also, clearly, as a direct result of worsening economic crisis and falling living standards.

Recent survey research has also investigated satisfaction with various aspects of people's daily lives. The findings are displayed in Figure 2.2.

Overall, the number of Russians who were very or mostly satisfied with their lives, 57 per cent in 1991, had dropped below half (48 per cent) by the end of 1993. As many as 43 per cent were to some degree or another dissatisfied. How does this compare with other European countries? Since 1985, the biannual *Eurobarometer* surveys of European Community countries has never averaged more than one in three not very or not at all satisfied with the life they are leading.[8] Twice as many as at the most stressed time in recent history in Western Europe are therefore discontented with their life in Russia today.

Russians' greatest source of satisfaction proved to be friends and family. The majority also found their work and their status in society satisfactory. There was clearly no alienated majority at this time. However, barely half were happy about the state of their health (51 per cent) or their living conditions (53 per cent), and under half felt that their family ate well (45 per cent), that the environment was in a good condition where they lived (38 per cent) or that it was safe to walk on the streets (a tiny 25 per cent by late 1993). Only three out of every ten Russians were satisfied with the amount of individual freedom in postcommunist Russia, and only 21 per cent had a sense of confidence in the future.

Figure 2.2 Quality of life, 1991–93
'How satisfied are you at present with ___?' (per cent very or mostly satisfied)

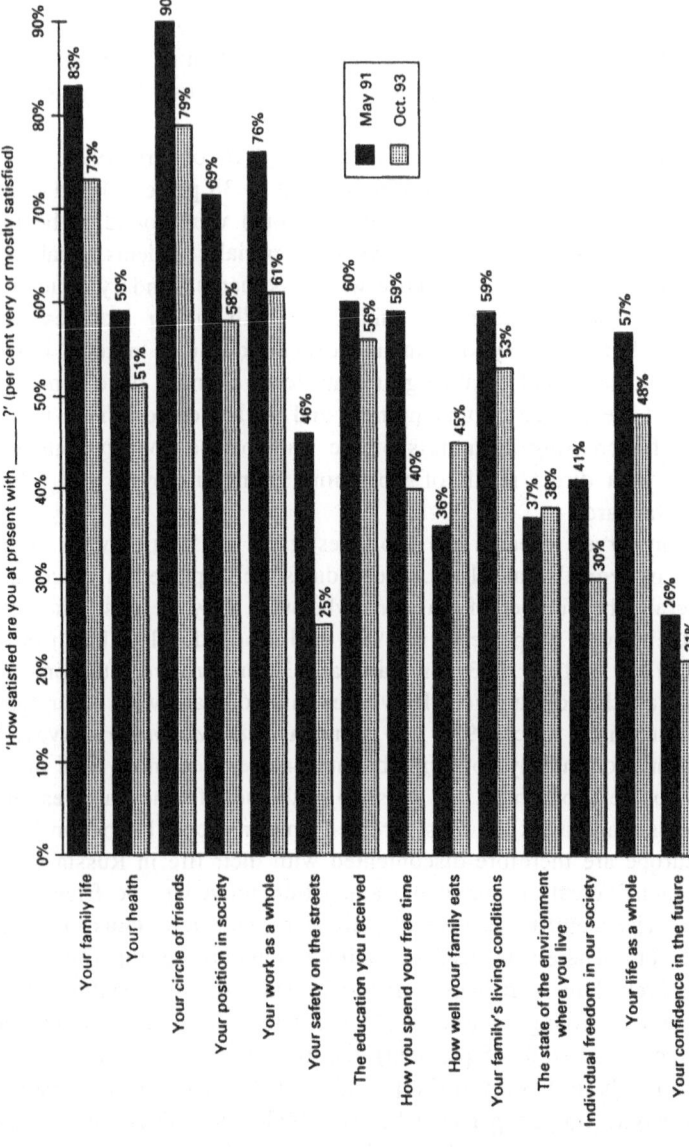

Source: Ekonomicheskie i sotsial'nye peremeny: monitoring obshchestvennogo mneniya, 3 (1994), p. 42.

The figure also gives a picture of rising dissatisfaction in most areas. Only satisfaction with how well their family ate had noticeably increased from 1991–93. This was a reflection of the way in which economic shock therapy had at least filled the shops with food. However, satisfaction with many other parts of their lives had sharply fallen. Almost one in five fewer were satisfied with their work or were happy about the way that they spent their spare time. Moves to a market economy had often required Russians to work harder or even to take a second job.

RUSSIAN STANDARDS OF LIVING

How well off, in a material sense, are Russians? Given the lack of reliable statistical data, understandable in a situation of rapid inflation and rising regional differentiation, nationally representative polls provide as good a way as any of judging the overall standard of living and changes in recent years in this area.

Let us look first at income. Background here is again provided by the 1981 and 1987 Academy of Science study. Its measure of standards of living is reported in Table 2.1.

As can be seen, while few Soviet citizens felt well off in 1987, just one in eight felt that their income was inadequate. Nearly half felt that they couldn't afford to buy clothes regularly, and just half felt

Table 2.1 Self-assessment of living standards, 1981–87

'How would you describe your standard of living?'	1981 (%)	1987 (%)
We live from wage to wage, often having to borrow	10	13
Our daily income is enough, but buying clothes is difficult	24	34
We have enough and sometimes even save, but need to borrow in order to buy luxuries (fridge, television, etc.)	40	37
We can buy most goods, but e.g. a car or a holiday is impossible	16	13
We can afford a few holidays, a car, a suite of furniture, whatever	7	3

Source: I.E. Ladygina, 'Mnenie naseleniya ob usloviyakh udovletvoreniya potrebnostei', in V.G. Britvin, S.V. Kolobanov and E.G. Meshkova (eds), *Obshchestvennoe mnenie v usloviyakh perestroiki: problemy formirovaniya i funktsionirovaniya* (Moscow: Institut sotsiologii AN SSSR, 1990), pp. 81–93.

Table 2.2 Self-assessment of living standards, 1989–90

'How would you describe your family's financial position? (Feb. 89)	(%)
We don't have enough money	18
We only have enough for the most basic necessities	16
We have enough money but no more	31
We have enough money	25
Anything is possible	10
How would you describe your family's living standard? (Oct. 89, urban)	
We live on the edge of poverty	3
We barely make ends meet	31
We have constantly to economise	52
We have enough	10
Can't say	4
How would you describe your family's living standard? (Dec. 89)	
Income is simply insufficient – we lead a hand-to-mouth existence	19
We only have enough money for basic necessities	31
We have enough but no more	38
We have enough	9
We deny ourselves nothing	2
How would you describe your family's material position? (June 1990)	
Money is barely sufficient, we live from wage to wage	20
Money is enough for the most basic necessities	47
We have enough money	23
We have enough money to buy almost anything	8
We have more than enough	1

Sources: For February, Yuri Levada (ed.), *Est' mnenie!* (Moscow: Progress, 1990), p. 45; for October, Valerii Rutgaiser *et al*. 'Otnoshenie naseleniya k ekonomicheskoi reforme', *Voprosy ekonomiki*, 4 (1990), p. 39 – survey of urban population of six republics, n = 1148; for December see Aleksandr Golov *et al.*, 'Godovoi balans dostizhenii i poter'', *Obshchestvennoe mnenie v tsifrakh*, 6 (1990); for June 1990 see *Mnenie naseleniya o tsenakh na tovary i uslugi* (Moscow: Informatsionno-izdatel'skii tsentr Goskomstat SSSR, 1991), p. 312, n = 30 000.

able to put money aside from time to time. The situation had clearly got worse over the preceding six years.

1988–90 was of course the period when Gorbachev first introduced major economic reform, for example allowing enterprises more freedom of action and some changes of ownership with the legalisation of co-operatives. The first of the new wave of surveys, begun at that time, offers a picture of how standards of living changed over the period. Some results are shown in Table 2.2. Evidently changes in the material well-being of the population were not great. Similar numbers of people thought that they barely had enough to live on or even that income was insufficient and that they were living in poverty, and similar numbers, around one in ten, felt themselves to be well off. Reforms had not yet begun to grapple with problems of price reform, and so the cost of living had not changed greatly for most people.

After the collapse of the Soviet Union, the new Russian Government of Yegor Gaidar introduced a programme of economic 'shock therapy'. Prices of many basic goods were raised, and wages for many did not keep up with inflation, if they were paid at all. The Government simply didn't pay the wages of many Russians working in the state sector.

It is not surprising therefore to discover, as is illustrated in Figure 2.3, that the number of Russians who saw themselves as being badly off appeared to have increased. The numbers who considered their family's material position to be good or very good were now somewhat smaller than during the communist period – between 5 and 8 per cent. By contrast, over four out of every ten people described themselves as poor or very poor.

However over the 1993–94 period, there has been little change in the picture. The proportions in each category – the well off, averagely off and poor have barely changed. Many people have in reality become poorer – according to official figures, by the end of 1992 37 per cent were living below the officially defined poverty line – but this has not changed the way Russians feel about their living standards.[9]

Just who are the people who have a high standard of living in the new Russia? Which social groups do they belong to? Evidence from the middle of 1994 suggests that workers in the private sector are over twice as likely to have a good or very good living standard, and that those with higher education and those living in large cities are also doing relatively well. Conversely, the old, the unskilled and rural inhabitants feel significantly worse off.[10]

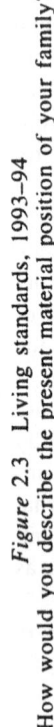

Figure 2.3 Living standards, 1993–94
How would you describe the present material position of your family?

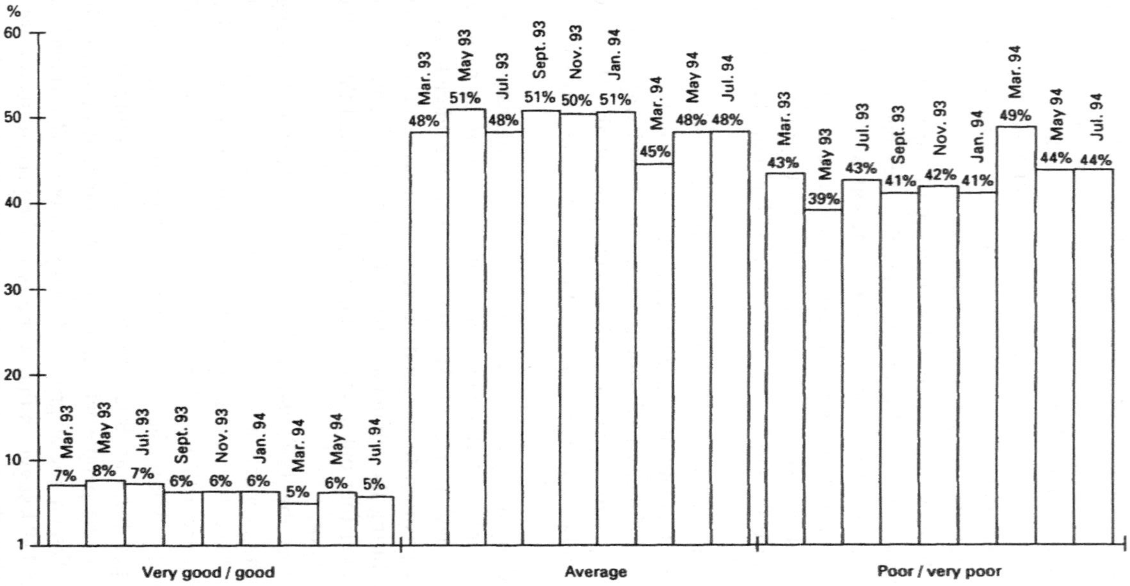

Source: Ekonomicheskie i sotsial'nye peremeny: monitoring obshchestvennogo mneniya, 5 (1994), p. 54.

Why are these the groups who are doing relatively well or badly? The answer relates to where money-making opportunities lie in the new Russia. Legalisation of private business in a predominantly monopolistic economy creates many opportunities for making large amounts of money very quickly. Those with some existing capital (in the main the old communist *nomenklatura* and those involved in black market activities before the changes) have been in a particularly advantageous position to acquire newly privatised assets at well below their real value. On the other hand, those groups dependent on the state for their income, and in particular pensioners, have suffered particularly badly as a result of the effects of rapid inflation and the Russian state's inability to find the resources to pay its employees adequately or on time. Rural inhabitants are suffering from the parlous state of Russian agriculture, where the collapse in the already inadequate investment in storage facilities and rural infrastructure has worsened an already problematic situation.

Poll data are also available on standards of nutrition. Here the state of affairs is again gloomy for many Russians. VTsIOM has carried out regular surveys on diet from the start of its operations. Thus, for example, in August and September 1989, just 18 per cent felt able to describe their diet as of sufficient quantity and high quality. Twenty-seven per cent said that the amount was enough but the quality inadequate, 9 per cent that the quality was satisfactory, but there wasn't enough, and fully 31 per cent said that their diet was deficient in both respects; 16 per cent couldn't say.[11] The same study found that, in detail, people felt that they had enough basics like bread, but not enough meat and fish (over three quarters), and insufficient fruit and vegetables (around two thirds).

The situation two years on, in August 1991, appeared broadly similar. In a poll of the urban population of nine republics, 16 per cent described their diet as good in terms of quality, variety and amount, 63 per cent as not so good, but adequate, and 16 per cent as poor in all respects.[12] In March 1993, too, surveys portray a similar picture: of Russians having in their homes enough subsistence foodstuffs such as bread and potatoes (overall 95 per cent and 91 per cent had these), but not so many having meat (70 per cent), fish (25 per cent), vegetables (61 per cent), or fruit (20 per cent).[13] However, one should perhaps not exaggerate. This is not describing a situation of famine. Newspaper reports about imminent starvation, the country not lasting the winter and so on are, to say the least, over-dramatised. The policy of allowing private plots and allotments has been an effective safety valve

Figure 2.4   Russian possessions, 1991

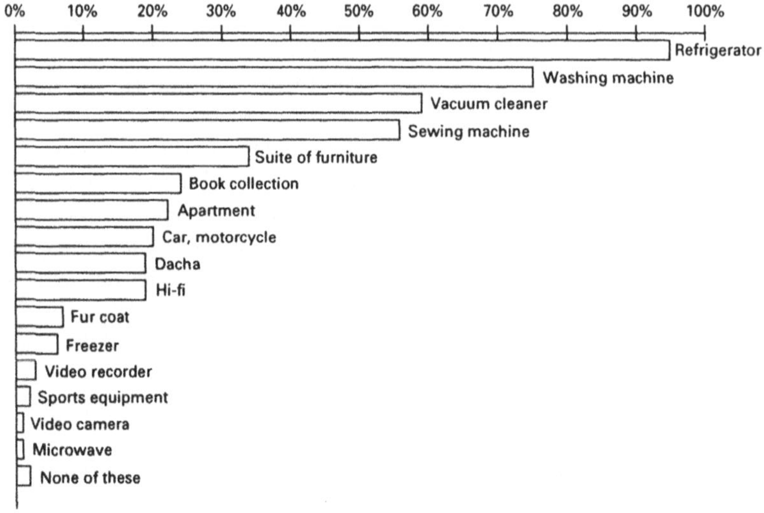

Item	%
Refrigerator	~95%
Washing machine	~75%
Vacuum cleaner	~65%
Sewing machine	~60%
Suite of furniture	~45%
Book collection	~40%
Apartment	~40%
Car, motorcycle	~35%
Dacha	~25%
Hi-fi	~25%
Fur coat	~15%
Freezer	~13%
Video recorder	~8%
Sports equipment	~7%
Video camera	~5%
Microwave	~5%
None of these	~7%

Source: Argumenty i fakty, 10 (1992), p. 2.

ensuring that many are able to produce their own food.

A similar description applies to the situation regarding possession of consumer goods. Towards the end of 1991 VTsIOM carried out a study related to ownership of various consumer goods. Figure 2.4 summarises the data. As can be seen, while many of the figures may appear on the low side to the Western observer, they are scarcely a picture of a population wholly deprived of such commodities: for example only 1 in 20 of the adult population does not own a refrigerator and three quarters have a washing machine.

THE RECENT PAST

The previous section looked at how Russians describe their standards of living. But politically what is most important is not the absolute situation. People can endure the grimmest of circumstances. It is the direction in which the country appears to be moving that often counts more. This relates to feelings about the recent past, considered in this section, and present concerns and expectations about the future, covered later.

Table 2.3 Views about change in the early 1980s

Compared to 5 years ago, would you say ——— better, the same or worse?

	Better		Same		Worse	
	1981 (%)	1987 (%)	1981 (%)	1987 (%)	1981 (%)	1987 (%)
Materially we have begun to live	68	60	25	27	7	11
We are eating	55	47	35	44	10	8
We are dressing	62	51	33	41	5	7
Our living conditions have become	52	40	32	46	15	14
Our holidays are	43	36	42	46	15	14
As a whole we are living	71	62	21	25	5	8

Source: I.E. Ladygina, 'Mnenie naseleniya ob usloviyakh udovletvoreniya potrebnostei', in V.G. Britvin, S.V. Kolobanov and E.G. Meshkova (eds), Obshchestvennoe mnenie v usloviyakh perestroiki: problemy formirovaniya i funktsionirovaniya (Moscow: Institut sotsiologii AN SSSR, 1990), pp. 81–93.

Views about the recent past can be conveniently examined in the areas of personal living standards, the general state of the country economically and politically, and changes in specific areas of social life. But first let us consider pre-*perestroika* views about the general situation. These can be seen in data from the survey by the Academy of Sciences Institute of Sociology cited previously, and shown in Table 2.3.

As we see, there is little sense of disaster evident in these responses. While quite large numbers did feel that various areas of life had not improved over the preceding five years, in every case in 1981 and four of the six categories in 1987, more felt that they had improved than stayed the same. No more than one in eight felt that these areas were getting worse, although how much this reflects self-censorship rather than honest description of reality can never be known. If one compares 1981 and 1987, one as before gets a sense of increasing stagnation. Not by a large amount, but to some degree, people were more likely to see no change in 1987. Overall assessments were, however, generally positive, with six or seven in every ten people saying that, overall, things were getting better.

Subsequent surveys present a wholly different picture. Figure 2.5 provides time series data for 1988–90 on four measures: overall personal position, income, material position of the respondent's family, and the

Figure 2.5 Views about recent change, 1988–90

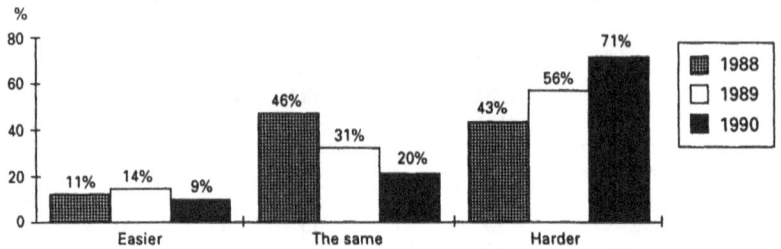

(a) How has [the current year] turned out for you in comparison with [the previous one]?

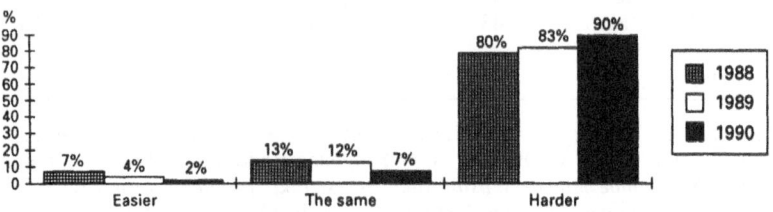

(b) And how has [the current year] turned out for our society in comparison with [the previous one]?

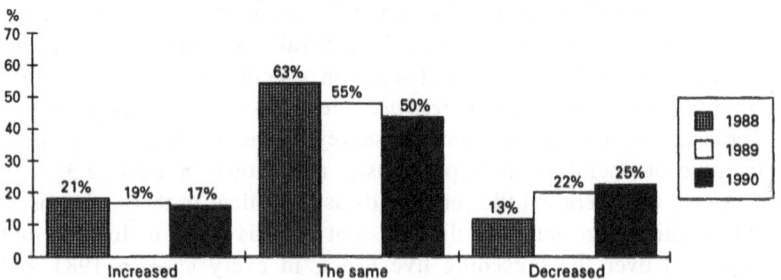

(c) How has your family's income changed in the [current year]?

Source: *Obshchestvennoe mnenie v tsifrakh*, 12 (1991). VTsIOM all-Union surveys.

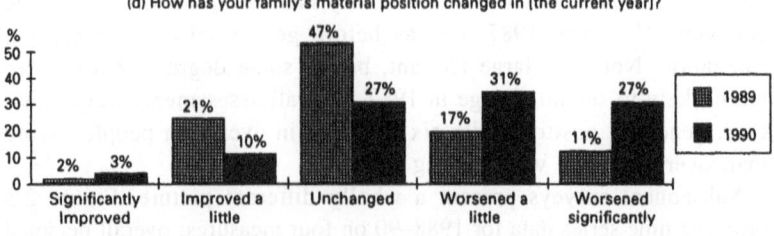

(d) How has your family's material position changed in [the current year]?

Source: *Obshchestvennoe mnenie v tsifrakh*, 10 (1991) and *Voprosy ekonomiki*, 4 (1990).

state of society over the previous year. They are from VTsIOM's annual end of year surveys. Taken together, they present a picture of a deteriorating situation over the period. Things were getting worse on all measures.

This sense among the public that matters were deteriorating was doubtless related to a combination of factors: economic decline, inflation, shortages, a growing awareness, as a result of the policy of *glasnost*, of just how grim the state of the country was, a sense among some that things were drifting out of control reflected in the secessionist movements in various parts of the country, the strikes of 1989–90, revelations about corruption among officials and so forth.

These trends in the public mood – the sense that personal living standards were declining and the national economy was out of control – are essential to understand as part of the background to the collapse of the communist system. While Gorbachev was massively popular abroad because of the changes he had made to Soviet foreign policy, the mood at home was getting worse all the time.

There are some significant features of the data beyond overall trends. It is striking how little the sense of how things had changed in the past year was related to changes in income. Even by 1990 only one in four had actually suffered a decrease in income, but 71 per cent said that the last year had been harder for them, and 90 per cent that it had been harder for the society. The final chart provides the key to the puzzle. It shows that while income had not declined for most, their material position had. The effects of inflation, which was a completely new experience for most Soviet citizens at this time, meant that real income was less even though they were being paid the same. Also, income in itself was often not the key to standard of living. In a shortage economy it was access to goods that mattered most.[14]

The demographics of these data are also interesting. Those sources that give breakdowns show that there was very little difference between any social groups in terms of their perceptions in this period on any of the four measures. Rural and urban inhabitants, men and women, those with higher or almost no education, Russians and other nationalities, all these groups appeared to have similar perceptions of what was going on, and similar experiences in terms of their own material positions.[15] The sense of growing crisis was a country-wide one.

It is also possible to look in detail at how Soviet citizens perceived changes in various areas of social life in the perestroika period. These are summarised in Table 2.4, again the result of VTsIOM end of year surveys. These give a clear sense of gains and losses over the course of the *perestroika* period, which provides a context for the more general questions of Figure 2.5.

Table 2.4 Perceptions of recent change

How have ——— changed in [the current year]?	Year	Better (%)	Same (%)	Worse (%)
Food supplies	1988	16	34	46
	1989	6	14	78
	1990	2	3	93
Supplies of manufactured goods	1988	8	27	59
	1989	3	10	83
	1990	2	3	92
The work of hospitals, pharmacies, and polyclinics	1989	5	37	40
	1990	3	23	63
The system of school education	1990	8	33	25
The work of the militsia and other law-enforcement agencies	1989	15	33	23
	1990	9	30	40
Activities of the press, radio and television	1988	86	9	2
	1989	72	13	6
	1990	56	17	13
Relations between people of various nationalities	1988	20	26	38
	1989	7	11	71
	1990	3	11	75
The possibility of earning more	1989	29	33	14
	1990	33	30	13
The influence of ordinary people on state affairs	1989	26	41	8
The personal security of the citizen	1989	5	21	59
	1990	3	13	72
The possibility of freely expressing one's opinion	1989	67	19	4
	1990	61	17	7
Fairness in the distribution of material goods	1989	7	43	28
	1990	6	31	48

Sources: Yuri Levada (ed.) *Est' mnenie!* (Moscow: Progress, 1990); *Obschestvennoe mnenie v tsifrakh*, 6 (1990) and 12 (1991).

The data show that, despite the overall feeling of things having become more difficult for society, there were important successes. In particular, large majorities felt that the activities of the media and the possibility of speaking one's mind had improved. Undoubtedly the policy of *glasnost* – telling the truth in public – had been a success for most Russians. Smaller numbers, but still around one in three, significantly more than thought the opposite, felt that it had become possible to earn more. The widening of opportunities, which was the main aim of the policies of introducing co-operatives and individual labour activity, again appears to have made a difference. Also, around one quarter said that the influence of ordinary people on state affairs had increased in 1989, whereas only 8 per cent thought that it had decreased. The policy of democratisation, reflected in the multi-candidate elections of 1989, had raised the sense among some people that they could make a difference to what happens.

Trends from 1988 to 1990 in these areas, though, show a falling number who thought that things were getting better. In the case of the media, this may be thought a combination of simply getting used to the new state of affairs and beginning to take it for granted, and also a reaction to increasing criticism of those limits on freedom of speech (for example freedom to criticise Gorbachev himself) that still remained. But overall, it seemed that there was majority satisfaction with the direction of political reforms.

However, in areas relating to the economy, rather than the way the country was governed, the opposite is true. Large numbers thought that supplies of various goods had got worse, with the amount increasing substantially over time. Soviet citizens felt that the fairness of distribution had fallen too, this perhaps reflecting a resentment of the 'excess' profits made by many of the new co-operatives. Hospitals and schools were seen to have deteriorated, although how much this reflected real change and how much simply increasing openness in the press about the true state of crisis in these areas is unclear. Personal security and inter-ethnic relations were also seen to have worsened by very large majorities. Other surveys found that this was also the way people felt about the state of the environment in the Soviet Union.[16] Therefore in many hugely important areas of people's lives – what was available in the shops, what happened when they fell ill, the state of the air they breathed – most saw only decline. And as the next section will show, these were very much the priority areas for most people. This helps explain why the general assessments of how things had changed during the *perestroika* period were so overwhelmingly gloomy despite some areas of improvement.

This mood of gloom is still more strikingly shown by a series of polls in 1991 which showed that most people would not have supported *perestroika* if they had known where it was leading. In December 1990 one third agreed and one third disagreed with this. By March 1991, after the bloodshed in the Baltic states that January, only 23 per cent would have supported the changes, while 38 per cent wouldn't, and that July, VTsIOM found that 48 per cent of Russians said that they would not have supported them if they had known the consequences.[17] This was the background to the coup of that August, and one certainly wonders if it was data like these that helped encourage the emergency committee to try to seize power.

What then of assessments by Russians of changes after the collapse of the Soviet Union? These assessments are of course in the context of the exceptionally harsh economic reforms introduced by the Yeltsin Government from January 1992. Since these reforms involved freeing prices without indexing incomes, and also permitted some degree of unemployment, it would be unsurprising if perceptions of the recent past had got gloomier still. But is this the case? Data from three survey organisations, shown in Figures 2.6 and 2.7, give us a picture.

Figure 2.6 shows how Russians feel the overall position of their family and of the country as a whole has changed in the recent past. As can be seen, the introduction of radical reforms changed the situation very little. VTsIOM had found 57 per cent in December 1990 saying that their standard of living had got worse to some degree. This remained the proportion at the end of 1991, and each of the surveys for the first half of 1992 shown in the charts finds virtually identical numbers saying the same. This suggests that perhaps commentators have overstated the effects of the Yeltsin reforms on the mass mood, and understated the effects of the disruption to people's living standards caused by the *perestroika* period. Survey data suggest very little discontinuity between these times.

It is also evident that matters were seen to be deteriorating less fast by 1993, and the numbers for whom things had begun to improve were slightly up. More Russians, then, appeared to be adapting to the changes, and beginning to feel that their lives were at least stabilising.

Figure 2.7 looks at how Russians felt that various parts of their lives had changed since the introduction of shock therapy at the start of 1992. As can be seen, very few Russians believed that matters had improved. Between one in six and one in eight felt that they had a

Figure 2.6 Changes in recent period, 1991–93

(a) Compared to 12 months ago, do you think that the financial position of your family has got a lot better, got a little better, stayed the same, got a little worse, or got a lot worse?

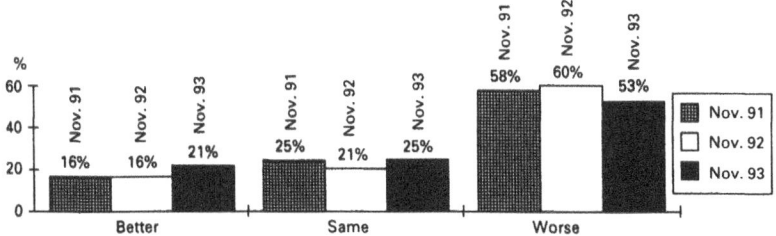

(b) Compared to 12 months ago, do you think that the economic situation in Russia has got a lot better, got a little better, stayed the same, got a little worse, or got a lot worse?

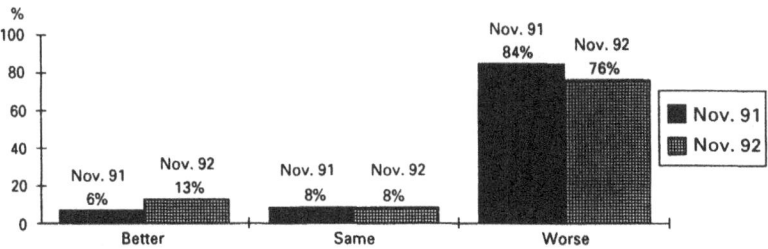

Source: *Central and Eastern Eurobarometer*, 2 (1991), 3 (1992) and 4 (1993). Surveys of European Russia by Institute of Sociology, USSR Academy of Sciences (1991) and ROMIR (1992 and 1993).

(c) How have the conditions of your life changed in the last few months?

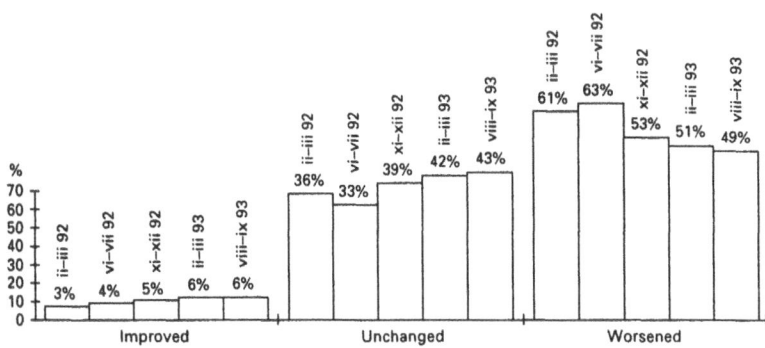

Sources: *Mir mnenii i mneniya o mire*, 9 (1992), 7 (1993) and no. 5 (1993). Polls by Vox Populi.

38 *Public Opinion in Postcommunist Russia*

Figure 2.7 Views about recent changes, 1992–93

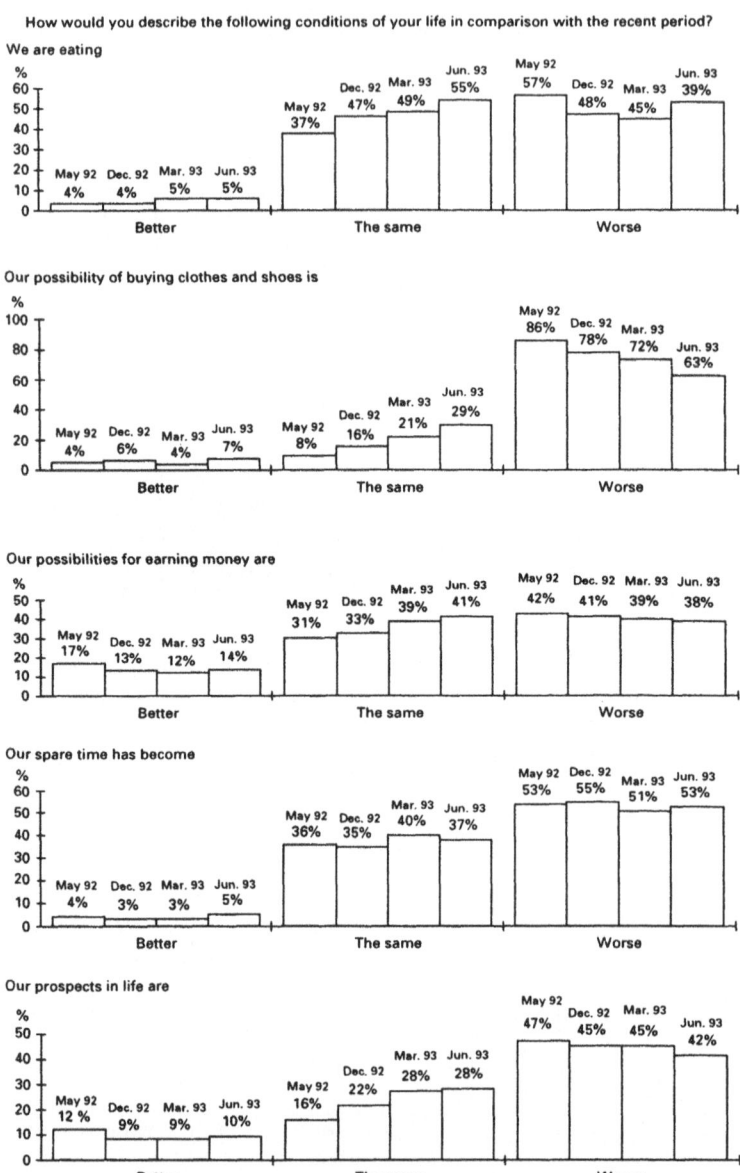

Source: Aleksandr Komozin, 'Shokovaya ekonomika: tendentsii obshchestvennogo mneniya naseleniya Rossii', *Sotsiologicheskie issledovaniya*, 11 (1993), p. 12. Surveys of Russia by Institute of Sociology, Russian Academy of Sciences.

chance to earn more money, and just one in ten that their prospects in life had improved. Just one in twenty said that their diet had improved, that they found it easier to afford clothing or that the way they spent their spare time had become more enjoyable. Much greater numbers in each case felt that matters had got worse or at best stayed the same. Again, though, as with feelings about overall standards of living, the trend appeared to be that fewer saw these matters getting worse as time passed. Russians were getting used to economic dislocation.

Which Russians were most likely to feel that matters were improving for them, and which that their living standards had got worse in the recent period? In February 1994, VTsIOM found that workers in the private sector were almost three times as likely (20 per cent compared to 7 per cent) as state sector employees to feel that their family's material position had improved in the last six months. Managers and specialists were also doing rather better than routine non-manual workers or workers themselves.[18] Supporters of the market economy might find this encouraging news since it suggests that the private sector is becoming a more lucrative place to be working, and also that skills are being more adequately rewarded than was the case with the Soviet policy of wage levelling. Managers, in particular, had often been able to take advantage of the privatisation of their enterprises to obtain ownership on favourable terms. These constitute the base for a new entrepreneurial class in Russia.

RUSSIAN CONCERNS

Now let us turn to the question of Russian priorities. What were seen as the most important problems facing individual Russians, and facing the country? How have these perceptions shifted over the period 1988–93, and what if any are the implications of these changes?

VTsIOM has carried out since 1988 regular surveys on this theme. Before 1992 they were samples from the whole Soviet Union, afterwards just Russia. Table 2.5 illustrates Russians' major concerns for the period 1988–90.

At this time, the centrality of material issues is evident. The shortage of food and consumer goods was stated as the most important problem people faced. Crime, environmental pollution, housing, health care: these were other major concerns of Soviet citizens in the *perestroika* period, as well as two problems relating to the socialist system, official privileges and corruption, and the humiliating sense of dependence on the whim of officials as the result of an over-powerful state. Almost

Table 2.5 Greatest problems for respondent's family, 1988–90

Which of these problems most complicates the daily life of you and your family?	1988 (%)	1989 (%)	1990 (%)
Poor supplies and quality of consumer goods	55	74	80
Shortages and poor quality of food	51	–	87
Low income, high prices	47	66	79
Environmental pollution	47	61	–
Widespread *blat* and unjust distribution of goods	49	51	–
Rise in crime	–	50	–
Housing shortages	35	38	–
Poor medical services	31	48	–
Depend on officials for solution of routine problems	27	38	–
Weakening of moral functions of society, widespread alcoholism, drugs, prostitution	–	38	–

Sources: *Kommunist*, no. 9 (1989); *Obshchestvennoe mnenie v tsifrakh*, no. 5 (1990); *Poisk*, no. 13 (1991). Each all-Union surveys by VTsIOM. Gaps indicate missing data in sources.

nobody talked about ideological issues such as the abandonment of socialism. By this time, the communist morality of sacrificing present prosperity for the sake of some glorious future was virtually dead. This is no surprise: moral principles are a luxury when you are short of food.

What of changes in priority after the collapse of the Soviet Union? While a number of the categories used are different, it is nevertheless possible to observe some trends. Data are shown in Figure 2.8. A noticeable feature is the extent to which shortages have ceased to be a problem: from being the most important issue for people, by June 1994 they were only named by 10 per cent, compared to 86 per cent who mentioned prices. Free pricing has helped to overcome shortage, but created a situation where few can afford the newly available goods.

Another apparent fall is in the relative position of environmental problems after 1988–89. There is no question that objectively the dire state of the natural environment in the former Soviet Union has not improved in the last few years. Large sections of the country remain an ecological disaster area. It may be that the observed fall is simply a function of the change in question wording – asking about problems for families in 1988–90 and social problems after that. While poisoned air and water are very real problems to millions of Russian families,

Figure 2.8 Greatest social problems, 1991–94

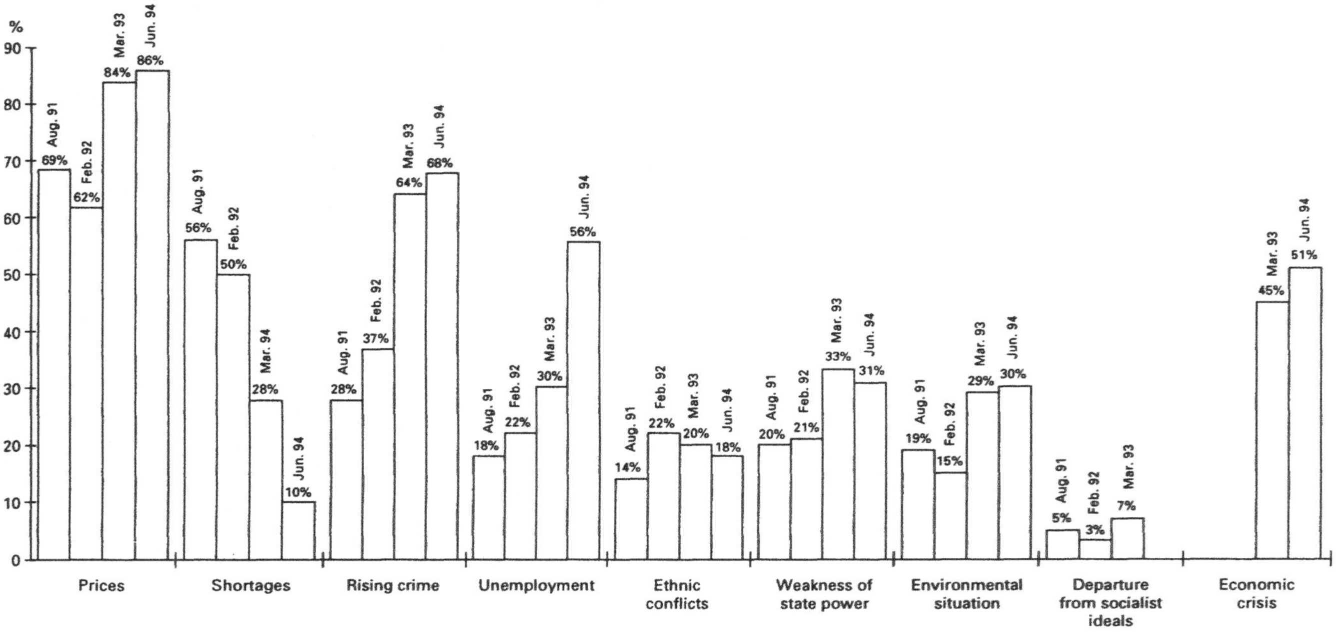

Sources: Moskovskie novosti, 38 (1991); *Nezavisimaya gazeta*, 7 March 1992; *Ekonomicheskie i sotsial'nye peremeny: monitoring obshchestvennogo mneniya*, 1 (1993), p. 54 and 5 (1994), p. 6.

people nevertheless see the most important social problem as the economic crisis, and the environmental crisis as only secondary to falling living standards.

Concern about crime has become much more prevalent over the recent period. This does reflect the real situation, with official figures showing huge rises in the numbers of serious offences, and many highly publicised murders, shoot-outs and other violent incidents. The number of homicides in a year, for example, had by 1992 risen to 22.8 per 100 000 people, three times what it had been in 1986, and comparing unfavourably with the rate of about 10 per 100 000 people in the United States.[19] There also appears to be a rising concern about 'the weakness and helplessness of state power', reflecting the increasingly evident lack of clear lines of authority and conflicts between various institutions, as well as the apparent inability to deal with problems such as crime or inflation.

Also striking is the way in which unemployment has moved from being an issue that was of major concern to few to a problem mentioned by well over half of respondents (56 per cent) by mid-1994. The economic shock therapy launched in 1992 at first did not involve major job losses as enterprises adopted moves such as putting workers on short time and there were few major bankruptcies. However, two years later, it was commonplace for workers to be on unpaid leave with little prospect of returning to their former employment, and little or no prospect of alternative work. By the end of 1993 around 5 per cent of the workforce were unemployed and another 5 per cent only partially employed.[20] Jobs were on the political agenda for the first time in recent years.

Figure 2.9 investigates which of the important social problems Russians feel the state should concentrate its efforts on solving. Material issues again stand out – over half mentioned social welfare and 44 per cent price control. However the fight against crime was as much a priority for Russians. Order and adequate living standards were vastly more important than nationalistic aspirations such as the re-establishment of the Soviet Union or the re-assertion of superpower status which have received so much attention following the electoral success of the extreme nationalist Vladimir Zhirinovsky.

What then of differences between social groups as to what is the most important problem? There is a clear gap between the sexes. Women are more likely to choose answers that refer to the specific problems faced in everyday life, men in terms of the abstract causes of these problems. The exception was the category 'moral and cultural crisis'.

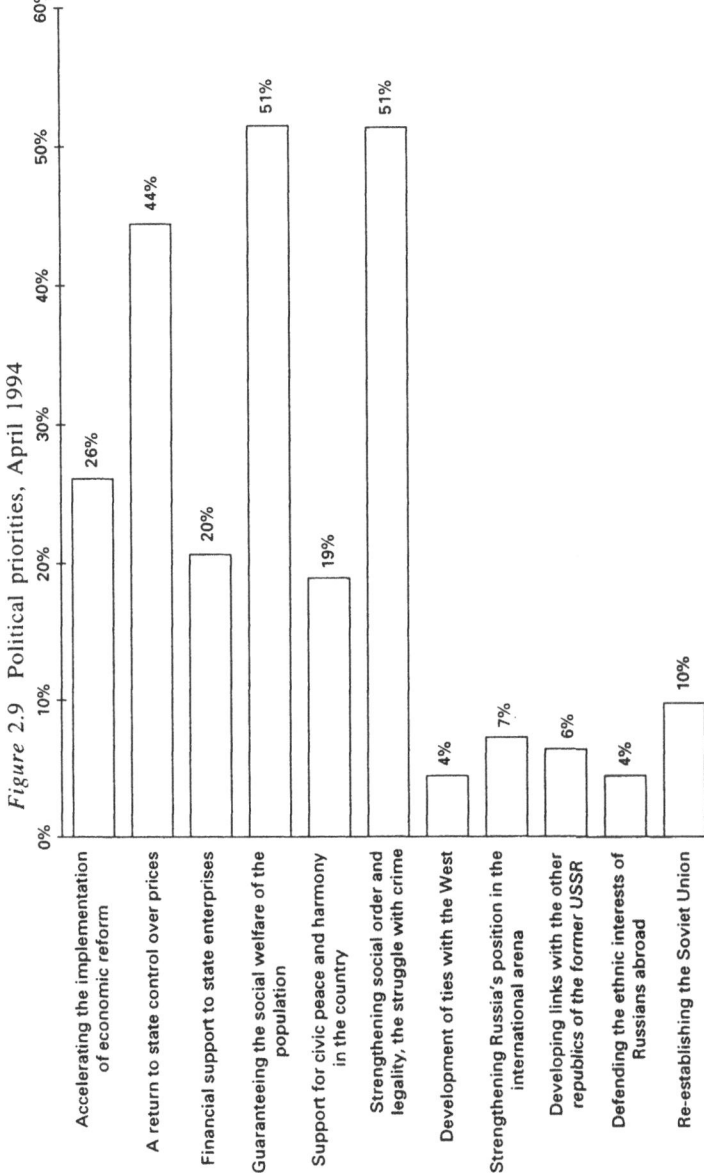

Figure 2.9 Political priorities, April 1994

Source: *Ekonomicheskie i sotsial'nye peremeny: monitoring obshchestvennogo mneniya*, 4 (1994), p. 45.

Women were much more likely to be concerned about this, reflecting a concern about the rise in alcoholism, pornography, suicide rates and other major social problems.

Age also makes a difference. Compared to the under thirties, Russians over 55 were 16 per cent more likely to mention crime as a problem, 10 per cent more likely to mention shortages, 7 per cent more likely to mention prices, and 18 per cent less likely to mention unemployment. Unemployment is more of a problem for young people, prices for the elderly.

Education, too, clearly differentiates social groups, in similar ways to gender. Those with higher education were 25 per cent more likely to mention the economic crisis, 31 per cent more likely to mention the crisis in morals and culture, and 8 per cent more likely to mention the weakness of state power, while those who hadn't completed secondary education were 16 per cent more likely to mention shortages, and 14 per cent more likely to complain about prices. A worker–intellectual gap in ways of perceiving the world, concrete versus abstract, is here evident.

THE FUTURE

Mikhail Gorbachev's accession was a cause for genuine optimism and enthusiasm in Russia. The Soviet Union's problems were only too evident to many of its citizens, and the new style and new priorities brought expectations of dramatic change for the better. So how long did this honeymoon period last? How long before optimism turned to gloom and despondency about the future? How did attitudes to the future compare with perceptions of the recent past? Were they more, equally or less positive? How did the collapse of the Soviet Union and Yeltsin's take-over of power affect expectations, and how has this changed in the course of the changes his government has introduced?

Since most people tend to link improvements with their standard of living, surveys usually approach the study of attitudes to the future by measuring views about the economic situation. Here one can again distinguish between expectations about personal position and expectations about the economy generally.

It is evident that before economic reforms had got underway people were very hopeful about future prospects. Thus, an Academy of Sciences Institute of Sociology study carried out in December 1988 found that fully 41 per cent expected their family's material position to improve 'in the near future', and only 16 per cent thought that it would deteriorate.[21] Expectations had been raised to quite a high degree.

Even by 1989 and 1990, according to VTsIOM, the number of optimists hoping for improvements was still the same as the number of pessimists, as shown in Figure 2.11. The watershed appears to have been 1991. Some time between the end of 1990 and August 1991, when the coup took place, there appears to have been a massive shift of mood among the people. Many more now expected to become worse off. The same is also true of expectations about the country's economy. While in February 1990, according to VTsIOM, just 27 per cent had expected the economy to worsen over the next year or two, and of these 24 per cent thought it would worsen only slightly, by February 1991 the number who thought it would get worse was fully 70 per cent, 43 per cent thinking that it would become substantially worse.[22]

In terms of Soviet politics, the two key events over this period were Gorbachev's rejection of the so-called 500-day plan for transition to a market economy, and the bloodshed of early 1991 in the Baltic states. These were the events that led many reformers to despair that any more good would come of the Gorbachev leadership. Opponents of change had abandoned Gorbachev long before this. The despair from both sides seems to have been reflected in public opinion.

It would hardly overstate the case to assert that we actually see here, in the numbers, a revolutionary moment in the sense meant by Tocqueville. For Tocqueville, revolutions were associated with that point in time when repressive regimes begin to reform. Change cannot satisfy the newly awakened aspirations of the people quickly enough, and as hopes turn to disappointment, people will no longer endure what previously they sullenly suffered. It was Gorbachev's failure, having raised expectations so greatly, to deliver tangible success which meant that his authority completely collapsed over this period.

What of expectations for personal prosperity after 1991? Figures 2.10 and 2.11 give an indication. As can be seen, the initial effects of the economic reforms were, unsurprisingly, to increase the number who expected things to get worse, both for themselves and for the country. Everyone knew that 'price reform' was a euphemism for price rises. However, this did not have the same political significance as in the Gorbachev period, since the Government had made it clear that their policies would make things worse before they made things better. Expectations were based more on what people were being told than on a sense of betrayal and hopelessness that efforts would be made to improve the situation.

Figure 2.10 Personal expectations, 1989–94

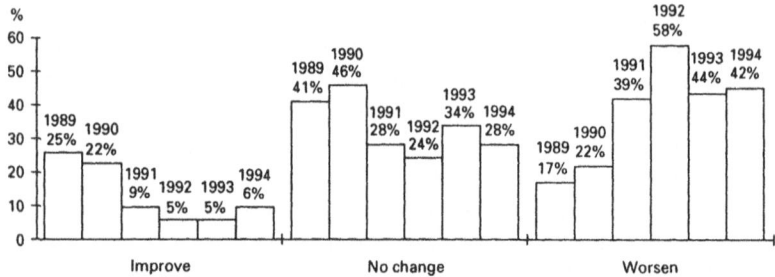

Source: Ekonomicheskie i sotsial'nye peremeny: monitoring obshchestvennogo mneniya, 1 (1993), p. 37; for August 1991 M. Krasil'nikova and T. Avdeenko, 'Potrebitel'skoe povedeniye naseleniya v krizisnykh situatsiyakh', *Voprosy ekonomiki*, 1 (1992), pp. 74–82; for June 1994 *Ekonomicheskie i sotsial'nye peremeny: monitoring obshchestvennogo mneniya*, 5 (1994), p. 56 – here the question said '6 months' not '12 months'.

Figure 2.11 Personal expectations, 1992–93

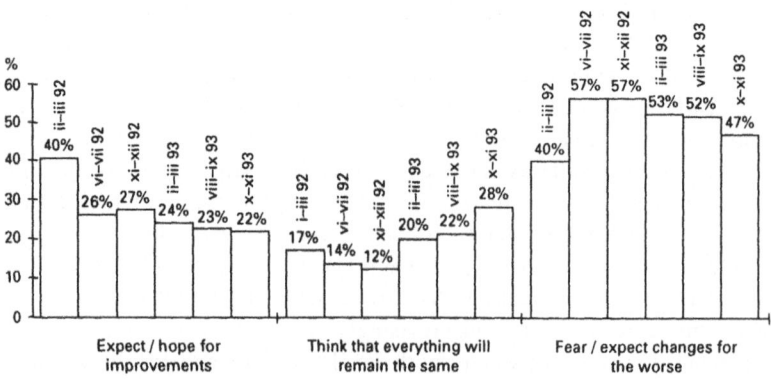

Sources: *Mir mnenii i mneniya o mire*, 9 (September 1992); 7 (57), July 1993, 5 (89), November 1993 and 3 (95) December 1993. Surveys by Vox Populi.

As was the case with assessments of changes in the recent past, it is also noticeable that the numbers expecting continuing deterioration steadily fell over the course of 1993, according to both VTsIOM and Vox Populi, whereas over 1988–91 they steadily rose. For the Russian authorities, the trend appeared to be in the right direction. In 1993 there was a slowing of inflation and some reduction in the budget deficit, which had a limited effect on public opinion. It is too early and the economic situation is too uncertain to state confidently that this trend is likely to continue, but it at least represented the first noticeable upturn in expectations since 1988.

Who were the optimists and who were the pessimists in Russia? Evidence from the *perestroika* period was that the young and the more highly educated were most likely to expect improvements in their position.[23] While in Russia one still gets the overall feeling of a crisis that will not go away, nevertheless more young people than old have confidence in the future. In this, incidentally, there was no education effect, and nor were there differences between workers in state and private sectors or various regions of the country. The poor and unskilled workers (overlapping categories) were somewhat more pessimistic, a realistic assessment of their prospects in an overmanned and collapsing economy.

How do expectations about the future relate to assessments of the past and the present? It is clear from all the survey evidence that the pattern follows a J-curve: that is things have got worse recently, but some whose standards of living have deteriorated are optimistic that they will improve in the near future. For example, while the 1993 *Eurobarometer* found 60 per cent saying that things had got worse over the previous 12 months, only 45 per cent expected them to get worse in the next year. Other surveys find similar results.[24]

Of course expectations are not made up solely of feelings about how living standards might change. We have all kinds of hopes and fears about what might happen to us. Different problems become important at different times. Russian surveys have asked people on a number of occasions to identify their greatest fears. Changes in the ranking of these, shown in Table 2.6, give a picture of how the changes of the recent period have affected the national consciousness.

Some of the Russian concerns are ancient human fears: of growing old, of losing loved ones, of illness. However, the extent to which in recent years man-made problems such as poverty, crime and unemployment have become just as central is striking.

Table 2.6 Greatest fears, 1989–94

When you think about the future, what do you fear most of all?

December 1989	March 1992	May 1994
1 Illness of those close to me	Crime	Poverty
2 War	Anarchy and civil war	Illness
3 Natural disasters	A death of someone close	Accidents affecting those close to me
4 Illness and loss of ability to work	Losing my job	Unemployment
5 Old age and helplessness	Illness in the family	Violence, crime
6	Poverty, destitution	Loneliness
7	Ethnic conflicts and pogroms	Family discord
8		Homelessness

Sources: A. Grazhdankin and B. Dubin, 'Tsennostnie orientatsii lichnosti i uroven' udovletverenosti zhizn'yu', Obshchestvennoe mnenie v tsifrakh, 3 (1990); Nezavisimaya gazeta, 26 March 1992; Ekonomicheskie i sotsial'nye peremeny: monitoring obshchestvennogo mneniya, 4 (1994), p. 60.

RUSSIANS' SPARE TIME

How do Russians spend the time when they are not working? What are their habits, what do they enjoy? This question has been investigated by presenting people with a list of common activities and asking how frequently they take part in them. The results are shown in Table 2.7.

The three most frequent activities among Russians of both sexes in 1994 were watching television, listening to the radio and visiting food shops. There had been considerable changes since 1990. Much less time was spent reading newspapers – in part a reflection of their rising cost, in part falling consumption of information in the postcommunist period. Russians also had to spend less time food shopping, but this was partly compensated for by the extra time that it was necessary to spend growing food, reflecting the situation where the shops were now full, but the prices too high. Both sexes also spent a lot less time shopping in general and in reading the 'thick journals' that had played such an important role in pushing back the boundaries of glasnost under Gorbachev.

Who did what? Men were in 1994 over three times as likely to have made something for the house or gone to watch a sporting event, and actually took part in sport or played games like chess or cards a lot more often. Women did half as much shopping again as men, spent

Table 2.7 Spare time activities, 1990 and 1994

Activity	Average number of days per year in which respondent does activity			
	Men		Women	
	1990	1994	1990	1994
Watch television	220	223	224	225
Listen to the radio	183	188	213	185
Visit food shops	146	112	209	169
Look after children	107	84	132	132
Visit garden or allotment	71	96	82	108
Read newspapers	200	109	167	95
Read books	65	88	62	75
Listen to records or tapes	78	73	64	75
Visit consumer goods shops	61	37	108	60
Have sex	*	33	*	36
Go out with friends	78	58	44	59
Have guests, visit friends	35	29	42	38
Knit, sew	3	4	42	38
Make something for the house	41	40	10	12
Take part in sport	40	37	18	23
Improve your professional qualifications	28	24	17	17
Read journals	81	22	75	19
Play cards, chess, etc.	36	27	18	14
Visit sporting venues	5	11	2	4
Play a musical instrument	19	6	4	9
Go to the cinema	17	6	18	5
Frequent bars and discos	10	5	4	5
Take photographs, paint or draw	5	2	2	2
Go to theatre or concerts	3	2	2	2
Go hiking	6	3	3	3
Visit restaurants	2	2	2	2
Attend political meetings	3	0.3	1	1

Note: * indicates category was not included in 1990.
Source: Ekonomicheskie i sotsial'nye peremeny: monitoring obshchestvennogo mneniya, 5 (1994), p. 29; Elena Dzhaginova, 'Povcednevnaya zhizn' Rossii: 1990–1994 godu', Segodnya, 15 September 1994, p. 6. The question read 'How often do you ———?' and possible answers were daily/almost every day; two or three times a week; once a week; one to three times a month; more rarely; never. The average number of days was calculated from this.

more time looking after children, and knitted or sewed on 12 times more days than men. Unmarried men did a lot less shopping: they normally lived with their parents. Unmarried women, by contrast, went shopping for consumer goods five times as much as the average Russian. They were the nation's 'window shoppers'. Young women under 30 were the main readers of literature. Young men listened to music the most often. Young people in general had the most fun – going out with friends, playing music, visiting the cinema, discos and bars a lot more often, and playing sport or having sex on average once per week. The middle aged, as we might expect, spent more time with children or doing things around the house. Older people, it seems, were very rarely able to go out, and only rarely invited guests to their homes.

Which activities did Russians most enjoy? The 1990 study asked just this. Table 2.8 shows the results.

While watching television was by far the most common spare time activity, it was far from being the most popular. Only around one in five Russians named it as one of their two or three favourite ways of spending their spare time. Family and home life seem to have been much more enjoyable. Earning money or getting job satisfaction appear well down the list. Very few people had as a priority any kind of social activities. 'Doing good works' was mentioned by just one in five, and political activities by almost nobody. It is true that most studies in most countries find that people place a greater importance on family life and health than work or public activity,[25] but this is so to an unusual degree here. A regime that 'encouraged' voluntary public service seems to have put many off the idea.

CONCLUSIONS

Is it possible to generalise about the mood of the Russian people over the recent period? The data cited certainly give a picture of change. In 1988, Russians were quite optimistic. Many expected things to improve in the near future, although their assessment of the recent past was less favourable. However, this mood did not last through 1989. The events of that year: strikes, the collapse of communism in Eastern Europe and the growth of independence movements in the Baltic states, bungled economic change, revelations about party corruption and nepotism, the humiliation of official candidates in the elections of that year, ever wider awareness of the environmental devastation, the collapsing health service and the horrors of Soviet history, all these com-

Table 2.8　Greatest pleasures, 1990

Which two or three activities give you the most joy and satisfaction?	%
Spending time with children	53
Reading interesting books and journals	40
Making things, doing work around the home	24
Working in the garden	23
Spending time with my husband / wife	22
Listening to music	22
Cooking good food	22
Travelling	21
Earning decent money	20
Working effectively	20
Strolling in the woods	19
Watching television	19
Eating good food	16
Studying and learning new things	12
Going fishing or hunting	11
Making love	10
Being on my own	10
Spending time with animals	10
Sport	9
Drinking in good company	9
Entertaining guests	8
Supporting my team	6
Doing good works	5
Doing nothing	1

Source: A. Grazdankin and B. Dubin, 'Tsennostnie orientatsii lichnosti i uroven' udovletverenosti zhizn'yu', *Obshchestvennoe mnenie v tsifrakh*, 3 (1990).

bined to create a change of mood. The number who thought things had got worse rose, the number who expected them to get better fell.

However, even as late as 1990, expectations were not overwhelmingly negative, and it appears that it was not until 1991 that more people thought things would get worse than thought they would get better. This gloom provides the backdrop for the final collapse of communism that year.

After the end of the Soviet Union, the mood initially became if anything grimmer. And it is only from this very low base that expectations appeared to begin to improve by 1993.

What are the implications of the sense of gloom about past, present and future for post-Soviet politics? They are in a way a source of both weakness and strength. Weakness in that governments lack enthusiastic support: one thinks of Western research showing that the best predictor of electoral success for regimes of any political persuasion is a sense of well-being and confidence in the future.[26] In parts of the former Soviet Union one could imagine a downward spiral where no government would be able to retain authority for long enough to change anything.

On the other hand, pessimism is a source of strength for reformers. If things are bound to get worse before they get better, then reformers have the opportunity to take the kind of measures that are necessary for economic transformation. The question is, how long can the public mood of endurance last?

Whatever the case, a dominant mood that things have got worse recently and are likely to continue to do so is the context in which one ought to understand attitudes to political institutions, the concern of the next two chapters.

3 Public Opinion and Soviet Political Institutions

The extent of legitimacy of the communist system in the Soviet Union has been much debated by experts, a debate which is likely to continue, since there is no way of going back and measuring it. The following is perhaps widely accepted. Whatever we are now told by violent anti-communists, there were many sincere believers in the system, who genuinely thought that society was on the road to communism. After the campaign of de-Stalinisation and the revelations about atrocities that took place after Stalin's death, levels of idealism were hardly to return to the levels of the 1920s, but it never completely died out. Such a belief was based on some undoubted achievements. While the extent and nature of the industrialisation achieved in the Soviet period is now under question, certainly the victories in the Second World War and in the space race through the launching of the first Sputnik, and the achievement of superpower status were considerable sources of Soviet pride.

However, there were also clearly a number of Soviet citizens who were actively opposed to the system. After Khrushchev ended mass terror, this opposition became increasingly visible with the rise of the dissident movement. This was not just an intellectual phenomenon. Nationalist movements and attempts to form free trade unions had somewhat deeper social roots.

Nevertheless, by far the largest group in Soviet society were those who had no publicly expressed attitudes at all about the system. It was simply not worth it for the majority. To speak against the official line might jeopardise one's job prospects, one's chances of better accommodation, the educational opportunities of one's children. It was far easier to mouth the official slogans, attend the 'political education' meetings, do one's civic duties by voting, participating in workplace commissions, citizens' courts, the Komsomol and the May Day celebrations. For the regime, by the Brezhnev era such outward compliance was enough. Gone were the days when it was a matter of heart and mind, when voters were expected to turn up at polling stations at 6 a.m., hours before they opened on election day, in order to demonstrate their enthusiasm for the single, imposed, candidate. The implicit deal was that people would be left free to pursue their own material interests, as long as they refrained from criticising the political status quo.[1]

Under Gorbachev, matters were transformed. Expressing one's views about the system lost its danger. Previously hidden critics could now speak freely, a change that was symbolised above all by the return of Andrei Sakharov from internal exile in Gor'kii in December 1986, and, later, Gorbachev's invitation to Sakharov to make the opening speech at the newly formed Congress of People's Deputies in mid-1989.

What was the effect of these changes on the legitimacy of the communist political system? Did they raise its prestige among the Soviet people, or did they fatally undermine it? How and when did public opinion about political institutions shift over once genuine political reform had begun at the end of 1988? These are the major concerns of this chapter.

When Gorbachev became General Secretary, decision-making power in the Soviet Union lay in the hands of a gigantic party–state apparatus which over the years, for a variety of reasons – some structural and some to do with the character of Brezhnev's rule – had become increasingly old, corrupt and unresponsive to the wishes of the leadership. Initially the new leader, like many communist reformers before him, saw the way to reform this as being a return to the principles of Lenin, 'that inexhaustible source of creative inspiration', as he described him in his book, *Perestroika*.[2] This basically meant three things. First, improved cadre policy: everything could be put right with the system of governing if only the right people were in the right jobs. Second, a discipline campaign: constant exhortations to the people to work harder, drink less and be more honest. Third, improved standards of honesty and decency in public life. The policy of *glasnost* can appropriately be described as 'no unnecessary lying'.

How did the public respond to these changes?[3] Unfortunately we have no survey data on Gorbachev's overall popularity before he actually began to change the institutional system, as survey organisations were reluctant before this time to ask such directly political questions. However, the earliest survey that was made public, in Spring 1989, gave him a 94 per cent approval rating.[4] Data from 1988 suggest further that Gorbachev's analysis of what was wrong with the way the Soviet Union was being run was broadly accepted by a majority. Thus VTsIOM, in their first all-Union survey, asked people what they thought had caused the country's present difficulties. The results are slightly distorted by the fact that, rather than being asked the extent to which they felt that the cause in question had contributed to the difficulties, they were

Table 3.1 Views about causes of Soviet social problems, 1988–89

What, in your opinion, is the cause of the country's present problems?	1988 (%)	1989 (%)
Corruption, alcoholism, speculation and theft	57	58
Technical backwardness	42	43
Dominance by bureaucrats	41	39
Lack of desire to work	28	27
Poorly qualified specialists	26	24
Mistakes by the country's leadership	24	31
Levelling, holding back of people with initiative	23	20
Incompetence among the leadership	19	18
Loss of faith in the ideals of socialism	16	18
Materialism, consumption	14	na
Consequences of Stalinism	13	14
Destruction of morals	13	16
Destruction of national traditions	11	15
Disregard for our own history	8	na
Loss of religious faith	7	10
Secret enemies	6	9
Degeneracy of the people	3	6
Policies of imperialist countries	2	2
Mafia, organised crime	na	36
One-party system	na	20
Lack of attention to problems of federalism and ethnic autonomy	na	13

Source: Yuri Levada et al., Est' mnenie! (Moscow: Politizdat, 1991), p. 281.

presented with a list and allowed to choose more than one answer from it. Nevertheless, the relative importance of various factors can be judged from the data. Results are shown in Table 3.1. For comparative purposes 1989 results are also shown.

As can be seen, few people identified the system itself as the cause of the problems (although one could make a plausible case that a factor such as corruption was itself systemic). The most popular answers were technological backwardness, over-bureaucratisation and corruption. The extent to which reported public opinion at this time still reflected what the leadership was saying is striking.

That this state of affairs altered was very much linked to the next stage in Gorbachev's thinking about how to reform the existing system of political institutions. It had become by 1988 increasingly evident that the bulk of the party–state apparatus was incapable of reforming itself and acting in the way its reform-minded leaders wanted. Party bosses preserved 'command-administrative' methods of running their fiefdoms instead of allowing scope for individual initiative. The solution was presented in Gorbachev's speech to the special nineteenth Party Conference in the summer of 1988, in which he outlined a plan for reorganising the party, separating the functions of the party and state apparatus, revitalising the structure of soviets, and introducing a system of competitive elections at all levels. This resulted in the predominantly multi-candidate elections of March–May 1989, and the formation of a new Parliament, the Congress of People's Deputies, which held its first session that summer. The initial popularity of this measure is demonstrated in Figure 3.1, which presents data from one of the first polls to explore attitudes to the political system as such, a VTsIOM study throughout the Soviet Union from that summer.

As can be seen, according to these data state structures – the soviets at all levels and the trade unions – were substantially the most popular institutions of those asked about. This was particularly the case in relation to the emerging challengers to communist rule, the popular fronts and non-political informal groups. What is striking about the various kinds of informal groups, even by the summer of 1989, is the high level of 'don't know' responses among respondents. Despite the political successes of the Sajudis nationalist movement in Lithuania and its equivalents in the other Baltic states, and despite the challenge to Party rule represented by the coal miners' strikes of that period, many people had not yet become aware of the existence of these new formations. It is also notable that the number who felt that informal groups should have more power (19 per cent) is somewhat less than the 24 per cent who felt that they should have less or none. It is possible that this reflected the bad press being given at the time to certain categories of informal group, such as youth *neformaly*, but it is more likely that it reflected a sense that groups that attacked the policies of the leadership were unacceptable rather than normal, which is a reflection of the lack of historical experience of such criticism.

Figure 3.1 also reveals a sense of overall acceptance of the CPSU at this time. Almost twice as many people said that the Central Committee and local Party leaders should be given more power than said that the power of these institutions should be reduced. This was so despite the fact that the Party remained the political institution very much first among equals. The answer, as Gorbachev was arguing, was for the Party to play the political role that Lenin had conceived for it.

However, even as early as mid-1989, the data give one a sense that the Communist Party, both centrally and locally, had become some-

Figure 3.1 Views about political institutions, summer 1989

Which organisations, in your opinion, should have more influence than now on political life and the taking of important decisions, which the same level, which less, and which should be totally deprived of influence?

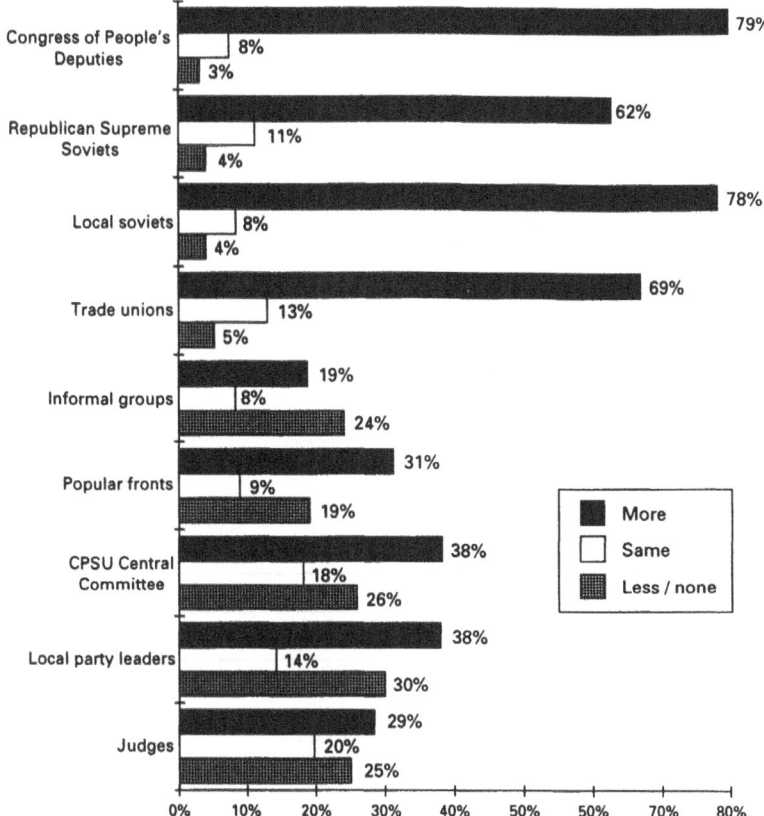

Source: *Obshchestvennoe mnenie v tsifrakh*, 1 (1989). VTsIOM survey, n = 1609. Don't knows included but not reported.

what unpopular in relation to state institutions. More than twice as many thought that the power of the new Parliament should be increased as thought Party organs at any level should have more power. The same survey illustrated the point still more starkly by asking directly about trust in the CPSU, as shown in Figure 3.2.

Here, by the middle of 1989, around one third of the Soviet citizens were saying that the CPSU had no trust among the people, and as

Figure 3.2 Trust in political institutions, summer 1989

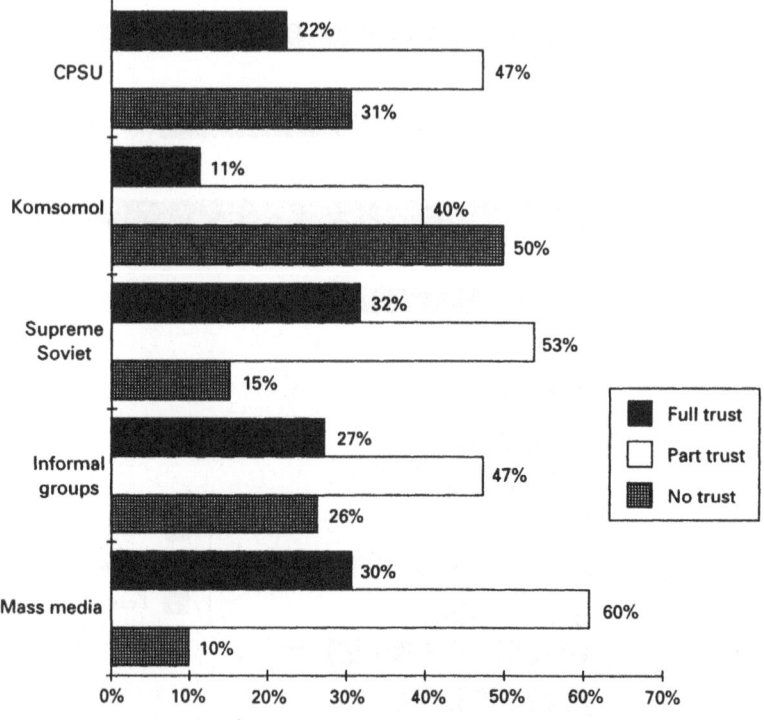

Source: Obshchestvennoe mnenie v tsifrakh, 1 (1989). VTsIOM survey, n = 1609. Don't knows excluded.

many as half thought the same of its youth wing, the Komsomol. Unquestionably the new, popularly elected institutions and the *glasnost*-influenced mass media were very much more popular than Party institutions. Again there was some ambivalence about informal groups, but unlike Party institutions, more people felt they were fully trustworthy than thought that they had no trust at all.

The sense of popular unease with ruling institutions was further illustrated by questions about the political system which were asked in the same survey. Particularly striking were the responses to questions about the Soviet Union's ruling classes. One forced-choice question was phrased thus: 'For many decades we have said that the people who are in power are servants of the people, fulfilling their wills and desires. In the light of *glasnost*, many doubts and objections have been raised about the truthfulness of this assertion. Which of the following fits your point of view most closely?' Only 14 per cent chose as their response the statement 'Our organs of power are of the people – they have the same interest as us'; 45 per cent felt that 'People we elect to positions of power quickly forget about our concerns and do not consider the interests of the people in their work'; 31 per cent chose the even more disillusioned view that 'The leadership is a special group of people, an elite who live only for their own interests; they are not concerned about us.' The remainder had no opinion.

So, at the very time when the new Parliament, the Congress of People's Deputies, was assembling for the first time in an atmosphere of widespread public interest, there existed a substantial reserve of hostility against the Soviet leadership as a whole. Boris Yeltsin had skilfully exploited this in his successful campaign for election to National-Territorial District Number One, the constituency representing the whole of Moscow, in the March 1989 elections. A constant campaign theme for Yeltsin was the issue of unjust official privileges.

Public opinion, then, approved strongly of Gorbachev's revitalisation of state institutions, but was far from being a stable situation. As with so many reforming leaders, Gorbachev faced the problem of rising expectations that went far beyond his conception of the desirable shape of the institutional system in the Soviet Union, and indeed beyond his ability to control.[5] This is well illustrated by looking at the way in which the popularity of a range of institutions changed after the middle of 1989.

THE COMMUNIST PARTY OF THE SOVIET UNION

Let us take the Party first. In Gorbachev's conception of the reformed political system the CPSU would retain its constitutional leading role. By virtue of the fact that it had introduced *perestroika*, and through the quality of its political leadership it would justify its position. However, the events of 1989 undermined these claims. Defeat for a number of Party leaders in the elections was a great shock and led to widespread public criticism of the political reforms from conservative forces. Meanwhile the Party came in for ever greater criticism in the radical press and from prominent liberals in the Congress, notably Yeltsin and Andrei Sakharov, both for its historical role under Stalin and Brezhnev, and for its current state. There were public scandals about the abuse of privileges by many senior CPSU figures. Striking coal miners called for an end to the Party's constitutional leading role – this from the very workers in whose name the Party was supposed to be ruling. On the ideological front, the collapse of communism in Eastern Europe helped undermine the theoretical base for the Party's power. By the end of that year it seemed to many to be irreparably split and incapable of reforming itself in the ways that Gorbachev had hoped.

Detailed information about how public opinion responded to the ongoing challenges to the CPSU's role can be obtained from a series of VTsIOM surveys from the end of 1989 and the start of 1990. In an all-Union poll from December 1989 they asked their sample what had been the main cause of the defeat of a number of important party and soviet leaders in the elections of March–May of that year.[6] The largest proportion (39 per cent) said that the people had already opposed the leaders before the election, which had only allowed the popular mood to be revealed. Twenty-eight per cent chose the slightly less damning condemnation that 'Candidates from the Party and soviet leadership were not prepared for the activity displayed by the population or prepared for new forms of electoral struggle'. Twenty-five per cent didn't know, leaving 6 per cent who blamed the opposition by speaking of 'the smart propaganda campaign and sharp criticism from supporters of the other "informal" candidates', and 5 per cent who praised the opposition by selecting the option 'effective agitation by groups of supporters of the informal candidates guaranteed them a majority and victory'. The numbers give a sense of just how profoundly unresponsive to the people the Party was seen as being at that time.

A February 1990 VTsIOM poll illustrates a number of other aspects of this process.[7] As mentioned above, the Party was seen as being profoundly split. Indeed it was, between the liberal forces who were at that time forming the so-called Democratic Platform and calling on the Party to admit its historical mistakes and completely change its nature, and conservatives in favour of the status quo. Thus, when asked to describe the current state of the Party, only 11 per cent selected the position that 'the Party retains its ideological and organisational unity', while 40 per cent thought that 'there are ideological and political splits in the Party' and a massive 34 per cent that 'the Party has exhausted itself and its collapse is threatened'.

Public opinion also felt that the Party was not acting as an effective governing institution. Thus, asked again to select from a pre-prepared list, only 25 per cent chose answers favourable to the CPSU – 11 per

Table 3.2 Attitudes to the Communist Party, February 1990

Do you agree that ———	Fully (%)	Partly (%)	No (%)	Can't Say (%)
Without the CPSU our country wouldn't be a great power?	26	37	26	12
The Party is a genuine association of the forces of our society?	21	37	34	8
The Party's mistakes have braked the country's development?	58	32	6	5
The Party has all the time led the country down the wrong road?	18	43	32	7
The Party should be dissolved?	21	na	52	27
Do you think that Article 6 is necessary?	24	na	57	20

Source: *Obshchestvennoe mnenie v tsifrakh*, 10 (1990). N = 2150.

cent that it was 'leading the country on the road to democratic transformation', 9 per cent that it 'supports the initiative of democratic social strata' and 14 per cent the Gorbachevian position that it 'balances the extreme positions of conservatives and radicals.' The option, 'the Party is braking the process of democratic transformation', was chosen by 14 per cent and by far the largest group, 49 per cent, chose 'the Party has lost the initiative and is allowing events to get out of control.'

One should not overstate the case though. What is also clear is that at this time only a small proportion of the Soviet population was prepared publicly to admit that it had dismissed the whole experiment with communism. This is shown in another battery of questions from the same survey, shown in Table 3.2.

What stands out from these data is that although a substantial majority of 58 per cent fully agreed, and 90 per cent fully or partly agreed, that the Party had made mistakes, only 18 per cent were prepared to say categorically that it had led the country down the wrong road, while 32 per cent disagreed with this, and 26 per cent fully and 63 per cent fully or partly credited the CPSU with making the Soviet Union a great power. Evident too is the groundswell of public opinion against Article 6 of the Constitution, which outlined the leading and guiding role of the Party in the Soviet political system, only a few months after Andrei Sakharov had organised the first demonstration against it in Moscow. Under one in four of the population agreed that Article 6 was needed.

Surveys from later on in 1990 reinforce the view that although the Party at that time was seen as a corrupt and reactionary body, and people thought that it would be a good thing if it faced political competition, nevertheless there were good things about the Soviet period too. Thus a survey during May and June 1990 by the Institute of Marxism-Leninism and the Academy of Social Sciences (plausible in that it is consistent with information from elsewhere, and the given sampling data are consistent with census figures) found that 52 per cent described the October Revolution as a 'natural stage in the country's development', compared to 22 per cent who felt that it was 'an inescapable accident' and 23 per cent a historical mistake. The same survey, asking about the attempt to put socialism into practice, found 5 per cent taking a determinist line, that at the time of the October Revolution there were no alternative paths of historical development, compared with 11 per cent who chose the option that the chosen path was correct, but there could have been more favourable variants, and the choice by 59 per cent that the idea of socialism was correct but impossible to put into practice. Only 24 per cent felt that the path chosen at that time was incorrect.[8] The proportions of people who had written off the whole Soviet period were pretty much the same as in the VTsIOM poll discussed above, where 28 per cent disagreed that the Bolshevik seizure of power was historically necessary, and only 32 per cent thought that it would have been possible to achieve the progressive Bolshevik goals without revolution.[9]

In detail, the study attempted to investigate popular attitudes to various periods in Soviet history. Table 3.3 shows the results.

What we see then is a feeling that the Party had outlived its usefulness, not a sense that the revolution should never have taken place and had failed to achieve anything useful. This was a feeling that led to the abandonment of Article 6 in early 1990 and the adoption of the new Law on Associations later that year which made it possible to form opposition parties. How then did the Party fare in the public mind after this time? Figure 3.3 illustrates the process through 1990 and 1991, until after the failed coup of August that year.

These are striking data. As can be seen, what popularity it had, and apparently even gained after abolition of Article 6, drained away in the course of that year as the people were treated to a succession of Central Committee plenums and congresses, both of the CPSU and the new Russian Republic Communist Party which were dominated by hardliners opposed to everything that *perestroika* had stood for. By July 1991 only 16 per cent of people either fully or partly trusted it according to VTsIOM. Asked in that survey whose interests they thought it represented, 67 per cent said 'only the party–state apparatus', and

Table 3.3 Attitudes to Soviet history, 1990

What is your attitude to the following events in the history of Soviet society?	This was necessary (%)	This was not necessary (%)	Can't say (%)
The establishment of a dictatorship of the proletariat	44	29	22
The dissolution of the Constituent Assembly	17	36	40
The execution of Nicholas II and his family	8	72	16
The introduction of NEP	65	9	20
Carrying out collectivisation	16	60	20
Carrying out industrialisation	59	13	22
The conclusion of a treaty with Germany in 1939	28	36	32
The mass repressions of the 1930s–50s	2	81	12

Source: 'Vashe otnosheniya k istorii', *Informatsionnii byulleten'*, *tsentr sotsiologicheskikh issledovanii Akademii Obshchestvennykh Nauk pri TsK KPSS*, 1 (1991), p. 99. N = 2000.

Figure 3.3 Trust in the CPSU, 1989–92

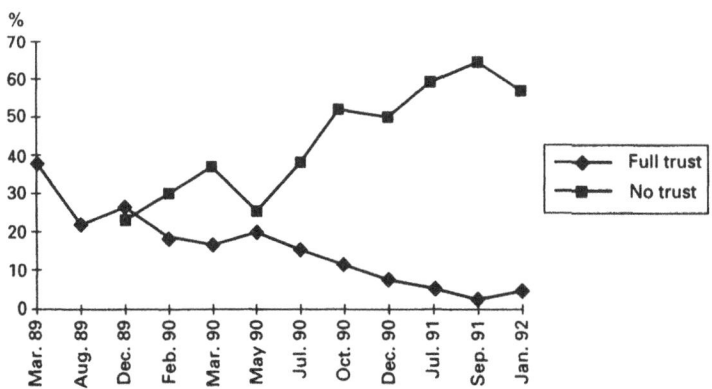

Sources: *Izvestiya*, 29 November 1990 and 1 October 1991, *Obshchestvennoe mnenie v tsifrakh*, 1 (1989), 7 (1990), 8 (1990), 9 (1990), *Moskovskie novosti*, 27 (1990), *Nezavisimaya gazeta*, 24 January 1991. Each all-Union polls, except for January 1992, which is of Russia only.

just 12 per cent 'the workers'. Similarly, only 8 per cent felt that it represented 'progressive social forces' compared to the 49 per cent who said that it was a vehicle for conservative ones.[10] After the coup in September 1991, only 2 per cent said that they fully trusted it.

What was the demographic basis for support in the Party? A survey in 17 regions of the Soviet Union in June 1990 found that people who 'believed the Party expressed their interests and hoped that its activity could end the country's crisis' were significantly more likely to be male, older than average, with higher incomes, living in rural areas and to have subordinates where they worked.[11] A Vox Populi poll the following month, again all-Union, asked the question 'Do you agree that the CPSU is the only political force which is able to lead the country over the next decade?' Overall 20 per cent fully agreed with the proposition, but among the over sixties, it was 34 per cent, 31 per cent among those with education of seven classes and below, and 33 per cent among unskilled workers.[12] The wealthy were those who had benefited from the existing system. Many of the older generation had devoted their lives to work on the communist project, and were understandably reluctant to abandon it and thus acknowledge that their lives had been in that sense wasted. Rural inhabitants had no wish to change the way they had worked all their lives, as reformers told them they should. Many managers owed their positions to Party patronage; and unskilled workers had benefited most from egalitarian wage policies in the 1970s and had much to lose from systemic change.

Let us move on to public opinion about the Communist Party in the period between the coup of August 1991 and the collapse of the Soviet Union. Clearly the facts that the CPSU had failed to condemn the attempt to seize power by the Emergency Committee, and that several leading figures had been prominent in the attempt further discredited it, creating conditions where Boris Yeltsin was able to issue his decree banning its activities as unconstitutional. A VTsIOM poll in 13 Russian cities in November 1991 found 61 per cent of their respondents supporting Yeltsin's ban on its activities.[13] The organisation, Mnenie, in two all-Russian surveys found that 47 per cent and 46 per cent of respondents respectively in September 1991 and March 1992 agreed that it should be banned, while 35 per cent and 32 per cent thought it should not.[14]

STATE INSTITUTIONS

Before *perestroika* it would have been pointless to investigate views about state structures separately from views about the Party. The two were inseparably intertwined, in such a way that it became normal to speak about the Soviet party–state. Memberships overlapped; the typical political career would involve periods in both party and state offices; and through the *nomenklatura* system the Party controlled appointments both to state institutions and Party committees, in particular the Central Committee apparatus, which oversaw the day-to-day operations of the Government. The Supreme Soviet was a rubber-stamp body which rarely met and when it did only endorsed decisions made elsewhere.

Gorbachev's reform proposals involved the separation of party from state. This involved the creation of a new two-tier Parliament, with a Congress of People's Deputies as the highest body above a new full-time Supreme Soviet. The Council of Ministers, first under Nikolai Ryzhkov and subsequently Valentin Pavlov, became at least partly independent from Party structures. Both began to be meaningful institutions in their own right, although their ranks remained dominated by Party members and it was unclear precisely what role Gorbachev foresaw for them in the new system.

So how were the reforms seen by public opinion? Again there appears to have been initial approval. Certainly the first meeting of the

Figure 3.4 Trust in state institutions, 1989–92

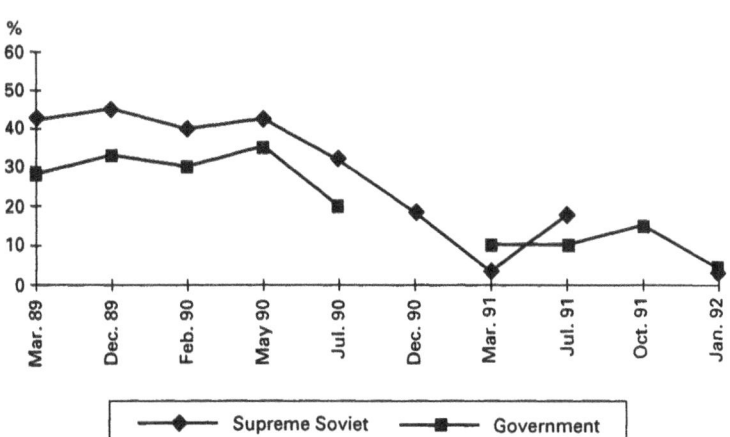

Sources: As Figure 3.3.

new Congress of People's Deputies caught the public imagination, with most of the nation tuned in to its opening proceedings. From the start there were, however, reservations about the composition of the new body, in particular the fact that one third of its membership was unelected. Nevertheless, as seen in Figure 3.4, large proportions of the population said that they fully trusted both the Supreme Soviet and Ryzhkov's government. If one adds in the numbers who said that they partly trusted these institutions, in all cases from 30 to 40 per cent, then it is clear that they had broad majority support as of mid-1989. And this even with the growing economic crisis.

However, during 1990 popular support evidently slipped away from the state organs, for reasons most closely connected with the emergence of competing republican institutions. The point at which the ratings of both institutions began to fall was precisely when the newly elected Russian Parliament first met, Yeltsin was elected as its chairman, and a new Russian Government under Ivan Silaev was formed.

However, there are other reasons why people began to become disillusioned with the new Parliament. These related partly to its lack of real powers. As an institution, it raised expectations beyond its ability to deliver. Furthermore, discussions were often conducted in vague and highly abstract terms, its sessions were frequently unruly, or dominated by seemingly irrelevant procedural argument. The absence of clear party structure within the legislature meant that patterns of support were constantly shifting, it was impossible for the ordinary citizen to make sense of where power lay, and the Congress was simply unable to make decisions on the most pressing issues of the time, in particular economic reform. Deputies were never really sure whether their role was to govern or to oppose. Most importantly, the Party establishment had been sufficiently strong at the time of the Parliamentary elections to ensure that the majority of deputies were broadly conservative, and the parliament therefore quickly lost touch with the public mood.

POLICE, COURTS, ARMY, KGB

The year 1989–90 saw a declining trust in the main Soviet decision-making institutions. But did the same apply to the institutions that were most responsible for maintaining state power and ensuring that central decisions were obeyed? Certainly all of the law-enforcement bodies came in for substantial criticism over the period: the Army not

Table 3.4 Trust in organs of social control, 1989-92

Organisation	Full trust (%)	Part trust (%)	No trust (%)
Army			
Dec. 89	44	22	14
Feb. 90	40	24	16
May 90	45	18	13
July 90	35		16
Dec. 90	41		13
March 91	40		
July 91	59	18	16
Jan. 92 (Russia only)	45		6
Security services			
Dec. 89	38	25	15
Feb. 90	34	25	17
May 90	39	23	12
July 90	24		16
Oct. 90	29		24
March 91	23		
July 91	38	17	27
Jan. 92 (Russia only)	15		24
Militsia			
March 89	14		
Aug. 89	10		
Dec. 89	22	40	24
Feb. 90	21	38	25
May 90	26	36	20
Sept. 90	20		
March 91	19		
Courts and Procuracy			
Dec. 89	22	36	20
Feb. 90	22	34	21
May 90	25	34	16
Sept. 90	20		
March 91	16		

Sources: *Obshchestvennoe mnenie v tsifrakh*, 1 (1989), 8, 9 and 14 (1990); *Nezavisimaya gazeta*, 24 January 1991, 16 October 1991; *Komsomolskaya pravda*, 30 October 1990 and 6 August 1991; *Moskovskie novosti*, 21 (1990); *Izvestiya*, 29 November 1990 and Darrell Slider, 'Public Opinion and the Political Process', in Stephen White, Graeme Gill and Darrell Slider (eds), *The Politics of Transition: Shaping a post Soviet future* (Cambridge: Cambridge University Press, 1993); Nikolai P. Popov, 'Political Views of the Russian People', *International Journal of Public Opinion Research*, 4, 4 (1992), pp. 321-34. All VTsIOM all-Union surveys, except Jan. 92 (Russia only).

least for the massacre of demonstrators in Tbilisi. Meanwhile the KGB was criticised for continuing surveillance of those who were politically suspect, and for its historical role in suppressing political opponents.

It is evident from the VTsIOM data shown in Table 3.4 that these bodies actually retained a surprising amount of support in Soviet public opinion. Several points are again worth emphasising. First, the Army and KGB were trusted by very large numbers indeed. It may be astonishing to Western readers that in none of the surveys reported from 1989–90 did the number who said that they had no trust at all in the security services go above one in four. Similarly, virtually all specialist attention at the time was focused on criticisms of the Soviet Army: about its treatment of recruits, its dominance by hardline conservatives, the possibility of its conducting a coup against Gorbachev, and understandably so, since these were such new phenomena. Yet from one third to one half of the entire Soviet population – not just Russians – said that they fully trusted it in 1989 and 1990. This shows us that many Westerners started from the wrong point when considering these institutions. Because historically they have been portrayed as threats to the West, and because we know so much about the less desirable activities of the secret police under Stalin and his successors, our instinctive response is one of mistrust or perhaps even fear. However, to many citizens of the Soviet Union they stood for something else entirely. The Army was a genuine source of pride. It had, after all, saved the world from Hitler – virtually single-handed if the regime was to be believed. It was what made the Soviet Union into a superpower. The absence of food in the shops was much more bearable if the compensation was a high standing in the world. Furthermore, the Army, unlike other institutions, was not dominated by bureaucrats. It was made up of the people – everyone's sons and daughters. As regards the organs of state security, these were protecting the right of the Soviet Union to determine its own future against those external forces that wanted to undermine it. The way in which they were also used against internal forces had become a great deal less obvious over the years immediately before Gorbachev.

Another interesting point relates to the public perceptions of the police and courts. It is clear that they were during 1990 substantially less popular than the Army and KGB. This perhaps relates to the day-to-day experiences of Soviet citizens. The *perestroika* period was one of rising crime, which the police were unable to combat successfully. Furthermore, law enforcement during the pre-*perestroika* era was highly politicised, 'telephone law' rather than rule of law. Party bosses decided how many cases should be resolved. It is perhaps not surprising that there was more mistrust of these institutions.

As for trends through 1991, they too are intriguing. Evidently there were substantial shifts in public perceptions about both the Army and the KGB, in opposite directions. The Army appears to have become much more trusted, despite the events in Latvia and Lithuania that January. This is perhaps because the armed forces were being increasingly seen as a sign of order in a chaotic situation. They represented virtually the only institution considered to be performing effectively in difficult circumstances. Many Russians had no objection to the use of armed force against non-Russians – if the figures are to be believed.

As regards the KGB, this was a time when its chairman, Vladimir Kryuchkov, was making increasingly sinister speeches about the necessity for bloodshed if order was to be restored. Bloodshed among Russians as well as others was the implication. This might contribute to an explanation of the rise in the number of people who completely mistrusted the KGB as an institution. However, there was no fall in the proportion who fully trusted it. It was only after the coup, masterminded, according to some sources, by Kryuchkov, that there appears to have been any noticeable decline of trust in the security services.

It is instructive to compare VTsIOM's data with the findings of two other organisations, Vox Populi, who investigated views about the armed forces in mid-1990, and the Institute of Sociology of the USSR Academy of Sciences, who carried out the a survey in May 1991 for the American Times–Mirror organisation.

Vox Populi asked their respondents in an all-Union survey at the end of July and beginning of August 1990 'To what extent do you trust the Armed forces?' Sixty-two per cent said that they trusted it either completely (30 per cent) or 'on the whole' (32 per cent).[15] The proportions are consistent with the VTsIOM data above, but a partial breakdown of these numbers by demographic group is also given. In particular they found that the armed forces were least trusted by the under thirties – less than a half, compared to more than two thirds of the over 55s. They also found that 82 per cent of people whose education was seven grades or less compared to 52 per cent of those with higher education trusted the armed forces to some degree. The two categories are no doubt related, since the younger group is better educated, but it nevertheless makes sense that young people, who were facing or had recently experienced compulsory military service (about which there had been, owing to *glasnost*, a large number of disturbing media reports), should be less trusting regardless of educational levels.

It also seems plausible that the old should have a greater degree of support for the Army than the young,. This may relate to direct memories of the Great Patriotic War, to a longer exposure to the patriotic rhetoric of the old regime, or because of greater suspicion of foreign countries in general, caused by less familiarity.

Information about trust in the Army among some of the peoples of the Soviet Union is also available. This is particularly intriguing, not least because the old communist regime had always seen the army and military service as a means of integrating the various nationalities. What stands out from the figures is the extent to which it was perceived as a Slavic Army. Thus 71 per cent in Belorussia (as it then was) and 70 per cent in Ukraine trusted it compared to only 54 per cent in Uzbekistan and 52 per cent in Turkmenistan, 20 per cent in Georgia and 2 per cent in Estonia, where fully 90 per cent mistrusted it, 77 per cent completely. In the two latter cases, the degree of hostility adds up to a perception of the Red Army as an army of occupation.

The Times–Mirror study of May 1991 did not ask specifically about trust, but asked people what kind of influence they thought that various institutions were having on the way things were going in the Soviet Union. The poll was carried out in European Russia, Ukraine and Lithuania (as well as several other European countries). Results are in Table 3.5. For convenience, the numbers who said that the institution in question was both a good and a bad influence, neither good nor bad or had no opinion have been combined.

The major difference between these and the VTsIOM data are in responses concerning the KGB, which people in all three republics clearly saw as a bad influence on the way things were going. This result is difficult to explain. It appears that while trusting the organisation, people didn't like what it was up to. Strictly speaking the two data are incompatible: perhaps support was much higher in the areas of the Union not covered by the Times–Mirror study? Perhaps question wording made a difference, since one questionnaire referred to the security services and the other asked about the KGB directly by name. Perhaps respondents knew that the survey was commissioned by an American organisation? But the inconsistency remains puzzling, the more so because of the similarity of appraisals of the other law enforcement agencies.

One other point stands out from the table: namely, the differences between the two Slavic republics and Lithuania. The latter had by this time declared itself independent and begun forming its own legal system, police forces and so on, clearly a popular move with the Lithuanian

Table 3.5 Trust in organs of social control, 1991

Which category on this card best reflects your opinion about the kind of influence the group is having on the way things are going in this country?

Organisation	Very/mostly good influence (%)	Both/neither/ DK (%)	Very/mostly bad influence (%)	Overall rating (%)
Army				
Russia	45	33	25	+20
Ukraine	42	32	26	+16
Lithuania	5	6	89	−84
KGB				
Russia	29	46	25	+4
Ukraine	26	46	28	−2
Lithuania	4	10	86	−82
Police				
Russia	35	39	26	+9
Ukraine	37	37	26	+11
Lithuania	65	23	12	+53
Judicial system				
Russia	27	49	24	+3
Ukraine	28	47	25	+3
Lithuania	61	28	11	+50

Source: *The Pulse of Europe: A survey of political and social attitudes* (Washington DC: Times–Mirror Center for the People and the Press, 1991).

public. The Soviet Army had also been involved in the deaths of a number of unarmed Lithuanian civilians in Vilnius that January. It remained hated. This is an early sign of a trend that became increasingly important: a higher degree of confidence in locally run institutions than national ones. This phenomenon is the concern of the next section.

TRUST IN REPUBLICAN INSTITUTIONS

Implicit in Gorbachev's moves to revitalise the state structure and introduce a more responsive and representative system was a reassessment of the nature of Soviet federalism. This involved an increase in the power of republican soviets and a corresponding reduction in the power of centralised institutions such as the Communist Party. This was necessary in order to reduce dependence on decisions being handed down from the centre and to increase local initiative.

However, in Soviet conditions, that is to say a highly centralised multi-ethnic state, such reforms faced two basic contradictions. First, as Nikita Khrushchev had discovered to his cost, decentralisation of power was a very risky business indeed. A view of the centre as predatory on the regions, as taking away far more than it gave back, was widespread. Privileges for armies of officials, funding subversion abroad, paying the cost of preserving superpower status, all of these meant that the standard of living in many regions was far lower than their contribution to the national economy. Increased local autonomy and control over resources – indeed moves towards autarchy – were therefore likely to be the demand raised through any democratic elections.

This was massively complicated by nationality issues. The basic feature of Soviet nationality policy had always been to avoid giving local elites the opportunity to gain power by appealing to nationalist sentiments among the titular nationality in their republic. Elites were always dependent on Moscow for their position and power. The consequence of carrying out democratic elections was to give non-Russian leaders precisely the opportunity to make such an appeal in order to consolidate their position independently of Moscow.

For these reasons, and also perhaps as a result of pressure from local officials who were reluctant to let go of power, Gorbachev avoided much change in the powers of republican governments. Khrushchev's fate – being voted from power after he had alienated the most important regional officials – was perhaps haunting the Soviet President. True, at the special Party conference Gorbachev did call for a reduction in the scale of the Party apparatus and a reduction in the amount of interference in state affairs (*podmena*), but this only really initiated a process by which officials from the Party apparatus shifted into state structures.[16]

Changes in the functions of republican governments were therefore something forced by these institutions themselves, rather than a process initiated and controlled by the central leadership. They resulted largely from the elections to republican parliaments that took place in 1990. In Russia these votes were between March and May of that year, and the results were enough of a victory for radical forces to enable Boris Yeltsin to be elected as chairman of the new Parliament. Pro-independence forces won majorities in Georgia, Armenia, Moldova and the three Baltic states.

Radical victories gave the impetus for attempts from below to change

Public Opinion and Soviet Political Institutions 73

the nature of the centre–republican relationship. Pioneering in this was the Lithuanian declaration of independence of 1990. This was followed by declarations of sovereignty by virtually all of the 15 republics that constituted the Soviet Union. Each announced that its laws were to be considered superior to all-Union ones. Precisely the arguments outlined above were deployed in many of the republics: the centre had shown itself to be bankrupt of ideas and had been exploiting the republics for its own ends, and therefore the people had to take power into their own hands. Even conservative leaderships in the Central Asian republics and in Ukraine and Belorussia were forced into such declarations, since to avoid them would leave the leaders open to attack from nationalists of various kinds.

How was this process related to public opinion? As can be seen from Figure 3.5, taken from various VTsIOM polls, before the 1990 elections the national Parliament was trusted to a considerably greater degree than republican ones. In part this reflects the reality that republican parliaments were toothless before the elections gave them democratic legitimacy. Thus the key point, where republican parliaments overtake the USSR Supreme Soviet, is precisely the time when the new freely elected parliaments meet for the first time.

However these data are somewhat misleading, since they report aggregate data for the whole USSR. That there were significant regional differences is well illustrated in one of the earliest studies involving Western scholars, carried out by Iowa University together with the

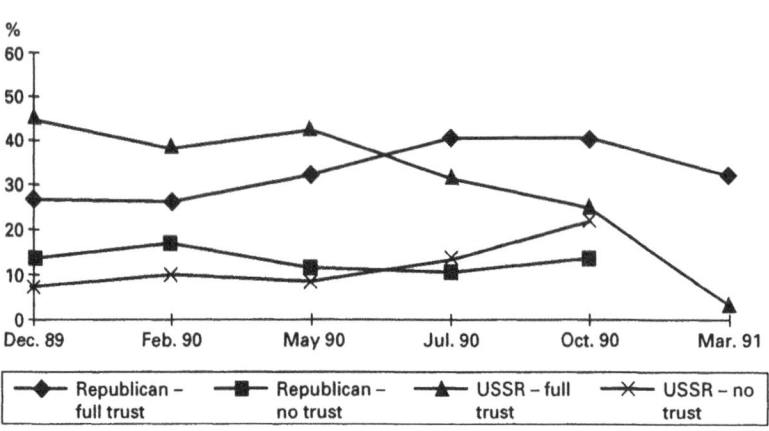

Figure 3.5 Trust in USSR and republican Supreme Soviets, 1989–91

Sources: As Figure 3.3.

Table 3.6 Positive appraisals of state institutions by republic, May 1990

Institution	RSFSR		Ukraine		Lithuania	
	Russians (%)	Ukrainians (%)	Ukrainians (%)	Russians (%)	Lithuanians (%)	Russians (%)
USSR Supreme Soviet	27	25	39	36	3	17
Rep. Supreme Soviet	37	44	33	24	71	20

Source: Arthur H. Miller, William M. Reisinger and Vicki L. Hesli, 'Public Support for New Political Institutions in Russia, the Ukraine and Lithuania', *Journal of Soviet Nationalities*, 1, 4 (Winter 1990–91), p. 95.

Centre for Political and International Studies of the Soviet Committee for the Defence of Peace, in the European part of Russia, Ukraine and Lithuania in May 1990. They asked respondents to appraise various institutions on a 5-point scale, with 5 being the most positive view. The proportions who gave each institution 4 or 5 are reproduced in Table 3.6.

As can be seen, the three republics could scarcely present a more different picture. In Ukraine, the Parliament and Government of which remained dominated by conservative forces, there was a greater degree of approval of the national Parliament at this time. This may be because that body was the more radical. However, Lithuanians had already begun to identify republican leaders as their legitimate government – something that clearly worried Russians living there. This latter group had little enthusiasm for leaders at either level. European Russia was in an intermediate position. More people rated republican institutions favourably, but not by large numbers.

A similar picture emerges in results to a second question in the same survey, 'Which political leaders do a better job of representing the interests of people like you?' The replies to this are shown in Table 3.7.

As can be seen, for most Russians and Ukrainians, with the exception of the minority population in Lithuania, once again little differentiation was made between centre and republics immediately after the elections, but there were a few who were beginning to prefer lower levels. It is clear that at this time there was in no sense a groundswell of opinion against the centre in either of the two Slavic republics.

The obvious conclusion that suggests itself from these data is that, for the Slavic republics at least, the elections were the beginning, not the end, of the process by which popular allegiance shifted from the centre to the republics. The first meeting of the new Russian Parlia-

Table 3.7 Views about leaders, May 1990

Response	RSFSR		Ukraine		Lithuania	
	Russians (%)	Ukrainians (%)	Ukrainians (%)	Russians (%)	Lithuanians (%)	Russians (%)
Republican leaders do a better job	22	22	18	13	86	22
No difference	58	53	54	59	10	33

Source: As Table 3.6.

ment, Yeltsin's election as its chairman in late May, and his appointment of a radical Russian Government under Ivan Silaev were key points, as was the Russian declaration of sovereignty which quickly followed. According to a VTsIOM all-union poll, 50 per cent approved of this sovereignty declaration at the time, while only 24 per cent were opposed.[17] As was shown above, it was during these events over the Summer months of 1990 that republican institutions became the more trusted. Even the Party-run Academy of Social Sciences found at that time that fully 54 per cent of a national sample had a positive attitude to the creation of an independent Russian state.[18]

This process had moved on considerably by the time of the Times–Mirror study of May 1991, shown in Table 3.8.

Table 3.8 Trust in national and republican authorities, May 1991

Which category on this card best reflects your opinion about the kind of influence the group is having on the way things are going in this country?

	Very/mostly good influence (%)	Both/neither/ can't say (%)	Mostly/very bad influence (%)	Overall (%)
National				
Russia	21	39	34	−13
Ukraine	21	37	40	−19
Lithuania	8	23	69	−61
Republican				
Russia	45	37	18	+27
Ukraine	45	31	24	+21
Lithuania	64	16	20	+44

Source: Times–Mirror survey.

As can be seen, according to these findings, by now in each of the three republics people felt overwhelmingly that republican parliaments were having a better influence on the way events were going. This transfer of allegiance from centre to republic was a major factor forcing Gorbachev and the central authorities to negotiate a new, decentralising, Union treaty, the event which was to provoke the coup of August 1991 and the final discrediting of the centre.

TRUST IN LOCAL GOVERNMENT

In discussing local government in the Soviet period, one faces the problem of where power actually lay at local level. Although the constitutional position was that the soviets had absolute authority, this was only exceptionally the case, for a number of reasons. Local soviets were bodies which met infrequently, were dominated by Party members, and usually only approved decisions made elsewhere. Power rather lay with the full-time apparatus of the local Party and soviet, which usually had an informal division of responsibilities between them. Frequently all local officials suffered from a problem of limited jurisdiction, with large factories and the ministries that controlled them being of far more importance.[19]

Public opinion was well aware of the nature of local power. An early example is a study by the Academy of Sciences Institute of Sociology in ten cities in three republics at the end of 1989, which asked respondents who had real power in their city. Results are shown in Table 3.9.

In the two Russian and two Ukrainian cities, then, most people felt that the Communist Party was in charge at this time. Only in Odessa did many people believe that their local soviet was influential. In fact this was the only place where more people thought the soviet had influence than thought black marketeers were in charge. The huge level of corruption in Uzbekistan is reflected in the more than half who said that black marketeers were in charge. (Of course there may have been little distinction between these and the local Party.) The importance of local enterprises, particularly huge military–industrial ones, in providing local services is illustrated by the numbers in the defence-dominated economies of Gor'kii and Odessa who named enterprise managers as being in power.

This is the context in which one has to consider views about local soviets, which are shown in Figure 3.6, again taken from regular VTsIOM polls.

Table 3.9 Perceptions of local government, 1989

Who has real power in the city in which you live?	Moscow (%)	Gor'kii (%)	L'viv (%)	Odessa (%)	Tashkent (%)
Party organs	51	55	65	37	46
Black marketeers	29	10	10	12	52
Enterprise managers	10	24	5	25	12
Local soviets	6	8	7	22	7
New social and political movements	1	0.4	6	0.4	4

Source: *Predvybornaya situatsiya: mneniya izbiratelei* (Moscow: Institute of Sociology, 1990), quoted in Darrell Slider, 'Soviet Public Opinion on the Eve of the Elections', *Journal of Soviet Nationalities*, 1, 1 (1990), p. 161.

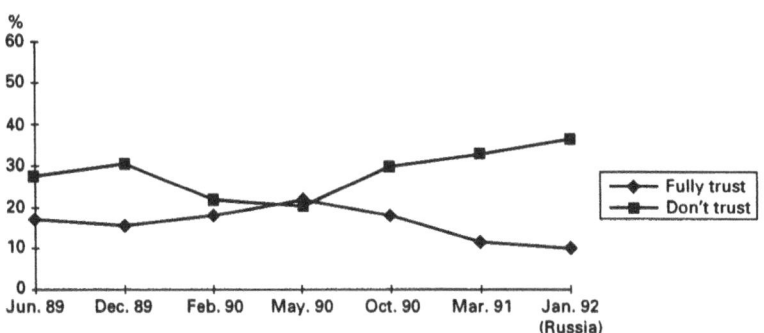

Figure 3.6 Trust in local government, 1989–92

Sources: As Figure 3.4.

As can be seen, the level of mistrust of local government over the period was extremely high. In fact, no institution with the exception of the CPSU was less trusted overall. This might reflect several factors. First, the fact that, for the reasons outlined above, many local governments simply could not be relied on to carry out their responsibilities effectively. Second, that they remained in many places substantially unreformed over the Gorbachev period. Corruption was often the norm. Third, the issue of the democratic gap, since voters had in many cases had no opportunity to choose their local leaderships freely. Fourth, many were aware that much resistance to change of any kind was based in this level of administration.

This lack of trust in local government, something which has been consistent throughout many different investigations, was significantly undermining Gorbachev's reforms. Untrustworthy local government implies that change has in many cases to originate from a higher level, from republican or national authorities. However, a large number of the changes that are implied by transition had, by their nature, to be implemented at local level. Policy changes such as privatisation of land or the creation of co-operatives were simply sabotaged by conservative Party officials.

TRUST IN THE MASS MEDIA

The most remarkable feature of Gorbachev's early years in power was evidently the policy of *glasnost*, usually rendered as openness, but more literally 'many voices'. Through it, part of the media was able to push back the boundaries of what it was acceptable to say, and tell some unpleasant truths about the state of the Soviet Union. It took perhaps around five years for the more radical newspapers and journals to lose all their taboos and finally feel free to say what they liked about, for example, Lenin's role in the Red Terror of the Civil War period and other highly controversial issues. Even the conservative parts of the media no longer had to speak in code.

However, more openness is not the only story. It is important to remember that many newspapers and, more importantly, Soviet television and radio, remained carefully controlled. Reporting on national television of the massacre in Vilnius as late as January 1991, for example, was mendacious. One of Yeltsin's priorities when he became head of the Russian republic was to achieve control of an independent Russian radio and television, showing how much he also understood that control over information was crucial to the consolidation of his own position. Even after the collapse of the Soviet Union, the battle for a free media had by no means ended. Unresolved issues of ownership, financing, legal protection of free speech and so forth remained important problems.

So how did the Soviet public react to *glasnost* and developments in the media? The data in Table 3.10 show how trust in the central press, radio and television changed over 1989–91. Perhaps the most notable feature here is the very low level of mistrust, at only around one in ten. Around one third said that they fully trusted these institutions, with slightly more saying that they partly trusted them. Evidently there

Table 3.10 Trust in the mass media, 1989-91

Date of survey	Fully trust (%)	Partly trust (%)	No trust (%)
June 1989	30	60	10
December 1989	36	44	9
February 1990	42	37	11
May 1990	36	36	8
October 1990	33		11
March 1991	22		
July 1991	29		

Sources: As Figure 3.3.

was a considerable satisfaction with changes in the way the media operated.

There were still, however, reservations. Over the period, many people were well aware that they were not necessarily being told the whole truth about what was going on. This is reflected in the high number of respondents who chose the option 'part trust' in the media, and is also well illustrated in a study by the Academy of Sciences Institute of Sociology in Autumn 1989 and Spring 1990.[20] It asked people (in a poorly worded question) how satisfied they were by the objectivity, completeness and usefulness of information from the country's 'hot spots'. In both 1989 and 1990 fewer than 10 per cent were completely satisfied, from 40 to 50 per cent were partly satisfied and the rest dissatisfied. The habit of scepticism about the mass media had certainly not died out.

The Times-Mirror survey of May 1991 tells a similar story. The majority, when asked what kind of an influence the print press and radio and television were having on the way things were going in the country, said that they were having a mostly good influence. The results are presented in detail in Table 3.11.

As can be seen, the most positive views were once again to be found in Lithuania. The effect of creating their own national institutions including a free press appears once again to have been a surge of enthusiasm. Respondents from European Russia and Ukraine appeared to be more sceptical, with large numbers offering the response both good and bad, which reflects the fact that there were both radical and conservative newspapers, and both hardline and liberal television and radio broadcasts. However, there was clearly at this time still a substantial level of trust in the mass media.

Table 3.11 Trust in the media, 1991

Which category on this card best reflects your opinion about the kind of influence the group is having on the way things are going in this country?

Response	Russia (%)	Ukraine (%)	Lithuania (%)
'Print press'			
Very good/mostly good influence	46	52	75
Neither/both/can't say	37	36	14
Mostly bad/very bad influence	17	12	11
Overall	+29	+40	+64
Radio and television			
Very good/mostly good influence	40	41	82
Neither/both/can't say	39	42	11
Mostly bad/very bad influence	21	18	7
Overall	+19	+23	+75

Source: Times–Mirror survey.

TRUST IN RELIGIOUS ORGANISATIONS

It needs little rehearsal to say that religious organisations were not encouraged under the old regime. Stalin in the 1930s waged an all-out war on religion, demolishing churches, closing monasteries, and murdering priests. Suppression continued in varying degrees subsequently, until Gorbachev's ideological shift from class to universal human values made possible a change. Many religious prisoners were released. The Russian Orthodox Church was able to reopen a number of its churches and monasteries, and to begin to separate itself from the state. A number of mosques were also revived, as were previously banned or suppressed denominations such as the Ukrainian Catholic (Uniate) and the Armenian Orthodox, and religions such as Buddhism. The *perestroika* years also saw an end to large-scale official harassment of Jewish culture and religion.

Subsequently, various religious organisations played important political roles. In many of the Soviet republics, the Church became a focus for nationalist revivals, particularly in Central Asia, Georgia, Western Ukraine and Lithuania. In the last, the reopening of Vilnius Cathedral in 1989 was a significant stage in the drive towards independence. In Russia itself, statements by the hierarchy of the Orthodox Church were given a great deal of attention.

So how did the Soviet people respond to the revival in religious activity? Had decades of 'scientific atheism' meant that there was no longer a place for religious organisations in social life? Was there active hostility or positive interest? Studies of public opinion have shed some light on these questions.

A simple, but no less striking for that, finding of these studies is that religion by no means died out over the Soviet period. VTsIOM carried out three studies over the period 1989–91, in each of which consistently only 20 per cent declared themselves to be outright atheists.[21] Of the rest, in the 1991 survey, 48 per cent identified themselves with a particular religious denomination. However rather fewer (39 per cent) said that they would like their children to be raised to be believers, that they believed in life after death (32 per cent), the existence of the devil (24 per cent), heaven (19 per cent) and hell (25 per cent). In other words central tenets of Christian religion were believed in by significantly fewer people. Furthermore, when asked 'Where, in your opinion, can man most of all find answers to the questions which concern him?', only 7 per cent answered religion, significantly fewer than those who replied 'a personal moral sense' (47 per cent) or 'art and literature' (10 per cent).[22] And fewer still were practising believers: that May, the Times–Mirror study found that only 3 per cent of people in the European part of Russia and 7 per cent in Ukraine attended religious services at least once a week.[23] Of course this might genuinely underestimate the number who would like to be practising but did not have the opportunity, but it nonetheless suggests that genuine believers are a lot rarer than those who are well disposed to religion.

As regards trends over time, the VTsIOM studies found no increase in the number who identified themselves as religious over the period 1989–91, and nor did studies involving researchers from the Russian Academy of Sciences in 1990 and 1991.[24] This would imply that the argument that there is a rise in the level of religious observance is questionable. What we are in fact seeing, these data suggest, is simply the open expression of previously hidden beliefs.

The demographic distribution of believers is interesting. According to the VTsIOM studies, from 70 to 80 per cent were women compared with 53 per cent women in the population as a whole, and 54 per cent were more than 50 years old. The Academy of Sciences research suggested that the highest proportion of people who believed in God was to be found among the oldest (60 and over) and the youngest (under

20) age groups. However, the oldest were also the most likely to be atheists, whilst the young were the least likely. By education, the highest proportion who believed in God was found amongst the least well educated, although they found the better educated were considerably more likely to believe in astrology, telepathy and other supernatural phenomena than the less educated part of the population.[25]

The geography is also intriguing. VTsIOM found that the most religious of all were Russians living in the Baltic states and Central Asia, and Georgians, Armenians and Central Asian peoples living in the European part of Russia, Ukraine or Belorussia. Being a member of an identifiable minority increases the need for attachment to the traditional culture of one's native people, as a reaction against the culture of the surrounding majority.

By any standards then, only a minority can be described as genuinely religious. But how did the non-religious majority regard the increasing prominence of religious organisations in public life? Figure 3.7 provides us with a partial answer. It shows VTsIOM data on trust in 'religious organisations of Christians, Moslems etc.'. A number of features stand out.

First, for the polls where the information is given, there were high proportion who said that it was difficult to say, nearly 50 per cent in each case. Two possible explanations suggest themselves. One is that many people trusted some religious organisations and mistrusted others. Anti-Moslem feelings, to say nothing of anti-Semitism, are not uncommon among many Russians, as will be discussed in Chapter 5. But another possible explanation is that the activities of the various religions simply passed many people by, having, as they saw it, no relevance to their lives.

That this latter explanation is more likely is strongly implied by another VTsIOM survey, from September 1989. It asked 'How much good will the more widespread distribution of religious beliefs do for you personally / for society as a whole?' Figure 3.8 displays the data. While few people think that increasingly open religious worship will harm society, 49 per cent say that it will have no significance for them personally. Adding the numbers who said that it was difficult to say, indifference was certainly the commonest reaction.

Another striking feature of the time series data in Figure 3.7 is the trend. Gradually but consistently more people were saying that they trusted religious organisations. This is perhaps an encouraging sign of pluralisation, with people more willing to respect the role of organisations with which they do not necessarily agree. But alternatively one

Figure 3.7 Trust in 'religious organisations of Christians, Moslems, etc.', 1989–91

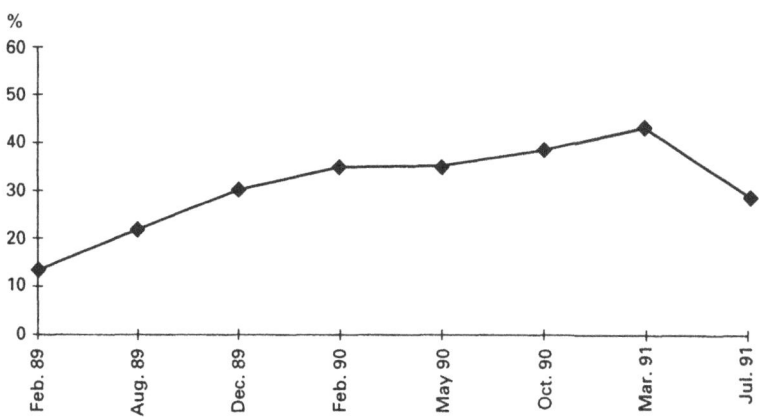

Note: Figure shows percentage who fully trusted religious organisations.
Sources: As Figure 3.3.

Figure 3.8 Views about religious revival, 1989

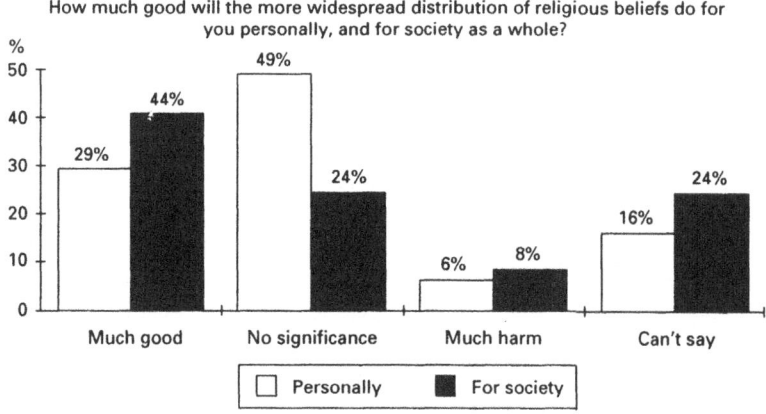

Sources: *Obshchestvennoe mnenie v tsifrakh*, 4 (1989). Exceptionally for VTsIOM, this source gives no details of the sample.

could see it as reflecting a crisis of confidence in the other institutions of society. It doesn't reflect greater trust in religion, but rather falling trust in politics.

TRUST IN LEADERS

A resource for any politician is clearly popular support. Obviously it is not the only important factor: the tasks they have set themselves, their relations with other parts of the political system and indeed with other political systems, pure chance, all these matter. Furthermore the leadership–public relationship is two-way, and leaders can shape opinion as well as needing its support. But popularity in the polls makes it very much easier for a leader to act.

Polling organisations in the Soviet Union were prevented in their earliest days from researching the popularity of the leadership. This was related to the desire to maintain the façade of monolithic support from the whole of society. The irony is that, at this time, this is precisely what Gorbachev had. As discussed earlier, the earliest published poll, carried out in the Spring of 1989, found that an astonishing 94 per cent approved of his activities.[26]

Figure 3.9a and b, reports trends in poll ratings according to VTsIOM for the period 1989–91.[27] A number of conclusions suggest themselves. Most strikingly, the critical period from the point of view of support for Gorbachev appears to have been May to June 1990. This is when Boris Yeltsin overtook him in the polls. This is a surprising finding. Yeltsin had managed to stage his political comeback at the elections of 1989, with his victory in National Territorial District Number One, the constituency representing the whole of Moscow in the new Congress of People's Deputies; 1989 was also the year when matters began to slip from Gorbachev's control as reflected in the wave of strikes, emergence of separatist movements and so forth. One assumes therefore that the change is not related to personality but to position. Yeltsin was elected chairman of the new Russian Parliament at the end of May 1990. This is the point at which he became a clear political alternative to Gorbachev. Clearly, this was of far greater importance in affecting the public mood than Gorbachev's appointment as Soviet President which had occurred that March.

The overall sense one gets from the data is of a steady draining away of support for Gorbachev, with none of the actions he took to try and revive his fortunes – in particular the various summits with

Public Opinion and Soviet Political Institutions 85

Figure 3.9 Views about leaders, 1989–91

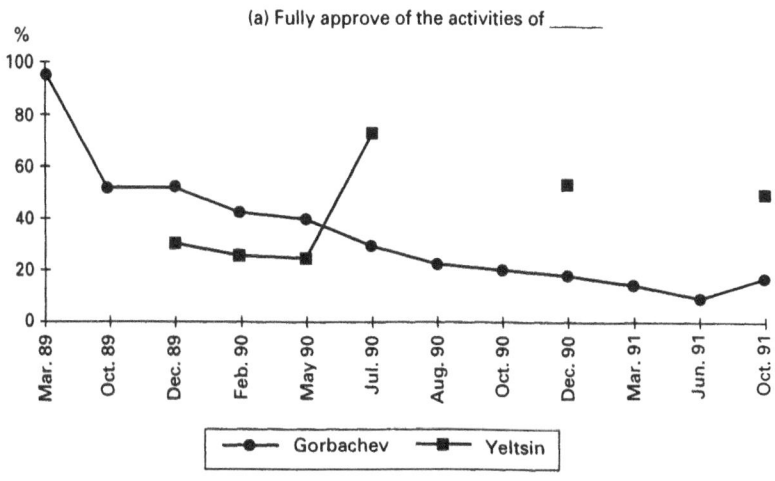

Sources: As Figure 3.3.

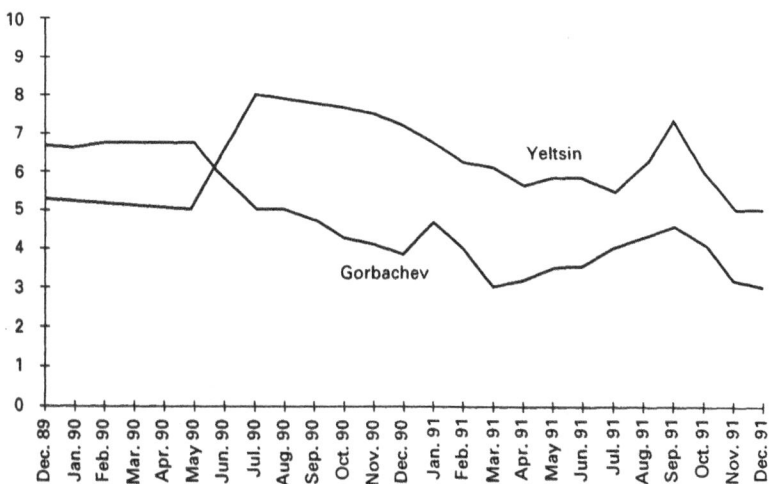

Source: Argumenty i fakty, 38 (1993), p. 2.

world leaders – having any impact on public opinion. Only a tiny minority still backed him at the time of the August coup. We should therefore interpret events after that as simply confirming a situation that already existed in public opinion: namely that Yeltsin not Gorbachev was substantially the most popular politician in Russia.

Yeltsin's personal rating during 1991 is also of interest. His popularity was boosted less by his election as President in a popular vote in June 1991 than by his reactions to the putsch of 19 August, and even then his popularity by no means returned to 1990 levels. Furthermore, the 'honeymoon period' was brief. By the end of 1991 disputes over the future shape of the Union, Yeltsin's personal humiliation of Gorbachev and fears about the consequences of imminent economic reform meant that the Russian President was no more popular in the polls than Gorbachev had been as late as mid-1990, which was not a promising position from which to launch reforms.

Survey data also give us the possibility of understanding something of the way in which the two men were perceived by Russians. A VTsIOM poll of 2000 Russians in January 1991 asked people which traits they thought were most typical for each. For Boris Yeltsin, the most commonly mentioned traits were 'openness and directness' (34 per cent), 'ambition and striving for power' (26 per cent), 'decisiveness' (24 per cent), and 'a willingness to consider the interests and moods of ordinary people' (19 per cent). For Mikhail Gorbachev, views were a great deal less complimentary, with 27 per cent saying 'two-facedness and hypocrisy', 20 per cent 'weakness and a lack of self-confidence', 19 per cent 'indifference to human suffering', and 18 per cent 'flexibility and skill at manoeuvring'.[28]

It is also possible to say something about the social base of support for each leader. For Gorbachev, support came relatively more from rural than urban areas, and from the old compared to the young. In this sense, the profile of the person who trusted the Soviet President resembled quite closely that of the supporter of the CPSU. Indeed Dobson and Grant have shown that at the start of 1991 Gorbachev's support was four times higher among communist loyalists than anti-communists.[29] This reflects how Gorbachev never really abandoned his position as a communist and his power base within the CPSU. As opinion moved away from the Party, it also moved away from him.

CONCLUSION: TRUST IN POLITICAL INSTITUTIONS 1989-91

So what actually happened to popular views about Soviet ruling institutions in the years after it had become possible to study them? Or to put it another way, what happens to views about rulers in a revolutionary period? There seems little doubt that the data above describe a revolution in attitudes. To describe it as a legitimacy crisis is not to exaggerate.

Polls from 1989 describe a situation where the main institutions of power: the Communist Party, the Supreme Soviet, the USSR Council of Ministers, and Gorbachev himself were broadly accepted. It is of course possible that this simply reflected the habit of self-censorship, with people saying what they thought their rulers wanted to hear. But by 1989 this seems unlikely: *glasnost* had by then reached the point where self-censorship was rarely necessary. In any event, what one is willing to say in public is the only part of one's opinions that can reasonably be considered as public opinion. A more likely explanation is that the vast majority of Soviet citizens thought that the best hopes for change for the better did indeed come from the existing institutions. For conservatives, they had always worked in the past, while those who desired change appreciated that resistance was great and thought that movement was in the desired direction.

Through 1990 however, the picture looks completely different. All the main Soviet ruling institutions, with the exception of the armed forces and the KGB, saw their popularity drain away. The Communist Party was forced to abandon its leading role, Yeltsin overtook Gorbachev in the polls and republican parliaments became more popular than the national one in most of the Soviet Union.

The obvious interpretation of this is that the central institutions had by this time ceased to be the representatives of change, and were rapidly becoming identified in the public mind with resistance to change. This was reflected in Gorbachev's insistence on a number of hardline appointments – indeed those people who were to attempt to seize power in the coup of August 1991. Furthermore, he failed to tackle adequately the two crucial issues of economic reform and the decentralisation of power. This created the opportunity for Yeltsin and his counterparts in other republics to cast themselves as the true reformers.

Crucial to this shift, as suggested in several sections of the chapter, was the emergence of a clear alternative in republican authorities. Legitimacy is by its nature a relative concept. Institutions only lose it when competing ones become more attractive. Poll evidence from 1990-91 shows precisely this. The middle of 1990, after the election of the republican parliaments, was when the popularity of the main institutions of the old regime fell most dramatically. The economy was shrinking at this point, but it had also been shrinking in 1989 and early 1990. The only plausible explanation, then, is that support for this particular regime was far more weakly related to actual performance than to the existence of plausible alternative arrangements.

4 Public Opinion and Postcommunist Political Institutions

The collapse of communist power in the Soviet Union in August 1991 did not leave a power vacuum. Republican institutions, which had managed to assert considerable power, as discussed in the previous chapter, were able to take over in most cases virtually unchallenged. But this did not solve the problem of where institutional power should lie. Should there be an executive form of government, with the President appointing a government answerable only to him, and elected parliaments playing a role merely as a 'sounding board'? Or should governments be formed from within Parliament, with the Head of State having more symbolic than real power? At a still deeper level, could the new institutions regain some of the popular trust and authority that political institutions in general had lost during the *perestroika* period? In Russia at least, postcommunist politics has focused just as much on these constitutional issues of who governs as on debates about policy.

So where has public opinion stood in these debates? Is it clearly supportive of one institution over the others? Is there a desire to return to the past? Are there any parallels between 1989–91 and 1992–93 in terms of the declining legitimacy of institutions of power? Or are Russians increasingly uninterested in political conflicts among their leaders?

A CONSENSUS ABOUT DEMOCRACY?

Following the collapse of communist power, there was little discussion about the nature of the new Russian institutions: they would of course be democratic. How many Russians oppose this, and from which social groups do they come?

It is clear that a substantial majority of Russians support a democratic form of government, and only a minority would like the old system back. This can be clearly seen in a series of polls by Vox Populi which have studied the kinds of rule that citizens feel to be appropriate for the new Russia. Results are shown in Figure 4.1.

Figure 4.1 Attitudes to socialism and democracy, 1992–93

(a) What role in Russia's fate – undoubtedly positive, mostly positive, mostly negative or completely negative – could today be played by a return to the principles of socialism?

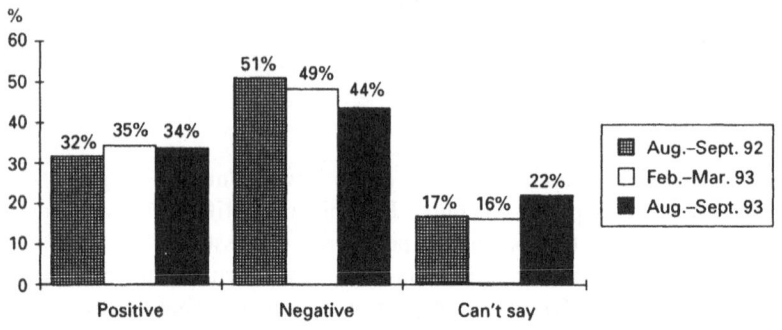

(b) And what role could be played by the consolidation of genuine democratic principles?

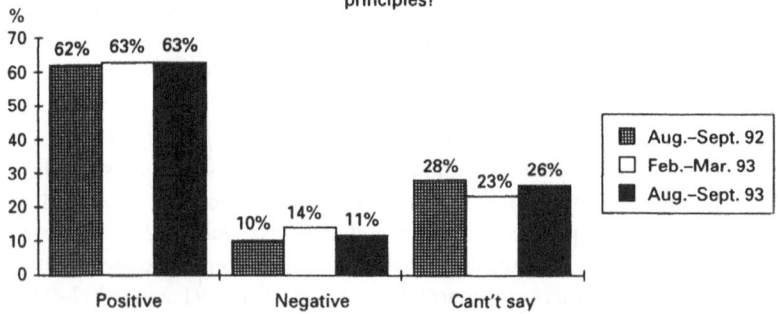

Sources: *Mir mnenii i mneniya o mire*, 4 (1993), 7 (1993), 10 (1993). Surveys by Vox Populi, respectively of n = 1590, n = 1996 and n = 1740.

It is clear from the histogram that a solid majority is convinced that some form of democracy is positive, although as the next chapter will show, this does not mean that Russians accept democratic values. Opposition to a return to socialism outweighs support. The most recent of the surveys indicates, however, that hostility to socialism may be falling somewhat, as memories fade, as the consequences of the moves to create a market economy become clearer, and as sections of the population become increasingly convinced that they have no stake in the new Russia. By the Autumn of 1993, there were only 10 per cent more people with a negative reaction to the idea of a return to socialism than people who reacted positively to it. The political success of parties with a much more interventionist attitude to economic policy in the elections of December 1993 reflected this trend.

Asking about communism rather than socialist principles produces a more negative response. The March 1993 study also asked 'To what degree do you agree that the communist system is the most appropriate for Russia?' Here just 21 per cent agreed, (8 per cent fully, 13 per cent partly) with 57 per cent disagreeing (21 per cent partly, 36 per cent completely).[1] There is much more limited support for a revival of the old system than for socialist principles.

Nevertheless this leaves a significant minority – around one in three – in Russian society still supportive of the old system. So who are the die-hard communists? Figure 4.2 illustrates the results of a January 1993 survey conducted by the Institute for Applied Politics.

As can be seen, the same pattern as prior to 1991 applies: people with a positive view of the communist cause are more likely to be poorer and older. The data also show that positive attitudes towards the communist cause are more often found among those with low levels of education and among women. This is hardly surprising: Russia's 'democrats' are clearly associated with an economic reform programme that harms these groups the most. Political identifications here reflect basic self-interest.

Figure 4.2 Positive attitudes to 'the communist political cause' by age and monthly income, January 1993

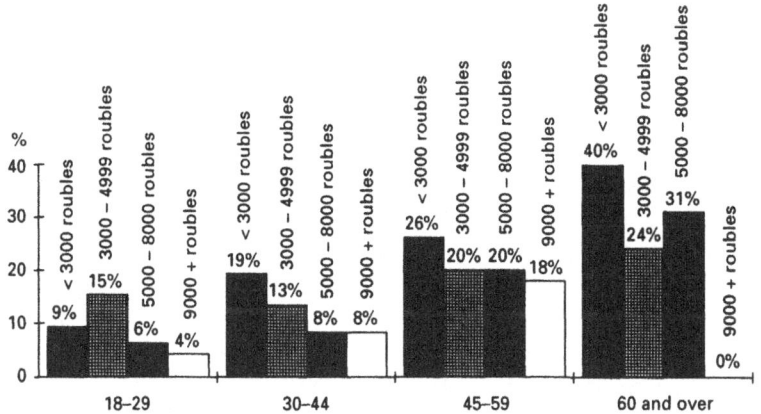

Sources: Unpublished survey by the Institute for Applied Politics, n = 1509. Cross tabulations calculated by the author.

SUPPORT FOR THE PRESIDENT

Figure 4.3 shows presidential ratings from 1989–94. As discussed in Chapter 3, Mikhail Gorbachev's popularity steadily declined over time, particularly after mid-1990 when Yeltsin emerged as a serious alternative, and further after the events in the Baltic states in January 1991 and the subsequent resignation speech of Foreign Minister Eduard Shevardnadze which labelled the Soviet President a dictator. Disappointed expectations were never reawakened. By 1991 few Russians still expected anything good out of the Gorbachev leadership. What then of the period since 1992? Has Boris Yeltsin suffered from a similar downward spiral where declining popularity reinforces political failures?

At the start of 1992, when the programme of rapid economic reform was launched, Yeltsin was considerably less popular than he had been in the aftermath of the coup. Before August, when Yeltsin had only limited power, he was able to assign blame for unpopular policies elsewhere. Inevitably, as soon as he gained decision-making power, his actions were unable to meet the aspirations of all Russians. The casualness with which he acceded to the dismantling of the Soviet Union, a move which had only limited support, and the price liberalisation of 1 January 1992, which had been rumoured for some time before that, appear to have reduced goodwill towards him quite substantially.

As can be seen, at least up until the Autumn of 1994, there was limited further deterioration in Yeltsin's poll ratings. What subsequent variation in popularity there was is clearly linked to the most central political events. The very end of 1992 saw something of a personal humiliation for the President when the seventh Russian Congress of People's Deputies refused to accept Yegor Gaidar, Yeltsin's nominee for Prime Minister, and instead appointed Viktor Chernomyrdin, a much less radical figure. Poll ratings fell correspondingly. The conflicts with the eighth and ninth Congresses in March 1993 over the powers that should be granted to the executive and legislative branches, culminating in Yeltsin's declaration of 'special rule', Parliament's attempts to impeach the President, and then the Referendum of 25 April saw a rise in sympathy for Yeltsin. Action to try to end the situation of dual power and political gridlock was popular. However over-zealous action was not. The aftermath of the October Crisis, in which a number of people died during the protests that followed the decision to dissolve the Parliament, saw a noticeable decline in the presidential rating. Public opinion approved of the initial decision to dissolve the

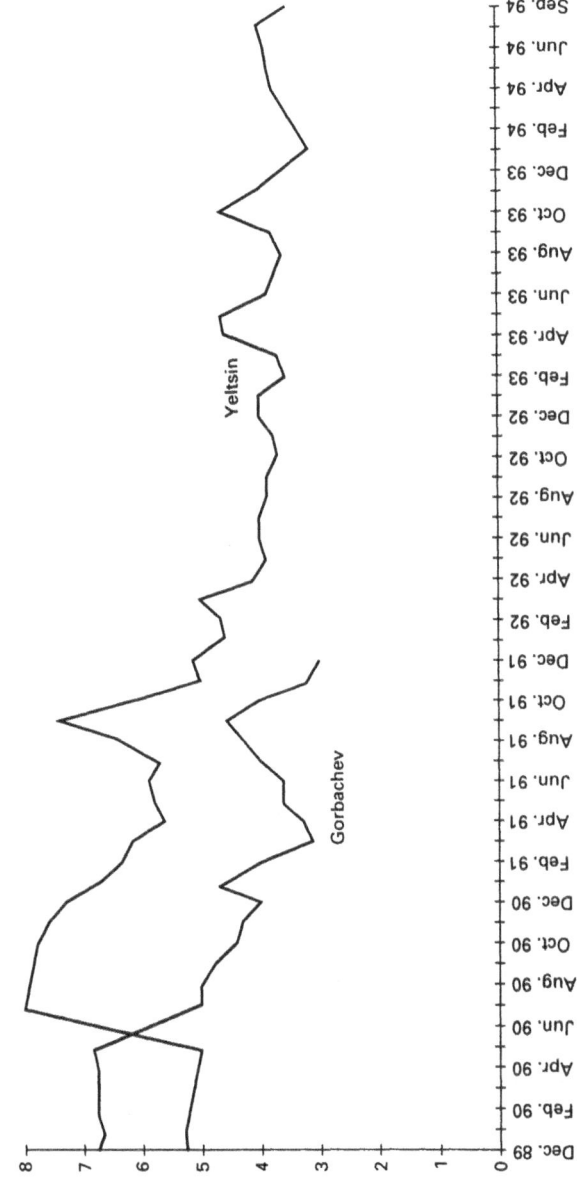

Figure 4.3 Ratings of Boris Yeltsin and Mikhail Gorbachev on a 10-point scale

Sources: Argumenty i fakty, 38 (1993), p. 2; *Ekonomicheskie i sotsial'nye peremeny: monitoring obshchestvennogo mneniya*, 3 (1994), p. 10; 5 (1994), p. 77 and 6 (1994), p. 50. Before 1992, the question wording was 'To what extent do you approve of the activities of ⎯⎯⎯?'. From January 1992, the question read 'What mark would you give Russian President B. Yeltsin if 1 is very low, and 10 is the highest possible score?'.

Russian Parliament. A typical national survey, carried out in October 1993, found that 53 per cent approved of this and just one in three disapproved. However, the subsequent bloodshed was not acceptable. Asked 'How would you evaluate the storming of the "White House" [the Russian Parliament building]: was this action necessary, should it have been avoided, or was this action unacceptable in principle?' just 14 per cent of Russians thought the act to be necessary, while 44 per cent felt that it should have been avoided, and 37 per cent that it was utterly unacceptable.[2] This blow to the President was reinforced by the political setback for Yeltsin of the elections of December 1993, which the calmer political atmosphere of the first half of 1994 did little to reverse.

However, in the context of falling production, high inflation and rising unemployment, crime and social tension, and continuing concerns about the President's health, the overall stability of Yeltsin's rating, albeit at somewhat low levels, is somewhat surprising. The very low popular expectations of possible improvement might contribute to explaining this. Perhaps as important as rational and structural explanations, though, is consideration of how effectively Yeltsin has been performing the functions associated with his role as Head of State, symbolically leading the people, that is the charismatic aspects of leadership. A sense that Yeltsin embodies typical Russian qualities – both good and bad – has always been a central part of his appeal.

Who are the Yeltsinites, and which groups oppose the President? And has the overall consistency of support disguised shifting demographic patterns in support over the period since his election in mid-1991? Figure 4.4 illustrates results of a poll in early 1993 which asked people to recall how they had voted in the presidential election.

As can be clearly seen, voting behaviour at least in Russian cities, was more strongly connected with political views than demographic factors. Those who were hostile to communism, those who believed that private property was necessary for economic progress and those who opposed the 1991 coup were most likely to have voted for Yeltsin; those who believed that private property was the exploitation of man by man, those who thought Russia should be a great power feared and respected by all or those who were positive about communism were least likely to have voted for him. Demographic factors such as age, sex and education were much more weakly connected: Yeltsin's voters were of all ages, of both sexes in approximately equal numbers, and were people from all educational levels.

Of course support for the President has fallen considerably since

Public Opinion and Postcommunist Political Institutions 95

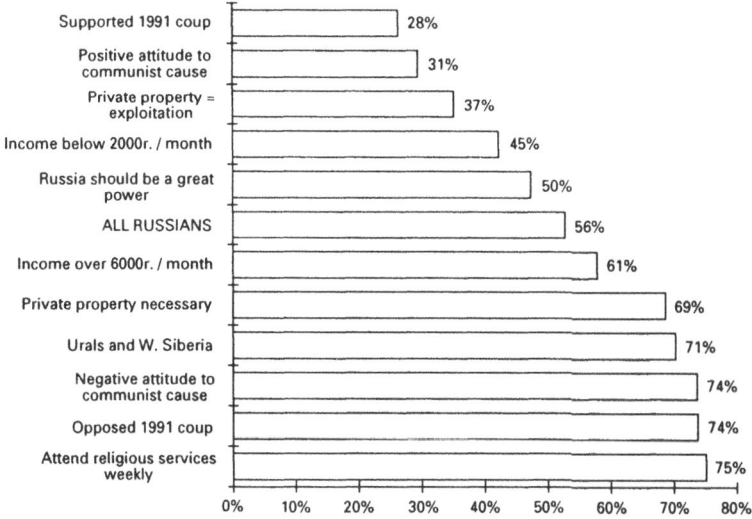

Figure 4.4 Yeltsin's supporters, June 1991

Source: Unpublished survey of urban Russia by the Institute of Applied Politics, Jan. 1993.

Note: Table shows percentage of each category who voted for Yeltsin in the June 1991 Presidential elections.

June 1991. Has this meant that the groups supporting Yeltsin have changed in any significant way?

When he was elected in 1991, it was possible to have a platform which was all things to all people, since he did not have the wherewithal to put policies into practice. However, after the Gaidar reforms began in 1992 it became increasingly clear that certain sections of society would be particularly adversely affected by change. Especially affected would be those whose livelihoods were dependent on state support – the elderly, rural inhabitants dependent on agricultural subsidies, unskilled manual workers employed in loss-making industries in the state sector – and these are indeed the groups in which support for the President has haemorrhaged the most since the height of his popularity in 1990–91.[3]

However, it remained the case that the President had, throughout 1992–93, substantially more support than his main political and institutional rivals, Vice President Aleksandr Rutskoi and the Russian Parliament. It is true that polls would occasionally find more people willing

Figure 4.5 Relative trust in institutions, June 1993

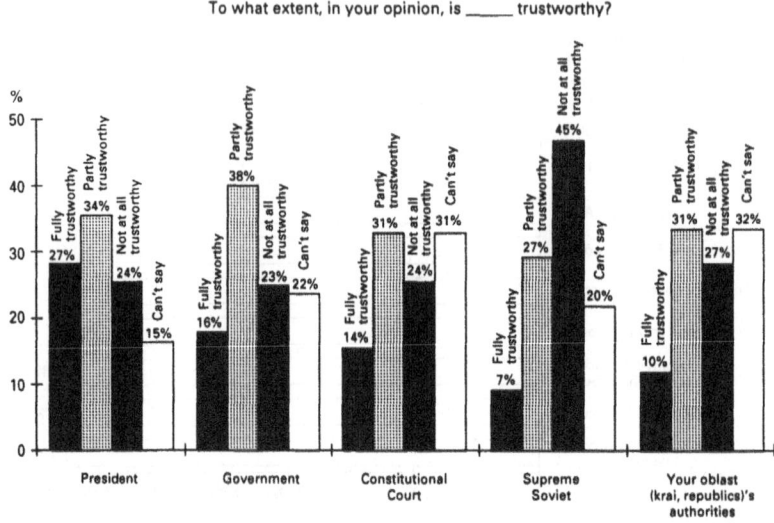

Source: *Ekonomicheskie i sotsial'nye peremeny: monitoring obshchestvennogo mneniya*, 4, August 1993, pp. 40–1.

to give positive reactions about Rutskoi than Yeltsin. Widely reported within and outside Russia were studies by ROMIR on behalf of Radio Liberty in October 1992 (confined to European Russia) and by the (hardly neutral) Russian Parliament's subcommittee for the study of public opinion in July 1992.[4] But national polls that asked about voting intention, or asked which politician respondents trusted most – of which a typical example is in Figure 4.5 – consistently found Yeltsin to be the most popular politician or the Presidency the most popular institution, although it was not uncommon for more people to say that they would vote for nobody or didn't trust any institutions.

The period after the October Crisis and the elections of December 1993, however, saw a change. From this point, the President was no longer the most popular and the most trusted of the various central institutions of government. As shown in Figure 4.6, more people now mistrusted Yeltsin than mistrusted the newly elected Parliament. It was no longer possible for the President to claim popular support as a justification for imposing his will, since allowing new Parliamentary elections had given new legitimacy to the legislature and allowed a more responsible opposition to emerge.

Figure 4.6 Relative trust in institutions, September 1994

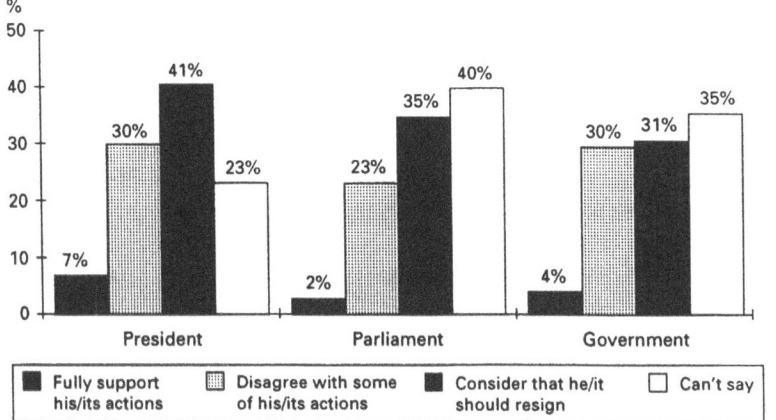

Source: *Ekonomicheskie i sotsial'nye peremeny: monitoring obshchestvennogo mneniya*, 6 (1994), p. 63.

SUPPORT FOR THE RUSSIAN GOVERNMENT

Since coming to power in January 1992, the Russian Government has been implementing a series of policies that have imposed considerable suffering on ordinary people. As discussed in Chapter 2, Russian gross domestic product had fallen during 1992–3 by 29 per cent and in 1994 by a further 15 per cent – a scale of decline greater than anything experienced even during the Great Depression in Western countries. At the same time Russian citizens have experienced unprecedented (for Russia) levels of inflation, with prices increasing 26-fold in 1992, although much less rapidly after that time. And by the end of 1994 even the Russian Government admitted that 5 million were unemployed. The Prime Minister, Viktor Chernomyrdin, admitted that by late 1993 three out of every four Russians did not have enough income to subsist on. Health and welfare services were in crisis, and crime had risen dramatically. Meanwhile, a small number of people were able to take advantage of the opportunities offered by economic reform to become very rich indeed, often by dishonest means.

Alongside the dire economic situation, the break-up of the Soviet Union has led to many difficult disputes with other former Soviet republics. In particular the arguments with Ukraine over the status of the Black Sea fleet and Ukraine's nuclear weapons, with many former Soviet republics about the status of the Russian Diaspora, and with the Baltic states concerning withdrawal of the Russian armed forces have been serious.

However, the Government has not been without its achievements. Relations with the West in particular have been relatively tension-free, and (until the crisis in Chechnya) to manage the various stresses in relations with the former Soviet republics without any conflicts having descended into the open use of force has been admirable (although there clearly remain issues around the desirable role of the Russian military in several former republics). There is freedom of worship, and the media (including television) reports a range of points of view. An end to omnipresent Marxist-Leninist ideology is a considerable relief to many. And there was also progress on the economic front: by late 1993, prices began to stop rising quite so rapidly as the Government took steps to control its enormous budget deficit; and privatisation has created a substantial private sector in important parts of the economy.

So how have ordinary Russians appraised their Government in the recent period? The time series in Figure 4.7 gives an indication. As can be seen, the extent of trust in the Government as an institution was not at all high. Only some two or three in every ten people trusted the Government to any great degree, whereas well over half in each case did not trust it much or at all. (Incidentally, these data illustrate also the advantages of using a four-point rather than three-point scale for this kind of question. In the VTsIOM data cited above the most popular answer was partly trust, but as we see, a more detailed choice shows that partly tends to mean not very much.)

It also appears that in the early part of 1993, the proportion of people who trusted the Russian Government fell somewhat. Particularly important in this is likely to have been the fiasco related to the confiscatory currency reform of the Summer of 1993, which exposed divisions between members of the Government and extreme lack of co-ordination of policies. The parallel with the collapse in popularity of the Soviet Government after the Pavlov currency reforms is striking. However, towards the end of the year, after the 'October Crisis' the government's popularity had begun to rise, as prices began to stabilise.

Figure 4.8, showing views about the Government during 1994, shows that the high degree of popular mistrust in the Government persisted. Over 1994, the Government was gradually becoming less popular, as time went on without any dramatic improvements in people's lives.

It is also possible to say something about popular perceptions of various aspects of Government policy, since Vox Populi regularly asked about these during 1992, using a 5-point scale. Their data are illustrated in Figure 4.9a–c.

Public Opinion and Postcommunist Political Institutions   99

Figure 4.7   Trust in the Russian Government, 1992–93

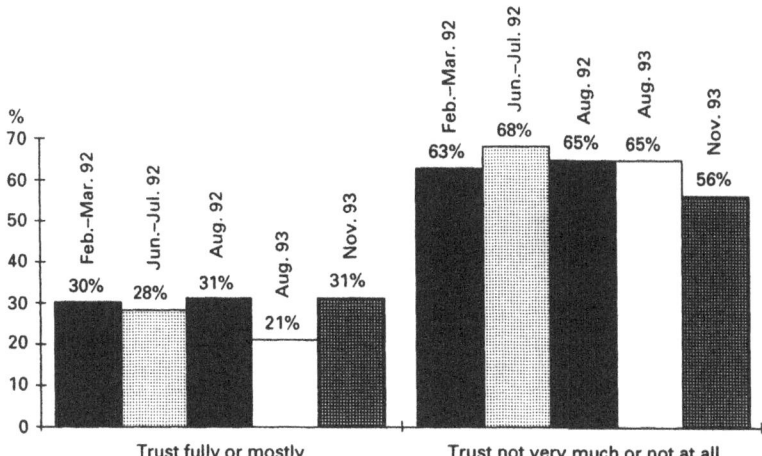

Sources: *Mir mnenii i mneniya o mire* 9 (1992) and 72 (1993) and 98 (1993); *Nezavisimaya gazeta*, 16 October 1992. Sample sizes respectively n = 1985, n = 1990, n = 1590, n = 1740 and n = 1718. Surveys by Vox Populi.

Figure 4.8   Attitudes to the Russian Government, 1994

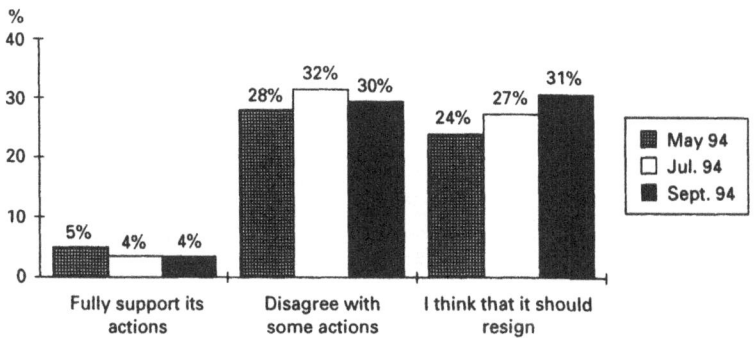

Source: *Ekonomicheskie i sotsial'nye peremeny: monitoring obshchestvennogo mneniya*, 4 (1994), p. 55; 5(1994) p. 78 and 6(1994) p. 63.

Figure 4.9 Assessments of Russian Government policies, 1992

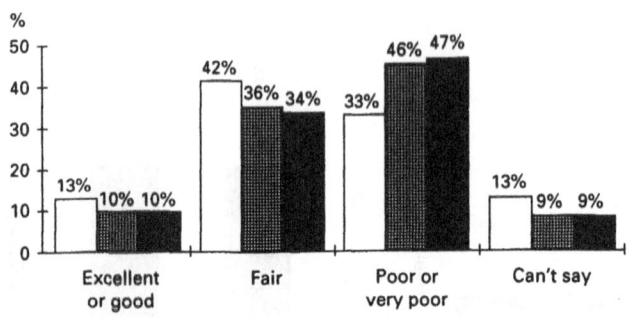

(a) How would you appraise the results of the government's activities in carrying out economic reform?

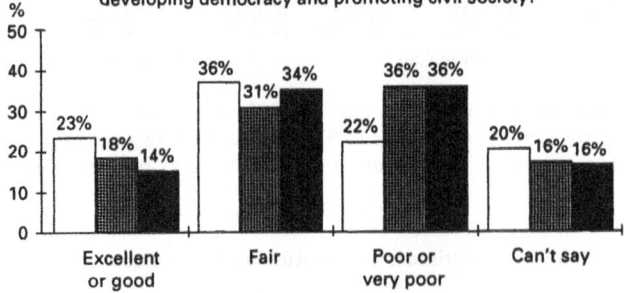

(b) How would you appraise the results of the government's activities in developing democracy and promoting civil society?

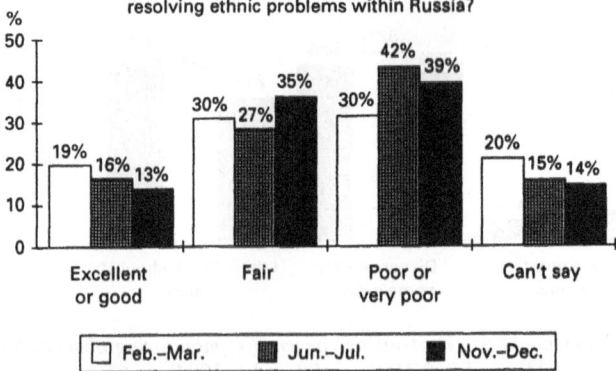

(c) How would you appraise the results of the government's activity in resolving ethnic problems within Russia?

Source: *Mir mnenii i mneniya o mire*, 1(7) and 2(8) (1993).

As can be seen, paralleling the overall degree of trust in the Government, assessments of the effectiveness of particular policies are not complimentary. This is particularly the case with economic reform, where half the population find the end results unsatisfactory. Only small numbers see Government policies as having been effective either in terms of developing political democracy or in managing Russia's multi-ethnic society, although the numbers believing that the results were good or fair are, in these categories, virtually equal or outweigh those considering matters to be poor, so perhaps assessments are not as harsh as they might at first appear. Over time, however, it is clear that assessments of Government effectiveness have fallen, as the honeymoon period – never as much of a honeymoon as was supposed – came to a rapid end.

THE RUSSIAN PARLIAMENT

Before the end of communist rule, the Russian Parliament and President Yeltsin were not perceived as particularly distinct. The Parliament had, albeit narrowly, selected Yeltsin as its chairman prior to his creation of the post of Russian President and election to that role in mid-1991. Before and after the coup of August 1991, both President and Parliament took the position that Russia's (and indeed their own) best interests would be served by a major reduction in the powers of the central soviet authorities. This disguised many of the potential differences between the two.[6]

However, differences there clearly were. The Parliament had been elected in the spring of 1990, when the CPSU had only just abandoned its leading role, and alternative political organisations had not had time to get organised. Consequently some 80 per cent of the Parliament were Communist Party members when elected (although of course this did not necessarily mean that all were sympathetic to communist views).[7] Radicals associated with the organisation Democratic Russia could only claim at best 350 out of the 1081 deputies who were elected. There were therefore clear ideological and political differences between the President and his advisers on the one hand and the Parliament on the other. These related in particular to economic reform, to the position of Russians living outside the Russian Federation, and to the constitutional debate over whether Russia should have a presidential or a parliamentary form of government.

These principled differences became more and more clear over the course of 1992–93, as the Parliament refused to pass the Government's budget and adopt important parts of the economic reform legislation, issued decrees supporting separatists in Georgia and Moldova and claimed parts of Ukraine as Russian, imposed a Prime Minister, Viktor Chernomyrdin, in December 1992, and, by March 1993 at the ninth Congress of People's Deputies, had stripped President Yeltsin of most of his executive powers and narrowly failed in attempts to impeach him.

So how did the Russian Parliament fare in terms of public opinion? Survey evidence demonstrates that the Parliament had very little popular support anywhere in the country. Thus, for example, in January 1992 VTsIOM in an urban survey found only 10 per cent prepared to say that they trusted it more than either the Government or the President.[8] In March the same organisation found that only 4 per cent fully trusted the Russian Supreme Soviet, and in May the figure was 6 per cent, with 36 per cent partly trusting and 40 per cent distrusting it.[9] In April and May the Institute for Social and Political Research of the Russian Academy of Sciences found that only 10 per cent of their sample said they would vote for the same people's deputies again, with 56 per cent saying that they would vote against them.[10] Similarly, the organisation ROMIR in a survey of the European part of Russia in October found only 18 per cent having any confidence at all in the Russian Congress of People's Deputies.[11]

Through the first nine months of 1993, when conflicts between the presidential branch and the Parliament were intense, the latter appears to have become still more unpopular. The Vox Populi data illustrated in Figure 4.10 are typical.

Clearly, then, by the Autumn of 1993, the Russian Parliament had become as unpopular as had been the reformed Soviet Congress of People's Deputies by 1991. The claim is confirmed by other survey organisations. VTsIOM's regular index asks respondents whether they think the activities of various institutions and individual politicians will help end the current crisis. It is not a particularly good measure, since it calls for speculation about the future rather than an appraisal of the present, but again it gives some sense of opinions and opinion trends. For the period from March to July 1993, according to this index no more than 7 per cent thought that the work of either the Supreme Soviet or its chairman, Ruslan Khasbulatov, was helpful.[12]

So how can we explain the unpopularity of the Parliament? And are there any similarities with the predicament of the USSR Parliament over the period 1989–91?

Clearly some of the Parliament's predicament did relate to its com-

Figure 4.10   Trust in the Russian Congress of People's Deputies, 1993

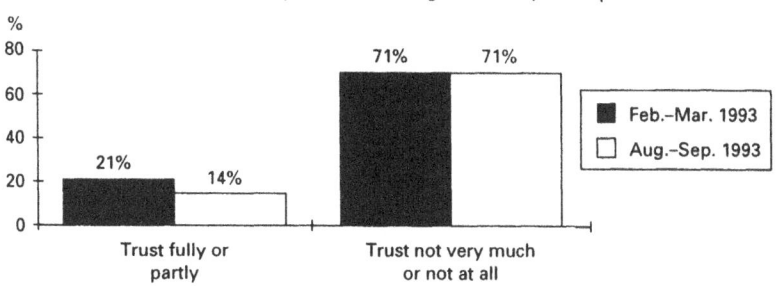

Sources: *Mir mnenii i mneniya o mire*, 20 (1993) and 72 (1993); samples were respectively n = 1996 and n = 1740.

position, and the perceived gap between the views of the deputies and those of ordinary people. On many matters, deputies were significantly more conservative than the Russian people as a whole. Furthermore their electoral mandate was not clear: at the time of their election the media was still controlled by the Communist Party and had virtually ignored the candidates of the Democratic Movement. Although the leading role of the Party had been abandoned, no other organisation had comparable organisation or resources to be competitive with official candidates.

Added to this was a lack of clarity about what the role of the Parliament actually was. The existing Russian constitution defined the Congress of People's Deputies as the 'highest organ of state power'. But at the same time it had granted the President temporary 'emergency powers' to rule by decree. What the procedure was to be if the two disagreed – as they often did – was unclear. The result was dual power and deadlock.

This constitutional issue raised still deeper questions about what the role of the Parliament in the political system should actually be. In established parliamentary and presidential democracies, the legislature is precisely where laws are approved, although its relationship with the government structures varies from country to country. However the Russian Parliament, like its Soviet predecessor, did not have this clearly defined function, as laws often originated elsewhere. It was thus easy to see it as no more than a 'talking shop', a rather pointless waste of public money.

Another structural problem the Parliament faced in attempts at establishing popular trust was the peculiar two-tier structure (in some senses three-tier) which it had inherited from the Soviet Congress. This meant that for most of the year, 80 per cent of elected deputies were not participating in parliamentary business. Even the members of the Supreme Soviet were not invariably involved, since some decisions were made by the praesidium of that body. Nevertheless all members of Congress had access to a range of privileges which caused considerable resentment.

The behaviour of many parliamentarians did not improve the institution's image. Fist-fights on the floor were shown on national television. Blatant abuses of procedure, such as deputies being allowed to vote on behalf of absent colleagues, did not inspire confidence in the legitimacy of its decisions. Parliamentary speaker Ruslan Khasbulatov wrote in his autobiography *The Struggle for Russia* of 'a lack of professionalism in governing bodies in general, many of which are unfit to serve'.[13] The association of compromise with betrayal which was typical of the attitude of many members of the Congress was in this respect a huge obstacle to its professionalisation and the development of a legislature able to offer legitimate opposition to ill-advised government actions.

The legislative output of the Parliament was also of dubious quality in that, like its predecessor, it proved unable to tackle the most urgent questions of ownership and economic reform. Its actions seemed to be designed to obstruct rather than to offer constructive alternatives. The absence of clear party structures within the Congress, with the exception of the hardline Russian Unity faction, was in this respect a great obstacle to the Parliament being able to play a useful role.

Furthermore, some of the decisions which did come out of the Parliament were deeply disturbing. This particularly related to some of the nationalist issues mentioned above. Decrees claiming the entire Black Sea fleet and indeed the port of Sevastopol as Russian were regarded by many as having the potential to provoke the 'nightmare scenario' of conflicts between Russia and Ukraine.

This combination of factors makes it unsurprising that the Russian Congress of People's Deputies was unable to establish popular legitimacy over the period 1992–93 before it was dissolved by presidential decree.

Parliamentary weakness is further emphasised by the nature of its support, illustrated in Figure 4.11. It is clear that hostility to the Parliament was characteristic of all social groups. Slightly more elderly and poor people were willing to trust it, but even among these groups there was not a feeling that the Parliament was standing up for their

Figure 4.11 Social composition of parliamentary supporters, May 1993

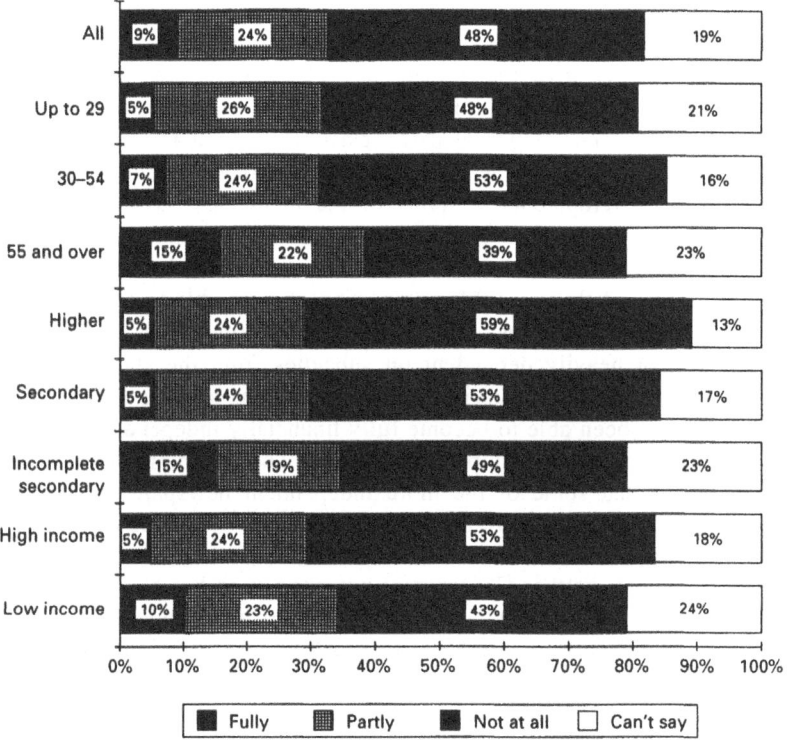

Source: *Ekonomicheskie i sotsial'nye peremeny: monitoring obshchestvennogo mneniya*, 4 (1993), pp. 47, 56. Poll by VTsIOM, n = 1993.

interests by the time of the referendum of 1993. Yeltsin's judgement that the Parliament was weak enough to be swept aside appears borne out by survey evidence.

TRUST IN THE MEDIA

As was discussed in Chapter 3, during the Gorbachev period the Soviet media were transformed. By the end of 1991, censorship had all but ceased, and there was virtually nothing outside the realm of official secrets which was closed to *glasnost*. However serious issues in terms of press freedom and the operation of television still remained. In particular, the traditional habit by officials at all levels of attempting to control what was said had not vanished. Furthermore, television and most newspapers remained under state ownership. This situation was reflected in public opinion. While very few people mistrusted the media, the massive trust that it had in 1989, when it was the leading force in the reforms, had fallen away by 1991, with most people taking an intermediate stance of partly trusting the media.

Since the collapse of the Soviet Union there have been a number of significant developments in terms of the media and issues of press freedom in general. One also observes significant continuities.[14]

The collapse of communism allowed for significant changes in terms of ownership of the press. Many newspapers were able to escape from state ownership. However, the dire economic climate has meant that most remain heavily dependent on subsidies from the state or from other organisations for survival. Only a very few, such as *Moskovskie novosti* have been able to become fully financially independent, thanks to income from sponsorship or advertising. The economic climate has also meant that some of the more independent newspapers, such as *Nezavisimaya gazeta*, have been limited to a very restricted circulation and are quite difficult to obtain outside the largest cities.

Furthermore, neither Government nor opposition has abandoned the habit of regarding the media as a vehicle for its own propaganda rather than as an independent check on state institutions. Notorious examples include the dismissal of the widely respected head of state television, Yegor Yakovlev, on the orders of Yeltsin's appointee as head of the Federal Information Centre, Mikhail Poltoranin. Ostensibly the dismissal was over the coverage of the Ingush–Ossetian conflict, but it was widely assumed that there was official displeasure at the increasing objectivity of news reporting.

Television coverage has remained rather one-sided. Opposition viewpoints are heard. Indeed few other countries would have tolerated shows like the nationalistic '600 Seconds'. But, for example, during the April 1993 referendum campaign, prime-time viewing was often interrupted in favour of pro-Yeltsin broadcasts. The opposition has found it difficult to get its opinions represented. Vice President Rutskoi was, for example, refused permission to display his alleged evidence of corruption within the administration at that time. The picket of the central television station Ostankino by hardline communists and nationalists in June 1992 was a protest against this situation.

Public Opinion and Postcommunist Political Institutions 107

However, the opposition, too, was not innocent of attempts to interfere with the media. The most widely publicised case was the attempt by Ruslan Khasbulatov and the Russian Parliament in July 1992 to gain control of *Izvestiya*, which remains Russia's newspaper of record, and subsequently to create an 'oversight council' which could make 'obligatory recommendations' to media organs. This was effectively an attempt to revive censorship.[15]

Nevertheless, what is indisputably true is that the Russian media continue to represent a wide spectrum of views. This remained true even after the events of September 1993, particularly as regards the written media. However, 85 per cent of Russians rely on television for political information, and the degree of Government control over its contents is a cause for concern. Obviously governments everywhere try to influence the media, but Russian television remains limited in its capacity to resist political pressure.

So how has the Russian public perceived its media in the post-communist period? Survey data suggest a number of interesting features.

The first relates to press circulation. There has been a clear decline in the number of readers of newspapers and journals. This is shown in Figure 4.12. Journals in particular have been extremely hard hit, with the proportion reading at least one falling from 43 per cent to 14 per cent of Russians. The numbers reading more than one newspaper regularly have also fallen substantially. Studies in 1994 suggested that people were much more interested in local newspapers that national ones. Only around one third regularly read national newspapers, with *Argumenty i fakty* (seen by 26 per cent, compared with 52 per cent in 1990) and *Komsomolskaya pravda* (10 per cent, down from 41 per cent in 1990) being by a long way the most popular. However, 52 per cent of people read a local newspaper at least once a week.[16]

What explains these trends? Clearly the answers are partly economic. The precipitous economic decline of 1992–93 has affected the printed media greatly, with costs rising massively. Readers often simply cannot afford increased prices, and many no longer have the time to devote to the 'thick journals' which used to be so popular.

In addition, an increasing sense of disillusionment with politics and an understandable desire to escape from grim reality has led to the increasing popularity of other forms of diversion: growing interest in the occult, religious sects, 'low-brow' fiction, television soaps, and even pornography. However, a study of television preferences in early 1994 still found that more people (59 per cent) watched news broadcasts more than any other types of television programmes. Next most

Figure 4.12 Newspaper readership, 1992–93

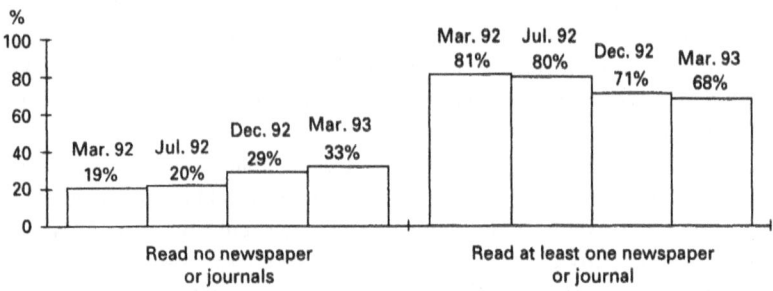

Source: *Mir mnenii i mneniya o mire*, 49 (1993). Vox Populi surveys, n = 1985, n = 1990, n = 1988 and n = 1996 respectively.

popular were soaps (55 per cent); music (43 per cent); and games and quiz shows (35 per cent). Around one in three (36 per cent) thought that there was too much news on television – hardly a majority view.[17]

To what extent do people see television and newspapers in Russia as deserving trust? Again there is some interesting poll evidence. Figure 4.13 reports VTsIOM data from 1990–93.

The category is of course rather broad. Central press, radio and television cover a wide range of media. Nevertheless, the data are intriguing. The media during 1989–90, when they were pushing back the boundaries of *glasnost*, constituted one of the most trusted institutions of Russian society, but a great deal of that trust was lost during 1991 when they once again began to appear as puppets of the leadership. Gorbachev's appointment of Leonid Kravchenko as television boss in late 1990 and the subsequent mendacious coverage of events in the Baltic states in early 1991 were key stages in this, as discussed in Chapter 3.

It appears that gradually over the 1992–93 period perceptions of the Russian media improved somewhat, however. The increased range of choice available to Russians and the greater degree of autonomy were viewed positively.

The time-series data do not, however, tell the whole story, since they only report the rather low numbers saying they fully trust the media. Far more, in the three-point scale offered, choose the option 'partly trust'. Russians have few illusions about the media. Research commissioned by Radio Liberty in European Russia in April 1992, for example, found that over half (52 per cent) agreed that 'the domestic media are not objective', compared to only 14 per cent disagreeing.

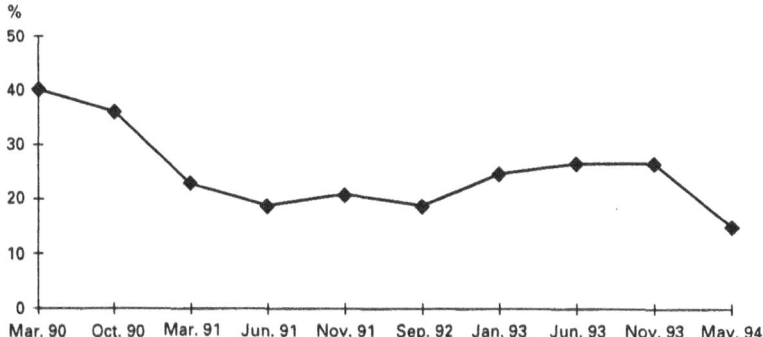

Figure 4.13 Trust in the mass media, 1991–94

Sources: *Ekonomicheskie i sotsial'nye peremeny: monitoring obshchestvennogo mneniya*, 4 (1993), p. 48, 1 (1994), p. 55 and 6 (1994), p. 52; *Radio Free Europe/Radio Liberty Research Report*, 11 April 1993, p. 51.

Similarly, only 28 per cent thought that 'the media are accurate', compared to 32 per cent who disagreed. The conclusions that some draw from these views are not comforting; 40 per cent agreed (against 32 per cent disagreeing) that 'the government should control the activities of the media'.[18] Perhaps this should not be overstated however. If it simply means legislation against dangerous actions (such as inciting racial hatred) then it is not a matter for concern. Refusing to allow opposition voices to be heard is, but only 7 per cent of respondents were willing to disagree that 'the media should report all points of view on controversial issues'. Russian public opinion in general, then, appears to remain supportive of a free media, and in general aware of the problems which exist in this area.

THE ORGANS OF SOCIAL CONTROL

As was discussed in Chapter 3, the Gorbachev period saw, somewhat surprisingly, a situation where the Soviet Army and the secret police retained high, if declining, levels of popular trust, whereas the ordinary police (*militsia*) and the courts and procuracy system inspired strikingly low levels of confidence. Explaining this, it was argued that it was necessary to see the Army and, to a somewhat lesser extent, the KGB, as sources of national pride and as institutions which were 'of the people' to a much greater extent than others. This despite the Army's role in events in Tblisi in 1989, Baku in 1990 and Vilnius in 1991. In comparative perspective this should not surprise us: in many countries the armed forces remain the most trusted national institution.[19] The police and courts were, however, associated with a failure to deal with the problems of corruption and rising crime, and popular confidence in them was low.

Through 1992–93, there were a number of important developments relating to the armed forces. Particularly relevant politically was the attempt by the Yeltsin administration, and primarily Defence Minister Pavel Grachev, to professionalise the armed forces. Legislation was also put in place banning political activity within the armed forces. At the same time, there were continuing problems relating to the redeployment of troops leaving Eastern Europe and other parts of the former Soviet Union, the treatment of conscripts, the reconstruction of the defence sector of the economy, and destruction of nuclear missiles. Perhaps the most important questions related to the desirable role of the armed forces in relation to conflicts in former Soviet republics such as the ongoing armed conflicts in Moldova, the Trans-Caucasus and Tadzhikistan. Protection of ethnic Russians living outside the Russian Federation was an emotive problem.

As can be seen from Figure 4.14, the Army still retained as of June 1993 a high degree of popular trust, although the evidence presented suggests that trust had declined somewhat since the Gorbachev period. It appears that despite the lack of clarity as to what the role of the Army should actually be after the collapse of the Soviet Union, Russians continued to have confidence that it would act responsibly. None of the difficulties it faced were great enough to undermine the sense of pride in it as an institution which was still felt by many.

The position of the security services after the end of communist rule in Russia was another area of controversy. Efforts were made to subordinate the new Federal Intelligence Service (FKS) and the Ministry of Security, the two main successors to the KGB, to Parliament, Government and the courts. The conception was that they should concentrate on matters such as fighting organised crime, security of nuclear weapons, and other major threats to the state, and no longer be used to damage political opposition (as had continued to be the case to some degree during the Gorbachev period). However, popular suspicions remained that the new institutions were old wine in new bottles, since the personnel, structures and organisation remained substantially the same. The failure to attempt to identify and punish those responsible for the abuses of the past did not inspire popular confidence,

Figure 4.14 Trust in the armed forces, 1992–93

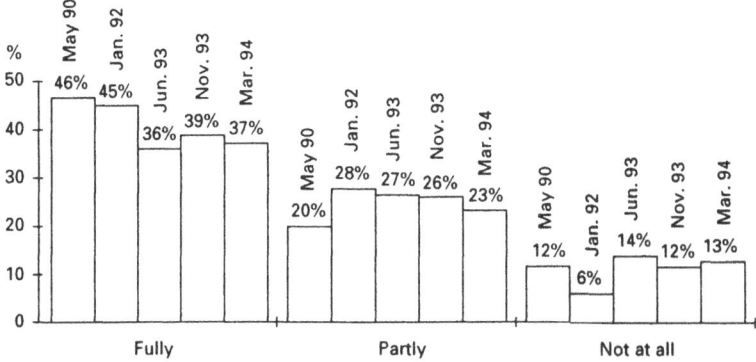

Sources: Obshchestvennoe mnenie v tsifrakh, 14 (1990); Darell Slider, 'Public Opinion and the Policy Process', in Stephen White et al. (eds), The Politics of Transition: Shaping a post-Soviet future (Cambridge: Cambridge University Press, 1993); Ekonomicheskie i sotsial'nye peremeny: monitoring obshchestvennogo mneniya, 4 (1993), 1 (1994), p. 55 and 3 (1994), p. 69.

although in practice such an attempt at revenge could have had damaging consequences.

Perceptions of the police were dominated by the alarming rise in crime which occurred during the early 1990s. Official figures showed that the number of reported crimes had risen from 1.62 million to 2.76 million from 1989–92, and of these, 420 000 were considered serious offences.[20] Under-funding and difficulties in recruitment meant that the police had conspicuously little success in fighting growing problems with drugs, racketeering and violent crime. While levels remain substantially below those in many other countries, the change in the recent period has contributed to a sense of rising disorder.

Reforming the legal system that Russia inherited from the Soviet Union is an awesome task, made more so by the absence of a tradition of legality through most of Russia's history, meaning that reformers have very little on which to draw. Law has traditionally been subordinated to the interests of the rulers of the day. Courts have traditionally operated with a presumption of guilt, and without adequate defence procedures or juries for even the most serious offences. Punishments have tended to the extremely harsh.

Reform attempts have been made in a number of areas since the end of communism. The last political prisoners were released from the

Perm-33 prison in February 1992.[21] Efforts are underway to increase the independence of the judiciary and improve the quality of its training. Procedural changes have involved moves towards a stress on the need to prove guilt rather than innocence, and the introduction of trial by jury. At the highest level, the creation of a Constitutional Court was intended to anchor laws within the framework of a higher 'legality' and consolidate the practice of judicial review.

So how has the public perception of these institutions shifted over the recent period? These institutions have been rather less thoroughly studied than others. However, some indicators are available. Figure 4.15 relates to the secret police.

As shown, surveys show a clear fall in the prestige of the state security services over the period. Efforts to bring their operations under control appear to have done nothing to improve their public image. Why should the KGB be more popular than its reformed successor? It is possible that suspicions about former KGB officials using long-established connections to line their own pockets or sabotage reforms might be a factor. Ultimately, though, a more convincing explanation is that in 1989–90 many respondents were simply not telling the truth in response to these questions. The fear of possible consequences had not vanished. Data from the postcommunist period, by contrast, shows more confusion, with around one in three unsure about the extent to which the former KGB deserves trust at present.

Unfortunately it is impossible to make direct comparisons of pre- and post-1992 perceptions of the *militsia* and courts, since the categories used by VTsIOM to measure this have changed. A rough idea can nevertheless be obtained from their data, in Figure 4.16.

As can be seen, while in 1990 there existed a reasonable degree of popular confidence in these institutions, to the extent that the data are comparable, we can observe a marked decline by mid-1993. The number who had no confidence at all in the institutions had risen from one in five to one in three, although this was still outweighed by the numbers who had at least some trust – around half of respondents.

Again these trends are rather puzzling. They could be taken as a response to rising crime, and reflect a feeling that the police and courts simply aren't doing the job they are meant to do. But this is not necessarily a matter of trust. Institutions could be trustworthy but under-resourced. It certainly does indicate that reform efforts have not improved the standing of these organisations. Rather than looking for rational explanations, then, these data should perhaps be seen as indicating a more widespread fall in trust in all state institutions in the recent period.

Public Opinion and Postcommunist Political Institutions 113

Figure 4.15 Trust in the state security services, 1990–94

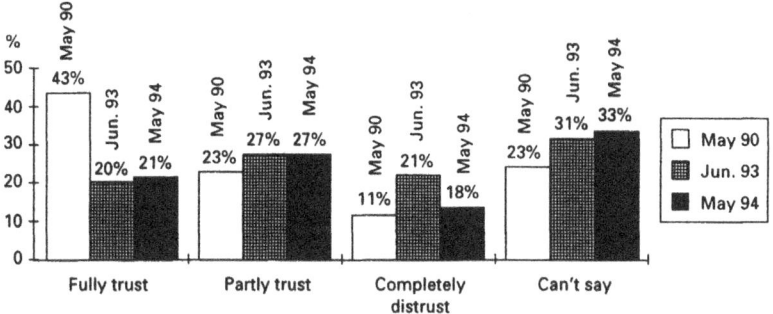

Sources: *Obshchestvennoe mnenie v tsifrakh*, 14 (1990); *Ekonomicheskie i sotsial'nye peremeny: monitoring obshchestvennogo mneniya*, 4 (1993) and 3 (1994), p. 69.

Figure 4.16 Trust in the police and courts, 1990–94

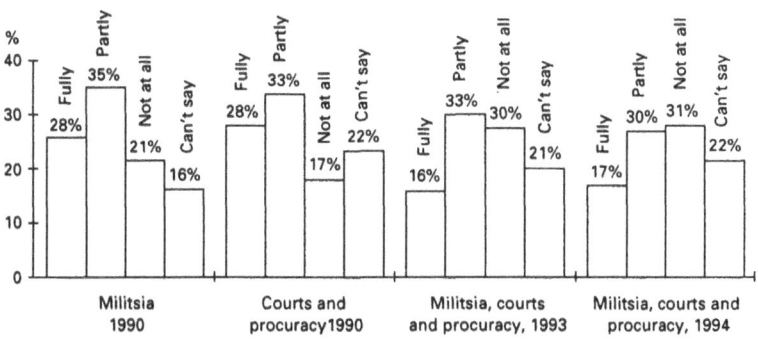

Sources: As Figure 4.13.

RELIGIOUS ORGANISATIONS

The previous chapter demonstrated that over the Gorbachev period there had been a pattern of increasing trust in religious organisations, and that the vast majority of Soviet citizens, including almost all Russians surveyed, felt that they were playing a positive role at the time.

Since the end of communism, there has been a continued growth in the role of the Orthodox Church, and of other religious organisations in national life.[22] New churches and monasteries have been opened and old ones restored. More religious programmes are broadcast on national television. Leading politicians have been eager to associate themselves with Orthodoxy. President Yeltsin himself has been in the habit of regularly meeting with the Patriarch of Moscow and All Russia, Alexei II.

At the same time, Russia's increasing openness has provided an opportunity for other religious organisations, ranging from other established Christian and non-Christian faiths to a wide variety of cults such as Jehovah's Witnesses, Hare Krishnas and Moonies, to become established. Paganism, illegal since the sixteenth century, has also revived.

Although it has become common to argue that such a religious revival – putting aside the more extreme elements – is able to fill the spiritual vacuum created by the collapse of communism, the developments nevertheless raise a number of political concerns. In particular many point to the danger of the Orthodox Church once again becoming an official state church, and of the interests of other denominations and faiths being ignored. Furthermore, while the Church hierarchy has been keen to stress its political neutrality and its ecumenical attitude to many Christian denominations and towards Judaism, it is clear that within the Russian Orthodox Church there also exists an isolationist and nationalist element whose views are more in tune with extremist forces in Russia. Many within the Church stress Orthodoxy's emphasis on collectivism and rejection of materialism, and its consequent moral superiority to other Christian denominations. This leads into views about the superiority of Russians to other nations. At its worst, this tendency is virulently anti-Semitic, and of course there has been no equivalent of Vatican Two in Russian Orthodox theology.[23]

So how have the Orthodox Church and other religious organisations been perceived in the recent period? Public opinion data are again suggestive. Figure 4.17 and 4.18 illustrate VTsIOM and Vox Populi data. Before 1992 the category used by VTsIOM was 'religious organisations of Christians, Moslems etc.' After 1992 this was subdivided, as shown.

Figure 4.17 Trust in the Orthodox Church, 1990–94

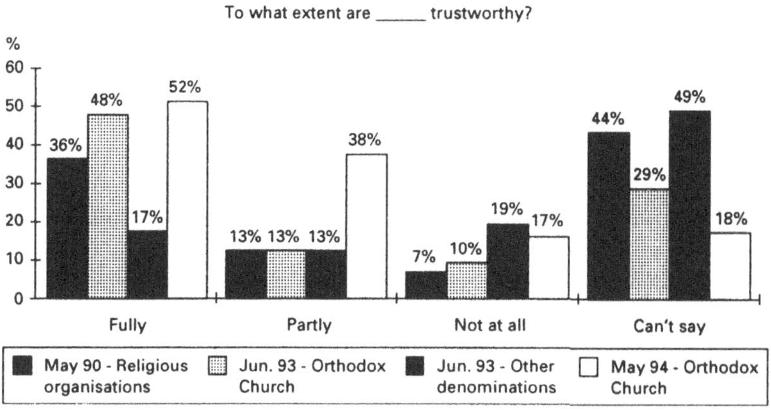

To what extent are _____ trustworthy?

[Bar chart showing percentages:
Fully: May 90 - Religious organisations 36%, Jun. 93 - Orthodox Church 48%, Jun. 93 - Other denominations 17%, May 94 - Orthodox Church 52%
Partly: 13%, 13%, 13%, 38%
Not at all: 7%, 10%, 19%, 17%
Can't say: 44%, 29%, 49%, 18%]

Sources: As Table 3.10.

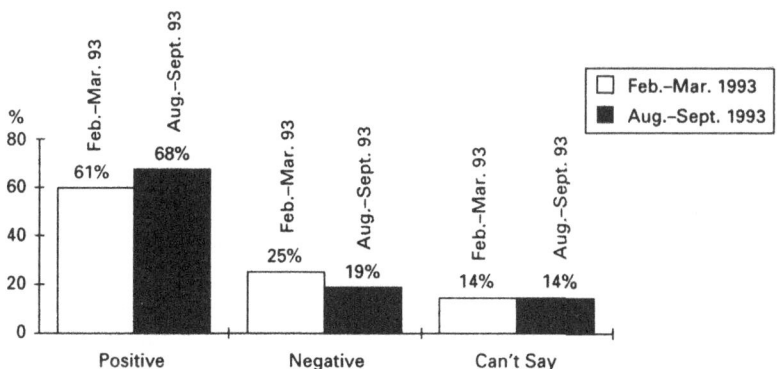

Figure 4.18 Attitudes to the revival of Orthodoxy, 1993

What role in Russia's fate – undoubtedly positive, mostly positive, mostly negative, undoubtedly negative or none at all – can the revival of Orthodoxy play today?

Sources: *Mir mnenii i mneniya o mire*, 37 (1993), 48 (1993) and 85 (1993). Surveys by Vox Populi, respectively of n = 1996 and n = 1740.

Clearly, over the recent period there has been a continuation of the trends that were seen in the Gorbachev period towards increased trust in the Orthodox Church, or at the very least no rise in mistrust. The Vox Populi data would suggest that more people mistrust the Church's role than mistrust the organisation itself, but in both cases, much greater numbers express a positive attitude. These feelings extend beyond those who consider themselves to be believers (around 40 per cent, as discussed in Chapter 3). Clearly, even for the non-Orthodox, there is an attachment to what Orthodoxy stands for in a cultural and historical sense.

It is difficult however to conclude much about religious organisations other than the Orthodox Church from these data, since the most popular response to the VTsIOM data was 'can't say'. The likelihood is that this represents positive attitudes to some other religious denominations or faiths, and negative attitudes to others. Or perhaps the word denomination was unfamiliar. One feature that is striking, however, is the fact that the number who distrust other denominations is around twice the number distrusting the Orthodox. This feeling is confirmed in other surveys. For example VTsIOM in August 1993 found that 38 per cent of Russians were in favour of restricting the activities of 'non-traditional religious tendencies', while only 27 per cent were against this.[24]

TRADE UNIONS

Clearly, the emergence of genuinely independent trade unions was one of the most important phenomena of the *perestroika* years. The miners' strikes of 1989–91 were devastating for the authority of the Communist Party and indeed for Gorbachev personally. However, the move away from their traditional role as 'transmission belt' for regime policies and the establishment of political autonomy was far from creating throughout Russia a situation where trade unions were able adequately to defend the interests of their members. In the postcommunist period there remained problems relating to organisation, financing and functions.

Organisationally, the new institutions, such as the General Confederation of Trade Unions which aimed to bring together all the new unions, remained embryonic, and there were suspicions that they were in many cases dominated by the same people who had run the old unions. The Government took over provision of social security and medical benefits, which had previously been a union responsibility, and few trade unions could afford to continue their role providing holidays, child-care and other welfare functions.

In terms of their ability to play a role more familiar to trade unions in the West, looking after the pay and working conditions of their members, unions faced major obstacles too. In a time of economic crisis, only those in the most essential industries, such as power generation, had the strength to achieve successful industrial action. For the majority of workers, pay and working conditions if anything worsened, and even if there was a union representing them, it made marginal difference.

So how has the perception of trade unions changed in Russian public opinion? As can be seen from the VTsIOM data in Figure 4.19, there is no doubt that public confidence has fallen dramatically in the postcommunist period. Clearly there is a widespread feeling that, indeed, unions are not playing a helpful role.

So is there a nostalgia for the past role of trade unions, or even for the days when unions were seen to be a vital part of the class struggle? And do attitudes to unions differ among the various sections of Russian society? Data from a survey of urban Russians in January 1993 provide some interesting information. Let us look first at perceptions of the old communist trade unions. Figure 4.20 is highly revealing.

Evidently there are significantly different perceptions of the old trade unions among men and women and between generations. Overall, 37 per cent agreed that the only function of the old unions was to collect money. However among the young the proportion was much higher, as shown. Older people can seemingly remember the time when unions did provide effective welfare services. There is also a huge gender gap. This is best explained by the fact that the services unions provided, in terms of child-care, holidays and so forth were of more benefit to women than men.

As regards the new trade unions, the pattern of older people being more positive remains, but here the attitudes of men and women are reversed. Women are somewhat less likely to agree that the new trade unions represent real power to the workers. The explanation remains the same, since the functions that did give women more power over their lives have been in general removed.

This question demonstrates a widespread social cynicism about trade unions in the current situation. Overall only 18 per cent of urban Russians felt that they represented power to the workers. According to the same survey, a greater proportion, 29 per cent, agreed that 'Unions are in general unnecessary'. This was to a great extent a political point.

Figure 4.19 Trust in trade unions, 1990–94

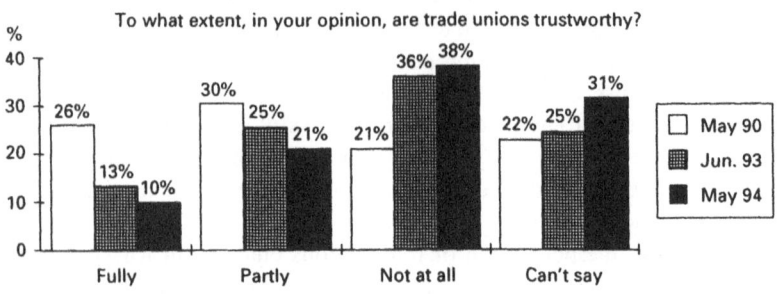

Sources: As Figure 4.15.

Figure 4.20 Views about trade unions in the communist period

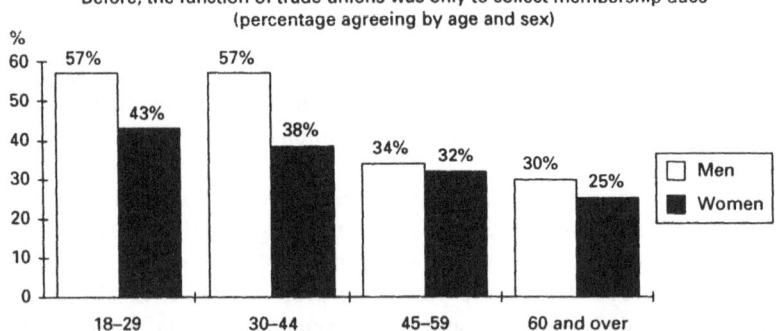

Source: Unpublished survey by the Institute of Applied Politics in Russian cities, n = 1509.

Figure 4.21 Views about postcommunist trade unions

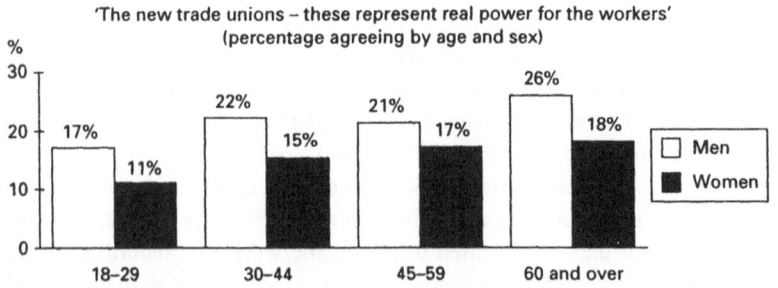

Source: As Figure 4.18.

Among those with a positive attitude to the communist cause just 17 per cent agreed, while among those who were negative about communism the proportion who agreed that trade unions were unnecessary was 37 per cent. There was, however, little relation with social class: workers were as likely to agree to the proposition as members of the intelligentsia or managers. Those who see the prospects for any kind of revival of workers movements in the new Russia will find little comfort in these figures.

CONCLUSIONS

The changes that occurred in the 1989–91 period in attitudes to institutions represented a transfer of allegiance among the Soviet people from Communist Party rule to the idea of political competition, and (in most of the country) from central to republican institutions. It was a legitimacy crisis for the old regime because these competing institutions were able to emerge.

Up to the winter of 1993–94, postcommunist Russia looks rather different. Previously, the battle between centre and republics had disguised the issue of presidential versus parliamentary rule at the centre. This rapidly became a central issue. And clearly poll data show that Russians disapproved of their Parliament so strongly that, in the absence of alternatives, by default the Presidency and Government were able to retain some degree of popular support.

However, disappointment with the performance of the Yeltsin administration appears to have led to a gradual decline in trust towards state institutions in general. This drifting is an extremely dangerous process, indicating that ever more Russians are becoming detached from the reform process. The presence of an alienated majority creates opportunities for those who want to fundamentally change the way in which Russia is ruled. This is the context in which the parliamentary elections of 12 December 1993, where anti-system parties gained almost half the vote, should be viewed.

5 Continuity and Change in Russian Political Culture

THE ISSUES

How does the experience of centuries of authoritarian rule affect Russian political culture? How important is it that decisions have for most of her history been taken from above, by an extremely narrow circle of decision makers, without popular involvement or discussion of alternatives? That there has never been much law in Russia, only a system of non-laws, or rather laws which are only arbitrarily applied? That regimes have only rarely respected the most basic rights of the citizen?

Traditionally, scholars of the Soviet approached these questions via the concept of political culture. The core of the argument of those who accepted the concept was that this historical experience was reflected in the set of attitudes and orientations to and norms and expectations about the political system that existed among the Russian people. For its proponents, the impact of Russia's historical experience has been to create a situation in which ideas such as freedom, self-government and equality before the law are simply absent from the collective consciousness. There is therefore little pressure from society for states to respect these things. Similarly, the extent to which the state has dominated Russian society is taken to have created an expectation that the state should have a very much greater role in areas of life from which it has become excluded in other parts of the world.[1]

In turn, supporters often argued, there existed some kind of 'fit' between Russian political cultural attitudes and the nature of the Soviet political system. The way in which rights were abused, the top down chain of command, the absence of law, the intolerance of opposition, all these things were familiar long before the Bolsheviks seized power. The drift towards presidential authoritarianism in postcommunist Russia represents a continuation of these long-run traditions.

This concept has caused a great deal of scholarly controversy. Criticisms have been directed at definitional problems, in particular issues of subcultures and of cultural continuity and change; difficulties of measurement; and also at the problem of what could actually be explained using the idea of political culture.[2]

The issue of subcultures recognises that political attitudes anywhere are not homogeneous, that there exist in any country groups divided by gender, nationality, language, region, beliefs, class, traditions, historical experiences. In a country as regionally and ethnically diverse as Russia this is particularly important. In some of the more extreme versions of the political culture hypothesis, one finds little appreciation of this.

Such criticism was fair, but should be qualified. Lack of attention to differences between various groups for the most part reflected the scarcity of useful information on the political attitudes of Soviet citizens. And where this was available, as for example with the surveys of Russian émigrés in the 1950s and again in the 1970s, clear differences between attitudes within different social groups were in fact identified by researchers.[3] The importance of generation and amount of formal education were particularly stressed by this work, a finding which clearly had significant implications concerning the likelihood of political change in Russia. However, the unrepresentative nature of the sample – people who had chosen to leave the country – always left the conclusions of this literature open to criticism. Furthermore, virtually nothing was known about some subcultures, such as those relating to nationality for example.

Concern about the issue of continuity versus change in political culture perhaps represented a more substantive theoretical challenge to the concept as a whole. Such criticism raised the issue of causality. How could it be justifiable to use attitudes to explain the nature of the political system when such attitudes were themselves determined by people's experiences of that political system?[4] However, in defence of political culture, this is surely a criticism that is best studied empirically: is it the case that one finds a significant legacy of the past in Russian attitudes or have urbanisation, rising levels of education, increasing awareness of the outside world, recent political experience and similar factors transformed attitudes? Are present attitudes sufficiently stable and deeply rooted for it to be meaningful to describe them as cultural attitudes at all?

Problems relating to measurement reflect many ongoing disciplinary arguments. In part they reflect familiar difficulties of survey research, and limitations of other methodologies. Such issues will form the concern of the next section of the chapter.

The final general line of criticism is directed to the question of what the concept can explain. How important are political culture type explanations in comparison with other influences in any political system?

In particular, the importance of the economic situation, the influence of large countries on small ones, the impact of particular individuals, changes in the social base of institutions, all of these can often form much more convincing explanations of what is going on than can arguments based on a particular reading of historical experience. But none of these can hope to provide the kind of long-term perspectives that the concept of political culture offers.

The new Russia is an ideal test case for some of the most important hypotheses of the political cultural literature. Furthermore, the extent to which the Russian people are determined to stand up for values of limited government and political rights is of critical importance in assessing the depth of democratic development in Russia. New possibilities opened up to political scientists by the development of survey research in Russia, of an acceptable standard, enable us to begin to judge these matters.

METHODOLOGICAL ISSUES

Is it acceptable to use data from public opinion surveys to study political culture? Some commentators feel strongly that it is not. The argument is that it is fallacious to equate political culture with public opinion. The survey method cannot adequately get at issues relating to individuals' orientations to politics, since these are much more complex than answers to structured poll questions.[5]

One could indeed go further down this road and also argue that the results of surveys of public opinion are not public opinion in the sense it was understood by the great theorists of the subject, people like Jefferson, Tocqueville or Lord Bryce. What these people had in mind was something amorphous, constantly fluctuating, even contradictory, just like individual political attitudes, but nevertheless something which acted as a social institution affecting what happened. Yet the survey method treats public opinion as fixed, constant, measurable. As one of the authorities on the subject, Leo Bogart, puts it:[6]

> The public opinion survey method requires that these elusive currents be treated as though they were static, that we define and measure what was formerly undefinable and unmeasureable. Once this is done, and done over and over again, it is easy to succumb to the illusion that the measurements represent reality rather than a distorted, dim, approximate reflection of a reality that alters its shape when seen from different angles.

Thus, using poll evidence to study public opinion is doubly removed from a country's political culture, even putting aside all the familiar problems of survey research: questionnaire design, accurate sampling, monitoring interviewers, interpreting what the results actually signify.[7] Yet to reject such evidence is to reject the only method we have that can get remotely close to representative data on political cultural attitudes. It also means rejecting data that give us the possibility of going beyond oversimplified generalisations about a 'subject' or 'participant' political culture, 'patrimonialism', to discover in detail which groups within society are more involved, which more apathetic and so forth. It allows the study of subcultures. Furthermore, it is useful for comparative purposes. This is not to reject other methodologies: depth interviews, content analysis, 'socio-pragmatics'. As one of the main participants in the political culture debate, Zbigniew Brzezinski, observes:[8]

> Alas in political science what is more easily 'proven' tends to be also more trivial. More significant propositions concerning the historical processes ... necessarily tend to be elusive of the reassuring precision of the statistical method, and require somewhat impressionistic and therefore also controversial judgements.

However, it is the challenge of the impressionist to explain results that do not fit in with his grand scheme, and statistical evidence can certainly add weight to such arguments. Eclecticism is therefore the best policy.[9]

POLL DATA ON RUSSIAN POLITICAL CULTURE

So just what is the balance of evidence on Russian political culture in the recent period? Do significant legacies of the autocratic experience exist? Or is there evidence of more change than continuity, in that significant numbers of people have become more supportive of democratic values?

Several Western scholars have already contributed to this debate, but limitations in the quality of their data and questions raised by their interpretations of them make many of the conclusions suspect.[10] Many interesting findings did come out of these studies. In particular, Gibson and Duch's propositions of support for majority rights and support for competitive elections, but lack of support for the rights of political opponents provide a challenge for future work to confirm or rebut. But their conclusions are contingent, and also only represent one point in time in a rapidly changing situation. It is worthwhile therefore, to contrast Russian evidence with this Western research. This has the advantage of giving a sense of trends in mass attitudes. Given the lack of data about attitudes before serious survey research began in 1988-89, seeing how a wide variety of measures of political cultural values work in the Russian context is also of interest. An examination of this Russian evidence suggests a number of interesting conclusions, several of which contradict published Western studies. In some respects it shows attitudes to politics which may indeed be supportive of democratic values. However, in many areas attitudes are revealed which are much less so, and which indicate that a base exists for a kind of politics that does show similarity to traditional forms.

Political Interest

Let us look first at political interest. An interested and aware electorate is traditionally taken by democratic theorists to be an important precondition for democracy to function. However, Russian political traditions are of a citizenry that is largely passive and uninterested in politics. The 'social contract' policies of the Brezhnev era required ordinary people to turn a blind eye to political corruption and accept political powerlessness in return for rising standards of living.

Evidence from VTsIOM, shown in Figure 5.1, demonstrates that the later part of the Gorbachev period saw a relatively high level of political interest, although even in 1990-91, while the communist system was collapsing, the number of people who were very greatly or greatly interested in politics – around one in five, was less than the number, about one in three, who were only a little or not at all interested. These sort of levels of political interest were broadly in line with Western democracies. One source found that political interest as of mid-1991 was as high in Russia as in, for example, the United Kingdom or the United States with respect to national politics, and higher for local politics.[11]

The period since the collapse of communism has, however, seen declining levels of political interest, with 60 per cent by late 1993 distancing themselves from politics, while just one in ten were interested to any great degree. This reflects a number of factors. The dire state of the economy and the degree of effort needed simply to subsist means that few have the time. Equally importantly, postcommunist politics has become much more complex. Towards the end of the *perestroika* period, issues were clear cut: one was for or against the existing system, and the outcome of the struggle would clearly affect

Figure 5.1 Political interest, 1990-93

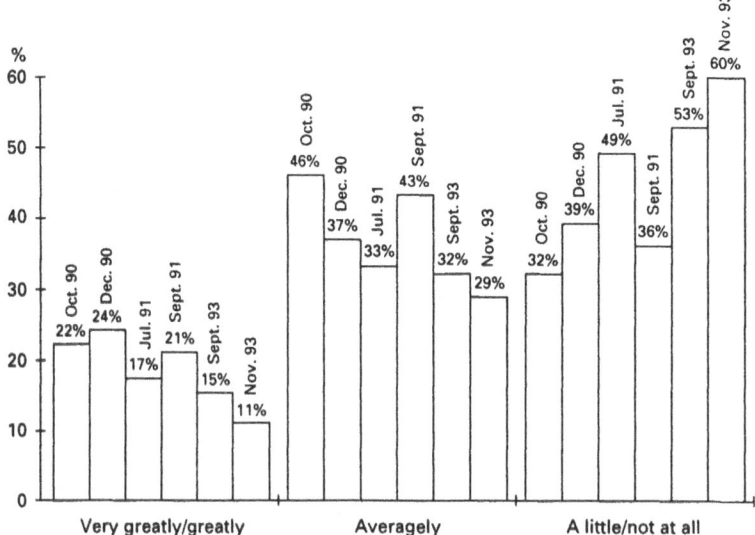

Source: *Ekonomicheskie i sotsial'nye peremeny: monitoring obshchestvennogo mneniya*, 1 (1994), p. 14.

the lives of every Russian. However, since 1992 political choices have been much less black and white, much more in shades of grey. The outcome of this 'normal' politics is much less exciting. Declining levels of political interest also reflect a disillusionment with Russia's political classes, exaggerated by the inflated expectations projected onto the new Russian leadership after the coup of August 1991.

Which sections of Russian society are most interested in politics? In a January 1993 survey by the Institute of Applied Politics, an overall average of 12 per cent were very strongly and 22 per cent quite strongly interested. However, for those who believed that the Communist Party had a very positive role in the history of the country, the totals were respectively 31 per cent and 21 per cent. Similarly, voters in the Russian presidential election for the highly nationalistic communist general, Albert Makashov, and the virtually official communist candidate, Nikolai Ryzhkov, were significantly more interested in politics than, for example, Yeltsin voters. Voters for the populist Russian nationalist Vladimir Zhirinovsky were the least interested. Education, age (with the older a lot more interested than young people) and gender (men more interested than women) all had a significant effect.[12]

Political interest in Russia is therefore strongest among those people who have traditionally been interested in politics under communist rule. The expansion of channels through which ordinary people can affect politics has not had the effect of mobilising a significant group of people who were previously uninterested. Falling political interest has accompanied the introduction of democracy in Russia.

Political Participation

The preceding section dealt with the extent of political interest in a passive sense. Perhaps more vital though for a system where there is some degree of popular control over government is active participation, where citizens are making an active effort to influence outcomes.

Political participation in the Soviet Union has been the concern of many previous studies, the most sophisticated of which went beyond the totalitarian stereotype of all participation under communist systems being merely ritualistic mobilisation by the regime. In fact a number found evidence that there was some engagement in many of the types of participation that were available to citizens, for example duties in citizens' courts or parents' commissions. These types of activity could make a difference, although there was no question that outright opposition political activity was suppressed until the *perestroika* period.[13] What then is the evidence of opinion surveys about the extent of political participation in the recent period?

This is a topic which has been approached directly, and also approached by investigation of the sorts of activities that could reasonably be described as participation. VTsIOM has since 1988 asked a standard question on the subject in end of year surveys. A time series of the results is shown in Figure 5.2.

Unfortunately, the results are somewhat distorted by the scale (or rather non-scale) that is used. The major problem is the category that has persistently been the most popular: 'For me, the most important thing is the fate of my native people.' It is unclear just how this relates to participation. Another ridiculous part of the scale is the final item: 'Politics doesn't interest me. I don't take part in politics.' Which is it? Are people not interested, or not interested in taking part?

Despite these flaws, however, it is still possible to draw some conclusions from the trends that are shown. First, there is evidence about the nature of the participation that occurred in 1988–89 as the politi-

Figure 5.2 Political participation, 1989-92

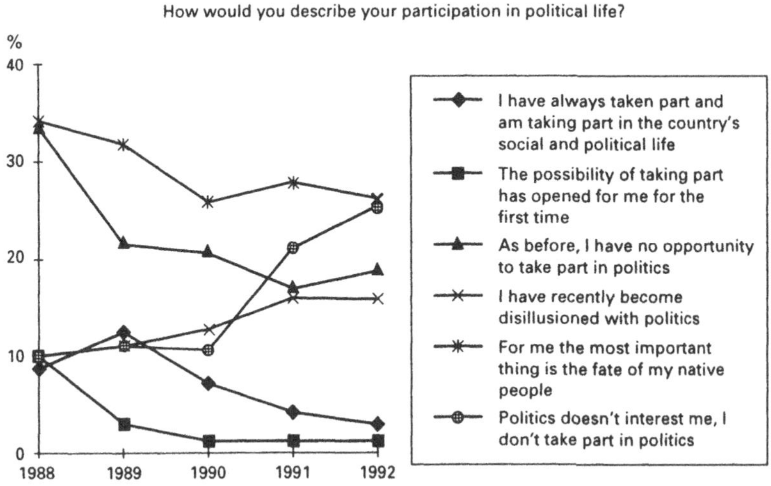

How would you describe your participation in political life?

- I have always taken part and am taking part in the country's social and political life
- The possibility of taking part has opened for me for the first time
- As before, I have no opportunity to take part in politics
- I have recently become disillusioned with politics
- For me the most important thing is the fate of my native people
- Politics doesn't interest me, I don't take part in politics

Source: Ekonomicheskie i sotsial'nye peremeny: monitoring obshchestvennogo mneniya, 3 (1993), p. 5. The surveys were of respectively, n = 1045, 1498, 2081, 2110 and 1771.

cal reform aspects of *perestroika* began. At this time, the 'explosion' of participation still only applied to about one in five, a number broadly comparably with the amount of participation identified in most studies of Western democracies.[14] Of these, half had begun to take part for the first time, and half had always taken part.

Clearly also there has been a substantial decline in participation since that time. It is unsurprising that the number saying that they were able to take part for the first time has fallen away. But the data also suggest that many people who had taken part in politics under the communist regime have now stopped participating. There has been a corresponding rise in the numbers who say that politics doesn't interest them or that they have recently stopped taking part in politics.

Western studies from the Gorbachev period on the subject all concluded that political participation in Russia was not at a greatly different level from that to be found elsewhere, and that therefore it was misconceived to regard Russian political culture as a primarily passive 'subject' one.[15] As can be seen, such conclusions were premature. A number of causes suggest themselves. Economic hardship means that people simply have less time to take part, and as the excitement of overthrowing a system begins to fade, begin once again to return to their old belief that individual actions can make no real difference. At the same time, many of the channels through which people tended to participate under communism simply no longer exist.

Overall, then, 1988–90 is appropriately seen as a time when, as with most revolutions, new groups became mobilised to take part in politics for the first time, and reduced levels of participation in 1992–93 are likely to be more typical for Russian politics in the near future. One should perhaps not overstate the case, though. The popular resistance to the coup attempt in August 1991 demonstrated that political action by very small numbers of people can make a huge difference to what happens.

Political participation has fallen a great deal since 1992, while political interest, although less than it was, appears to remain higher. This is a state of affairs characteristic of many contemporary societies. Democratisation perhaps has the effect of raising the sense of psychological commitment to the regime, while in normal times reducing the actual level of political activity.

Efficacy

Another characteristic often associated with a healthily functioning democracy is efficacy. This is normally taken to have two separate dimensions: internal efficacy, which is the subjective feeling that one is capable of taking part in politics; and external efficacy, which refers to the responsiveness of the state and of politicians.[16]

These issues, however, are not ones that have been much studied by Russian survey researchers. It is therefore necessary to rely on published Western research, although the information is partial and rather unconvincing.

Looking first at internal efficacy, the New Soviet citizen survey of mid-1990 found that only 10 per cent in the European part of the USSR disagreed with the statement 'If an unjust law were passed I could do nothing about it'.[17] It must be said that their measure is dangerously like a cliché, and also confusing in that it contains the word 'nothing', since disagreeing with negative statements can become rather confusing.

The only other measures of internal efficacy of which I am aware are from the single-city studies by Jeffrey Hahn and by Shiller, Boycko and Korobov.[18] Hahn found that inhabitants of Yaroslavl had similar levels of confidence that they understood what was going on in politics

Table 5.1 External efficacy, 1991

Response	USA (%)	UK (%)	Russia (%)
Generally speaking elected officials lose touch with the people pretty quickly			
Completely/mostly agree	78	84	89
Mostly/completely disagree	19	13	7
Don't know	3	3	4
Most elected officials care what people like me think			
Completely/mostly agree	44	35	18
Most/completely disagree	53	61	72
Don't know	3	4	10

Source: Times–Mirror survey.

to Americans in 1976; but that they were substantially less likely to think that they could influence unjust or harmful laws being considered by their local government. Shiller and his colleagues found that in Omsk (and Kherson in Ukraine), citizens were significantly less likely than Americans to think that they could influence how local authorities performed their duties (in this case street cleaning), or to be able to influence what happens at their children's school. However, these data inform us about Yaroslavl and Omsk, not about Russia.

System responsiveness is a factor which has been covered more. The two questions from the Times–Mirror survey reported in Table 5.1 are typical.

As can be seen, the evidence was that, as of May 1991, inhabitants of the European part of Russia were significantly more sceptical about politicians being responsive to ordinary people than was the case in either the United Kingdom or the United States. Only small minorities thought that elected officials cared about their views (18 per cent) or stayed in touch (7 per cent). Similarly, Shiller and his colleagues found that a much greater proportion of Omsk's citizens found dealing with public officials to be a humiliating experience.

The balance of evidence about efficacy, such as it is, then, suggests that Russians remain sceptical both of their ability to affect what happens and of the extent to which the system responds to them. Although it contradicts Jeffrey Hahn's thesis about growing similarity between Russian and Western attitudes, it should not come as a surprise. There is very little tradition of state responsiveness in Russia.

Views about Elections

An area in which there is some *prima facie* evidence that the Russian people appear to have accepted what are clearly democratic values is support for competitive elections. The chance to throw the rascals out periodically is, there can be little doubt, the single greatest check that any public has over its rulers. The experience of the multi-candidate elections of 1989 and 1990 was that elections were indeed a way of getting rid of unpopular figures, and the presidential election of 1991 proved that it was also possible genuinely to choose your rulers. A poll by VTsIOM in December 1989 showed that 90 per cent of Russians thought that 'deputies should be elected from several candidates', compared to just 5 per cent who wanted 'a return to the old system of voting'.[19] By the end of 1989 there was virtually unanimous support in Russia for the idea of competition, as opposed to the old system of a single candidate ('voting' rather than elections, as the Poles apparently used to insist on calling it). This reinforces similar findings in the Gibson and Duch study.[20]

However, there remained, according to survey data, some scepticism about the effectiveness of elections among significant numbers of Russians. This can be seen in responses to the statement 'Voting gives people like me some say about how the government runs things', asked in the Times–Mirror survey in May 1991. Just 47 per cent of Russians completely or mostly agreed with this, compared to 83 per cent of Americans and 55 per cent in the UK. There still remained a significant minority of over 40 per cent who were sceptical about the actual effects of voting. This could partly reflect the fact that elections up to this time really had not changed very much, despite how it appeared at the time. In both the 1989 and 1990 elections the results had produced parliaments that remained dominated by the institutional interests of the old regime. May 1991 however was in the middle of the campaign for the Russian Presidency, and cynicism at this time was only likely to increase at a greater distance from elections.

So it would appear that far from all Russians value their newly gained right to express their opinion on their rulers. This is reflected in turnout figures of just over 60 per cent in the referendum of April 1993, somewhat lower than for the elections and referendums of 1989–91, and of just 54.8 per cent in the elections of December 1993. However, in comparative perspective, many democracies get by with turnouts substantially below this figure. It would seem to be premature, therefore, to say that the culture is completely supportive of free elections,

Continuity and Change in Russian Political Culture 131

particularly in an environment where their outcome may only seem to lead to a worsening of economic crisis.

The Russian Autocratic Tradition

Related to support for free elections is the issue of democracy versus a strong hand. The 'Russian autocratic tradition' of support for a strong highly personalised form of leadership unaccountable to the people or to other institutions, and of an equation of political disagreement with chaos are almost clichés of the political culture literature. Figure 5.3 presents the available evidence about this.

As can be seen, the extent of popular support for transferring power to a single individual revealed in survey data depends very much on the way the question is worded. In the first of the polls, given a choice between an 'iron hand' and a democracy equated with anarchy, it is perhaps not surprising that just over half chose strong leadership and only 30 per cent democracy. However, when the choice is posed for or against the very much more loaded term 'dictatorship', the results are a mirror image, with only one quarter in favour and 50 per cent against. When the choice is not posed in such polar terms, order *or* democracy, as in Fig. 5.3f, it can be clearly seen that there is a strong desire for both.

It is also noteworthy that there appear to be no clear trends over time. Continuing economic decline and political gridlock has not since 1992 led to an increase in the numbers tempted by the strong leader who ignores democracy. The implication for Boris Yeltsin's attempt in late 1993 to impose a firm hand is that the public does not wish to see this at the expense of all democracy.

But on all measures, however worded, it can be seen that a substantial proportion of Russians choose the non-democratic option. It is interesting to note, in comparative perspective, that only slightly smaller numbers were in favour of a strong leader in the United States. It seems there exist in each of these countries substantial numbers impatient with the confusion of the democratic process, and who are tempted by the false saviour who pretends to know the answers to the nation's problems. A breakdown of the data shows that such people are significantly more likely to be female, older, less educated, poorer, living in rural areas or smaller cities, in Southern or Central Russia, and engaged in agriculture or unskilled manual labour.[21]

Figure 5.3 Support for autocratic leadership, 1991–94

(a) With which of the following do you most agree: (A) in the country today everything is falling apart and therefore it needs a strong power – the so called iron hand – to allow the re-establishment of order; or (B) the country needs greater democratisation and further weakening of the central authorities?

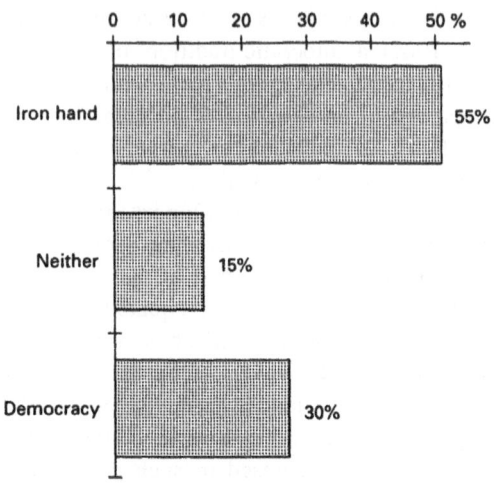

Source: *Mir mnenii i mneniya o mire*, 6 (1991). Vox Populi survey, February 1991, n = 1989.

(b) Some feel that we should rely on a democratic form of government to solve our country's problems. Others feel that we should rely on a leader with a strong hand to solve our country's problems. Which comes closer to your opinion?

Response	USA	Russia	Ukraine
Democratic form of government	64	51	57
Strong leader	27	39	30
No opinion	9	10	13

Source: Times–Mirror survey (May 1991).

(c) Which is now necessary for our country, democracy or a strong hand?	
Democracy	51
Strong hand	35

Source: *Argumenty i fakty*, 41 (1991).

(d) Do you agree with those who say that the only way out of the situation in which the country finds itself is the establishment of firm dictatorship?

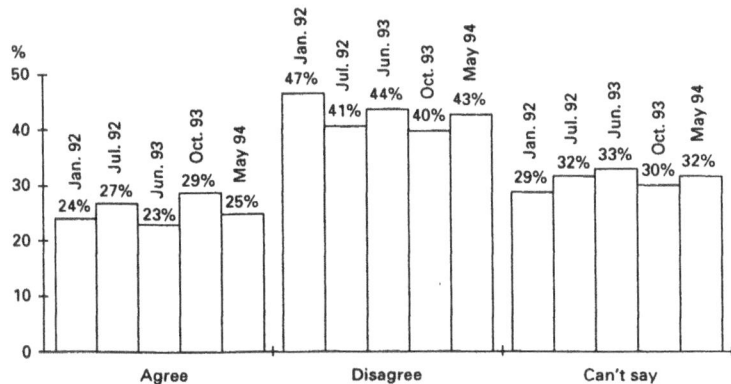

Sources: Nezavisimaya gazeta, 14 February 1992. Moskovskie novosti, 33 (1992); Ekonomicheskie i sotsial'nye peremeny: monitoring obshchestvennogo mneniya, 4 (1993), p. 45, 1 (1994), p. 51 and 4 (1994), p. 46. All VTsIOM polls.

(e) In the press the idea of the need to establish an authoritarian form of rule with strong personal powers for the president and simultaneously to limit the powers of representative organs at all levels is repeatedly addressed. What is your attitude to this idea?

I support it	43
I oppose it	43
Can't say	14

Sources: Nezavisimaya gazeta, 4 April 1992. Poll by VTsIOM, March 1992, n = 3490.

(f) What role in Russia's fate could the following play today (a) the idea of strong unlimited state power, (b) a return to the principles of socialism, (c) consolidation of genuine democratic principles, (d) calculation of what is the most useful, practical thing (e) flourishing of Russian nationalism, (f) a rebirth of Orthodoxy

Response	Undoubtedly positive %	Mostly positive %	Mostly negative %	Undoubtedly negative %	Can't say %
Strong state power	23	21	27	8	21
Return to socialism	12	23	31	18	17
Genuine democracy	29	34	10	4	23
Pragmatism	77	17	2	0	4
Russian nationalism	6	15	26	32	21
Orthodoxy	23	38	3	22	14

Source: Mir mnenii i mneniya o mire, 38 (1993). Vox Populi survey, March–April 1993, n = 1996.

Figure 5.4 Russian views about various nationalities, May 1991

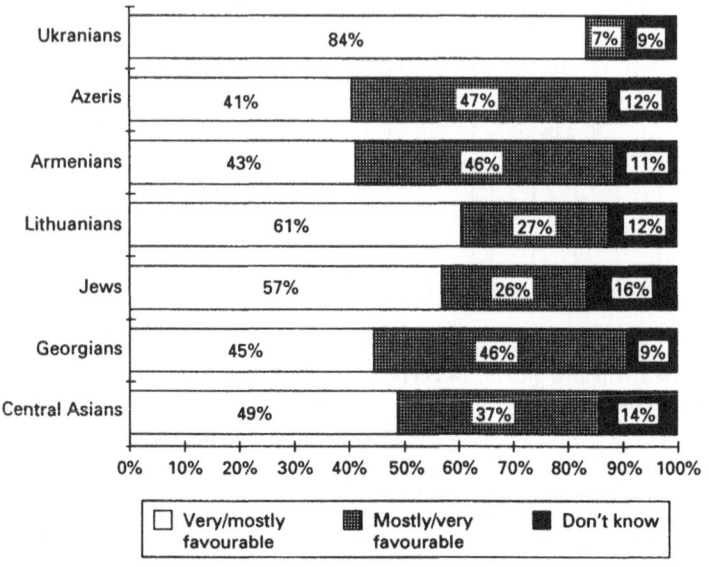

Source: Times–Mirror survey.

Tolerance

The idea of a leader who knows the answers evokes an image of the state abusing the rights of those who disagree politically, or just those who don't fit because of their ethnicity, religion or social position. Democracy, on the other hand, is clearly related to tolerance and protection of minority rights. It is for this reason that political scientists conventionally measure tolerance by asking people about rights for those groups that they dislike.

So how tolerant are Russians? Figures 5.4 and 5.5 provide us with a picture of views about various ethnic minorities. The picture is one of a high degree of racial prejudice. In both studies, around one third of the inhabitants of European Russia were prepared to admit to interviewers that they disliked inhabitants of the Caucasus and Central Asia. The true situation is likely to be worse as many tend to be unwilling to admit their prejudices to interviewers.

When it comes to social 'misfits', those who are in some way different

Continuity and Change in Russian Political Culture 135

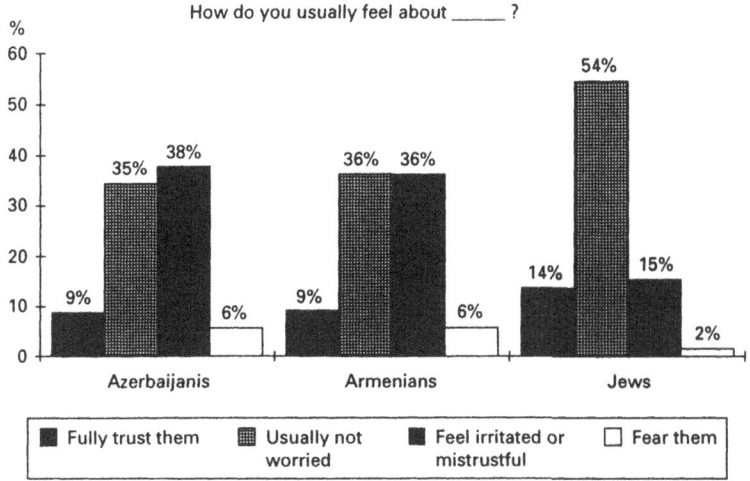

Figure 5.5 Russian views about ethnic minorities, October 1993

Source: *Ekonomicheskie i sotsial'nye peremeny: monitoring obshchestvennogo mneniya*, 1 (1994), pp. 56–7.

from the norm, the picture is still bleaker. The data in Table 5.2 are some of the most chilling material to come out of postcommunist societies. They give a sense of a significant minority of Russians who fear and hate all those who are different, and think that it is acceptable to oppress such people. The table portrays a huge degree of intolerance for social deviance, with, for example, one in three believing that homosexuals should be exterminated, another one third that they should be isolated from society, and only 10 per cent that they should be left alone. Russian society is scarcely more tolerant of prostitutes, AIDS victims or even rockers. What stands out strongly is the unwillingness to let people be, applied almost as much to people whose actions are only harming themselves as those whose actions might reasonably be considered to harm society. The expressed desire among almost one in four to see the physically handicapped liquidated is frightening.

Tables 5.3 and 5.4 illustrate Russians' views about the political rights of disliked groups. They suggest that many are prepared to see ideas with which the majority disagrees censored from the media and excluded from the educational system. Evidently postcommunism sees a danger of the abused themselves becoming abusers. Only narrow majorities were in favour of protecting the rights of holders of controversial

Table 5.2 Views about the socially deviant, 1989

How, in your opinion, should we act with regard to people whose behaviour deviates from social norms?

	Liquidate (%)	Isolate from society (%)	Give help (%)	Leave to their own devices (%)
Prostitutes	28	33	8	16
Homosexuals	34	31	6	10
Drug addicts	28	25	41	1
AIDS victims	17	25	51	1
Murderers	72	22	1	0
Mentally ill	3	37	56	0
Tramps, the homeless, social dregs	10	23	46	6
The poor	4	3	82	3
Alcoholics	8	25	56	4
Hippies	7	12	6	40
Rockers	21	15	8	27
Physically handicapped	23	9	50	1
Members of sects	5	7	3	55

Source: *Obshchestvennoe mnenie v tsifrakh*, 2 (1990). VTsIOM survey, December 1989, n = 2696. For further details and analysis of these data see Yuri Levada et al. (eds), *Sovetskii prostoi chelovek: opyt sotsial'nogo portreta na rubezhe 90-kh* (Moscow: Nauka, 1993), pp. 117–26.

views at the end of 1989 (the height of *glasnost*). And in May 1991 overwhelming numbers favoured banning books containing ideas dangerous to society from school libraries. Not that the USA and UK appeared much more liberal – perhaps this reflects a need among many for a system of morality more attractive than the moral relativism of liberal democracy where virtue means what we like doing and vice is what we dislike (as Ernest Hemingway once put it).[22]

A very difficult problem in a situation of such social and ethnic intolerance, though, is the question of what should be done about people who actually preach fascist ideas. Perhaps this is a conceptual problem with the way in which these things are measured? Democrats should not be too hasty in condemning those who want to ban fascists – as Russians evidently do – although surely a lesson of the Soviet experience is that you can't simply suppress such problems. Preventing someone from doing what they want often intensifies their desire to do it.

Table 5.3 Views about minority rights, 1989

Question	Yes (%)	No (%)	Can't say (%)
Should people who have opinions which are controversial to most people have the right to express their views on television?	51	41	8
Should people who have opinions which are controversial to most people have the right to publish in the newspapers?	52	41	7
Should people who have opinions which are controversial to most people have the right to teach in educational institutions	42	47	11
Should people who speak about the inequality of various nationalities have the right to publish in the newspapers?	22	72	6
Should people who speak about the inequality of various nationalities have the right to appear on television?	22	73	5
Should people who speak about the inequality of various nationalities have the right to teach in educational institutions?	17	76	17

Source: *Obshchestvennoe mnenie v tsifrakh*, 7 (1990). VTsIOM all-Union survey, December 1989, n = 2063. Results for Russia only given.

Table 5.4 Views about minority rights, 1991

Response	USA (%)	UK (%)	Russia (%)	Ukraine (%)
Books that contain ideas dangerous to society should be banned from public school libraries				
Completely/mostly agree	50	47	47	65
Mostly/completely disagree	45	49	35	25
Difference	+5	-2	+12	+40
Freedom of speech should not be granted to fascists. (US – ... should not extend to groups like the Communist Party or Ku Klux Klan.)				
Completely/mostly agree	35	32	65	73
Mostly/completely disagree	59	58	27	14
Difference	-24	-26	+38	+59

Source: Times–Mirror Survey

Rights Consciousness

Let us move on to more general questions about civil rights. These questions must of course be seen in the light of the intolerance towards minorities which has just been discussed, since the key issue in this area is the treatment of minorities, whether social or political. Again this should be taken in the context of a historical absence of such rights in Russia.

The first point to be made is about the dubious reliability of several attempts by Western political scientists to measure the depth of rights consciousness. Particularly poor was the measure used in the 1990 University of Houston survey. It gave respondents a list of rights, and asked whether they should always be observed, or whether it depended on the situation.[23] Unsurprisingly, in every case except that of free assembly, majorities exceeding 90 per cent said that these rights should be respected. It is difficult to be against rights in the same way it is difficult to oppose motherhood.

What then of Russian evidence on civil rights? A traditional way of posing the question is the equation of freedom and rights with anarchy and chaos. In order to preserve order, the state is therefore justified in depriving citizens of basic rights. The problem seems especially relevant because of the way in which political liberalisation has indeed been accompanied by rising crime, social tension, separatism and other phenomena which concern many Russians greatly. Tables 5.5 and 5.6 illustrate VTsIOM questions from late 1989 and from mid-1993 on the issue.

As may be seen, while consistently large numbers refuse to accept a separation between the issues, a large minority is willing to accept the suspension of democratic rights in order to 'solve' these problems, which is invariably part of the dictator's justification for abuses conducted under his rule.

What, then, of attitudes to specific rights? These are illustrated in the series of poll questions in Table 5.7a–h.

It is interesting – given their historical absence – to see the extent to which Russians do respond in a way which is supportive of various political rights. Thus Table 5.7a has 56 per cent wanting full freedom of movement, Table 5.7b has 66 per cent against restrictions on the freedom of the press, and Table 5.7h has 56 per cent saying that groups they disagree with have the right to demonstrate in their city or village. It would appear that the effect of historical experience for most people is not to create a norm that the state is entitled to restrict the freedom of the individual, but rather to make many people appreciate

Table 5.5 Views about freedom of speech, December 1989

With which of these statements do you most agree?	(%)
In order to improve the state of affairs it is necessary to give everyone the possibility to express everything they want to	57
The main effort should be directed at the preservation of calm	36

Source: *Obshchestvennoe mnenie v tsifrakh*, 7 (1990), n = 2063.

Table 5.6 Views about order versus democracy, June 1993

Which in your opinion, is more important: the preservation and further development of democracy (freedoms of speech and press, a guarantee of voting rights and other civil rights) or ensuring economic and political stability in the country?	(%)
Preservation and further development of democracy	7
Ensuring economic and political stability	39
They are both important	41

Source: *Ekonomicheskie i sotsial'nye peremeny: monitoring obshchestvennogo mneniya*, 4 (August 1993), p. 45. Poll of Russians, n = 1993.

how important it is that the state does not interfere in these areas. This directly contradicts any thesis of cultural continuity. It is noteworthy how many more were prepared to countenance restrictions on newspapers in the UK than Russia, according to the Times–Mirror survey, although the comparison is perhaps spurious, since the historical degrees of press freedom in the two countries are so different.

However, these data once again leave a significant majority who did actually accept restrictions on freedoms by the state even in the abstract: 36 per cent prepared to see restrictions on freedom of movement, 24 per cent in May 1991 and 40 per cent in April 1992, with a more popular government in office, prepared to see the media more restricted (Table 5.7b and c), 45 per cent (Table 5.7f) willing to have force used if a demonstration is (in whose judgement?) potentially violent.

One can thus distinguish degrees of rights consciousness. When one looks at a range of rights, then significantly more Russians think that they should be applied than not. However, a large minority dismisses them in any circumstances, and substantial majorities are prepared to deny the rights of disliked groups. To talk, therefore, of 'a broad and unconditional demand that rights of every sort be unconditionally protected' is somewhat overstating the case.[24]

Table 5.7 Rights consciousness

(a) In your opinion how should the problem of visits abroad by Soviet citizens be solved?	%
It is necessary to allow full freedom of action for everyone	56
It is necessary to restrict visits for some categories of people, such as qualified workers	27
Nobody should be allowed this possibility	9
Can't say	7

Source: Mir mnenii i mneniya o mire, 9 (1991). Vox Populi survey of Russia, September 1991, n = 2000.

(b) Would you approve or disapprove of placing greater constraints and controls on what newspapers print?	UK (%)	Russia (%)	Ukraine (%)
Approve	54	24	19
Disapprove	40	66	70
Difference	+14	−42	−51

Source: Times–Mirror survey.

(c) Do you strongly agree, agree, disagree or strongly disagree that the government should control the activities of the media?	%
Strongly agree	26
Tend to agree	14
Undecided	13
Tend to disagree	15
Strongly disagree	17

Source: Radio Free Europe/Radio Liberty Research Bulletin, 31 July 1992. Vox Populi all-Russia poll, carried out in April 1992.

(d) What is your attitude to mass protest?	%
Any meetings, demonstrations and other forms of protest are acceptable irrespective of whether they are allowed or forbidden	30
Only those meetings and demonstrations not forbidden by law should be allowed	37
Only those permitted by local authorities should be allowed	8
None should be allowed	14

Continuity and Change in Russian Political Culture

(e) What should be the authorities' position regarding protests if the protest is peaceful and quiet?	%
They should not interfere	24
They should engage in dialogue with its organisers	65
They should intervene using the police and army	4

(f) What should be the authorities' position regarding protests if the protest is accompanied by a threat of violence or force?	%
Not interfere	3
Engage in dialogue with its organisers	43
Intervene using police and army	45

(g) What should be the authorities' position regarding protests if the protest disrupts the normal life of people or paralyses a city?	%
Not interfere	2
Engage in dialogue with its organisers	31
Intervene using police and army	57

Source: *Obshchestvennoe mnenie v tsifrakh*, 9 (1990). VTsIOM all-Union survey, December 1989, n = 2521.

(h) What would be your attitude if people gathered to demonstrate on the streets of your city (village) under slogans with which you disagree?	%
I would try to prevent it	12
I would be opposed, but not try to do anything	16
This is their right	56

Source: *Obshchestvennoe mnenie v tsifrakh*, 9 (1990). VTsIOM all-Union survey, March 1990, n = 2505. Answers for Russia only.

Attitudes to a Multi-Party System

Many researchers have seemed to treat the question of a multi-party system as relatively simple. The fact that respondents to surveys say that they prefer a multi-party system to Communist Party rule is taken to provide a basis for it.[25] And indeed the data cited in Table 5.8a–c show that over the course of 1989–91 the reservations many people had about admitting support for multi-party politics vanished. There only remained one in four opposed to the idea by May 1991, according to the Times–Mirror study.

However, it is misleading to take this as indicating that Russia is smoothly progressing towards multi-party politics. It is striking how little impact any of the hundreds of parties that have emerged since the collapse of communism have had on Russian politics. Until the parliamentary elections of December 1993 these institutions had no clear function in the emerging Russian political system, and therefore seemed marginal to large sections of the population.

Russian survey research before the end of 1993 concentrated on attempts to demonstrate the marginality of most existing parties. Numerous studies showed that even the best-known parties were recognised by only around a quarter of Russians. As of September 1993 the most recognised, according to VTsIOM, was the Liberal Democratic Party of Vladimir Zhirinovsky, which just 30 per cent had heard of.[26] Many arguments were cited to explain this: the experience of Communist Party rule has discredited the concept of party itself; party leaders are unrepresentative and out of touch; parties are just after power.

However this research – or at least the way in which it is interpreted – may well have understated the depth of party recognition in the new Russia. Analysis of data from a survey by the Institute for Applied Politics makes the point. They asked respondents in early 1993 to give their assessment, positive, neutral or negative, of 20 of the best-known parties. As with the later VTsIOM study, this research confirms that no one party had made a big impact. The party most were willing to give an opinion about was the All-Union Communist Party of Bolsheviks of Nina Andreeva, with two thirds recognition, followed by Nikolai Travkin's Democratic Party of Russia, the All-Russian Union of Cossacks and the fascist Pamyat at around half, and the remaining parties recognised by well under one in three. However, when the number of parties each individual respondent felt competent to give an opinion on is considered, the interpretation changes. Only one in five of the population had no views at all on any of the 20

Table 5.8 Attitudes to multi-party politics

(a) With which of these statements do you most agree?	%
A multi-party system is completely necessary as a natural development of democracy	27
A multi-party system will have no benefits – it will just mean more bureaucracy and talking shops	19
We have a one-party system historically – a multi-party system would be artificial	11
Many opinions already exist within the CPSU, and therefore other parties are unnecessary	20
The idea of a multi-party system is essentially anti-Soviet and is raised by anti-socialist elements in order to split our society	3
Within the Party there already exist many factions and groups and so we already have a multi-party system in practice	5
No opinion	23

Source: Obshchestvennoe mnenie v tsifrakh, 1 (1989). VTsIOM all-Union survey, June 1989, n = 1609. Respondents were allowed more than one answer.

(b) Is it necessary to retain Article 6 of the Soviet Constitution?	%
Necessary	24
Unnecessary	57

Source: Obshchestvennoe mnenie v tsifrakh, 10 (1990). VTsIOM all-Union poll, February 1990.

(c) Overall do you strongly approve, approve, disapprove or strongly disapprove of efforts to establish a multi-party system in our country?	Russia (%)	Ukraine (%)
Strongly approve	21	21
Approve	39	51
Disapprove	19	15
Strongly disapprove	7	3

Source: Times–Mirror survey.

parties asked about. It is therefore misconceived to assume that parties had completely failed to make an impact. People had heard of at least some of them, and were prepared to vote for them when they got the opportunity in 1993. All the evidence from other transitions is that this is a vital stage in forcing parties to coalesce into a manageable number of blocs, forcing them to adopt real policies which can attract votes and so forth.[27]

As regards actual positive identification with political parties, the study found that only 22 per cent of respondents were willing to answer in the affirmative the statement 'Are there any parties in Russia which you are ideologically close to or which express the interests of people like you?' However, fully 52 per cent were willing to give a positive assessment of one or more of the existing parties. The case should not be exaggerated. Around a half assessed none of the parties positively. But the number who identified with at least one was greater.

The absence, until late 1993, of a 'presidential party' was also significant in explaining low levels of party identification, since supporters of the Russian Government were left without a group with which to identify, except the constantly splitting Democratic Russia.

What then of party identification after 1993? Did the fact that parties gained at least some role in the political system mean that identification with them rose? Figure 5.6 shows party identification through 1994.

While between 52 per cent and 58 per cent over the period did not feel that any of the parties mentioned did reflect their interests, the remainder did. Levels of party identification of over four out of every ten adults are broadly comparable with levels of party identification in more established democratic systems. Furthermore, it has been shown that the parties that competed in the December 1993 elections were able to begin to establish a social base, representing particular sections of Russian society.[28] Russian parties still faced significant obstacles. Alternative means of campaigning via television meant that politicians could consolidate power without reliance on party organisation. Russia's size and diversity made constructing national party organisations very difficult indeed. However, parties had been able to consolidate themselves to some degree.

Figure 5.6 Party identification, 1994

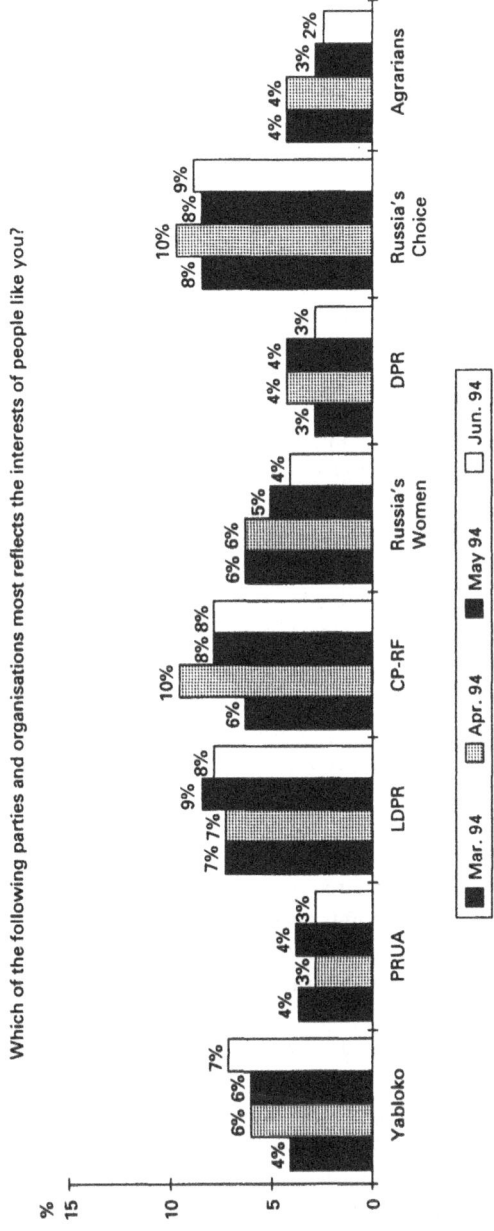

Source: Ekonomicheskie i sotsial'nye peremeny: monitoring obshchestvennogo mneniya, 5 (1994), p. 18.

Inter-Personal Trust

Another cultural trait which political scientists have traditionally associated with democracy is the existence of a reasonable level of interpersonal trust. This is a precondition for the kinds of compromises that have to characterise democratic politics, and for the formation of the kinds of civic links that act as a counterbalance to state power. Table 5.9a, b below shows how little postcommunist conditions are conducive to such a feeling.[29]

What might explain these low levels of trust? In the political sphere one sees in the postcommunist period a culture war between those holding conservative and radical views. Conservatives see progressives as selling out to the corrupt and depraved West, while radicals see their opponents as a useless leftover of the old and discredited regime. The split is based on incompatible systems of moral understanding, which is why the issues that arise out of it become so charged, relating as they do to people's most basic identities and the most important decisions they have taken in their lives. Widening the schism, marketisation leads to intense deprivation for the majority while creating a new class of winners whose conspicuous consumption offends many. The collapse of the old system of values has created conditions where anything goes. It is hardly surprising that rising social tension and crime lead to falling trust in other people.

CONCLUSIONS

Jeffrey Hahn ends his study of Yaroslavl by arguing that his evidence demonstrates that a set of recognisably democratic values existed, at least (he is careful to point out) among inhabitants of Yaroslavl in May 1990. The burden of proof, he says, lies on those who seek to claim that there is more continuity than change in Russian political culture.

However, examination of a wider range of studies from the period 1989–94 shows that the evidence is at best deeply mixed. Disturbing levels of social intolerance and lack of respect for the whole democratic process exist among sections of the population. Many Russians feel that their political opponents or social groups they dislike should not have any political rights at all. This is not surprising given the historical experience. Communist rule, in line with pre-Revolutionary Russian political traditions, inculcated a complete, if distorted, system

Table 5.9 Inter-personal trust

(a) With which of the following judgements do you most agree?	Dec. 89 (%)	Jan. 91 (%)
You can trust people. They won't let you down	54	36
You can trust some, but you shouldn't rely on people	40	41
Can't say	6	23

Source: Yuri Levada et al. (eds), *Sovetskii prostoi chelovek: opyt sotsial'nogo portreta na rubezh 90-kh* (Moscow: Nauka, 1993), p. 81.

(b) To what extent do the people around you have an irritable, malevolent or even hostile attitude to each other?	1992 (%)
Almost all have such an attitude	12
The majority have such an attitude	58
A minority have such an attitude	21
Almost nobody has such an attitude	5
Can't say	4

Source: *Mir mnenii i mneniya o mire*, 6 (1992). Vox Populi all-Russia survey, February 1992, n = 1985.

of values and ways of behaving on its subjects. Politics was crudely about imposing your will, not about negotiating compromises in a pluralistic structure. Laws were not to protect individuals but to enforce the will of the state. Participation barely affected outcomes, and politicians were not responsive to popular demands. When this structure collapsed people simply couldn't absorb a new structure and set of values immediately. Expectations retain a reflection of the communist period. As Havel writes, 'The human mind and human habits cannot be transformed overnight.'[30]

This raises a number of other questions. What is it that causes political cultures to change? It is certainly not a simple function of education and urbanisation, although as the cited evidence demonstrates, it is the educated urban population that expresses the most obviously democratic views. To what extent is it connected with regime performance? To put this another way, is the chain of causation, for many, subjective material satisfaction leading to identification with a particular regime, and only then with regime values? This is simply way of saying that democracy requires an effective market economy, a common conclusion of the literature on democratisation. Or is it more important to stress elite attitudes and behaviour? Here elite actions precede mass attitudes. In this respect what is crucial for Russia's democratic prospects is the behaviour of her political elites. Or should we consider what is the starting point of people's identity – in terms of family, nation, class, gender and so forth – and what is the importance of this in shaping people's orientation to politics? Information about political socialisation in the absence of many of the institutions that perform this function in the West is scarce.

If it is the case that attitudes to the fundamental political values discussed in this chapter do continue to change, are we justified to continue using the term political culture at all? Would it not be preferable simply to talk of public opinion as an independent entity pulling Russian politics in various contradictory directions?

6 Russians and Non-Russians on the Collapse of the USSR

For Russians, having an empire was natural. For centuries, well before the rise of nationalism as a political ideology, many peoples were subject to Russian rule. Some had been assimilated relatively peacefully, others with a great deal of suffering and loss of life. Russification of nations whose cultures differed – that is, the imposition of the Russian language and cultural norms and the Orthodox religion, was frequent.

In this respect the Soviet period represented an extension of Tsarist practices, although the empire-building was in the name of proletarian internationalism rather than Russian national glorification. Many peoples were assimilated by force (Baltics, Western Ukraine, Georgia, parts of Central Asia, Moldavia), although this time Russians as well as non-Russians were forced to adhere to a largely alien set of values: those of Marxism-Leninism. But for many Russians, and some of the non-Russians, the sacrifice was worth it in order to achieve superpower status and the respect of the world, even for those who didn't believe that they were building paradise in the Soviet Union. The suffering undergone during the Second World War was particularly influential in this respect. A Russian-controlled buffer zone on her western and southern borders was necessary in order to ensure that the experiences of the Great Patriotic War would not be repeated, and it was justified by the sacrifices of that war.

For many non-Russian peoples, however, the situation was quite different. They had never asked to join the Soviet Union, and many felt they had suffered greatly as a result. Many did: one thinks of the deportations of the Volga Germans, Crimean Tatars, Chechen, Ingush, Meshketians, Kalmyks, Balkars and Karachais, not to mention large numbers from Galicia and the Baltic states during the Second World War, the effects of the 'Harvest of Sorrow' particularly in Ukraine and Kazakhstan, official anti-Semitism, harassment of Islam and attempted destruction of Buddhism.[1] This is not to mention the automatic repression of manifestations of nationalism, suppression of national cultures and histories, and the constant humiliation of domination from Moscow through the Russian-run Communist Party, armed forces and secret police.[2]

Despite such suppression, though, for most of the empire's peoples the Soviet era was also one of progress. Near-universal education meant substantial rises in literacy, with some nations gaining a written language for the first time. As economic development proceeded, life expectancy and the standard of living rose, dramatically for many of the Asian peoples. The federal structure (in the famous phrase, 'federal in form, unitary in content'), industrialisation, and the cultural autonomy given to some peoples (limited of course by the demands of ideology) created jobs in government, administration and culture which in turn led to the emergence of genuine national elites. Furthermore the USSR was unusual in being an empire where the metropolis (Russia) was poorer than some of the peripheral nations (the Baltics, Georgia). Such a situation may have led to some degree of support for the Soviet Union, particularly among Asian peoples who were comparing themselves not with Europe but with other Central Asian countries.

However, what did not happen to any extent was a drawing together of the nationalities. This is indicated by the low levels of inter-marriage between Slavs and non-Slavs, and the hostile views of many of the peoples of the Soviet Union towards each other, some of which were illustrated in Chapter 5.[3]

Thus when he became General Secretary, Gorbachev inherited a precarious situation. Many of the subject peoples no longer wanted to remain part of the country, but most Russians could not imagine its fragmentation. His policies only made the situation worse. Paul Goble judges that Gorbachev comprehensively failed to understand the potential political importance of nationality and thus neglected to design policies that would take it into account. This was due largely to a combination of the lack of experience on the part of himself and his closest colleagues and advisers in dealing with national problems, and constraints on his thinking imposed by his ideological beliefs.[4] The decline in coercion, the policy of *glasnost*, and most importantly the holding of free multi-candidate elections thus created conditions where the elites in various non-Russian parts of the country could come to power on platforms advocating at first massive decentralisation of power, and then, when it became politically feasible, full national independence. Gorbachev failed to respond intelligently to this challenge, manifestly unable as he was to understand the process through which independence was becoming the magic word, the answer to all the problems facing a nation, the escape from coercion and bullying by an alien central authority and the reassertion of personal and national identity.[5] As a result, a process began during which many republics declared their 'state sovereignty', and then, in the aftermath of the failed coup of August 1991, their full independence from the Soviet Union. So what did Russians and non-Russians alike make of this process? What was the balance of support for and opposition to the preservation of the Soviet Union? Among the supporters, was it necessary to reform the administrative structure of the Union at all, was all secession ruled out, and was the use of force to hold the country together justified? Among the opponents, was a complete breakdown (such as occurred) or just a substantial decentralisation envisaged? And how did views change after the collapse of the Soviet Union? Did previous opponents become reconciled to the change, or has there been a latent desire to reverse the break-up? What kind of relationship did Russians and non-Russians envisage between the former Soviet republics? Should such linkages be abolished, be restricted to economic ties, or include political and military decisions? And has the Russian attitude towards the constitutional position of republics within Russia changed since 1991?

A few Western scholars have addressed these questions.[6] In general their work has been consistently interesting, but it has not covered all the areas in which one might be concerned. Hesli and Barkan, analysing the results of the New Soviet Citizen survey of May 1990, found widespread (from 87 per cent to 98 per cent) support for increasing the autonomy and independence of union republics in each of their six groups (Russians and Ukrainians in European Russia and Ukraine, and Russians and Lithuanians in Lithuania). Looking in detail at where people thought decisions ought to be taken, in Russia and Eastern Ukraine the consensus of opinion was that most decisions ought to be taken at republican level, in Western Ukraine the population was evenly split as to whether most or all decisions should be taken by republican authorities, and in Lithuania an overwhelming majority thought that all decisions should be taken by the republican government. In a convincing regression analysis of support for republic-level decision making, they found that it is most strongly correlated with mistrust of central Soviet institutions and support for republican ones and urban residence in Lithuania, nationality, support for the local popular front and living in rural areas in Western Ukraine, and (much more weakly) with negative feelings about central institutions in Russia and Eastern Ukraine. Interestingly they found no significant link between support for decentralisation and bad appraisals of Government economic policy, with the implication that decentralisation was not desired for technical reasons to do with more efficient administration. It was rather an end in itself (independence acting as the magic word again).

John Dunlop, in a brief survey of the poll evidence about Russian attitudes, also drew some strong conclusions. He argues that 1989–91 saw 'a "de-imperialisation" of the Russian psyche'. This is on the basis of discussion of several polls by VTsIOM, the All-Union Centre for Public Opinion Research. These showed in 1989 that Russians were very much opposed to the break-up of the Union, but by September 1990 were in favour of a decentralisation of power to republics and the right to secede on the basis of a majority vote for both republics and autonomous formations within republics. Furthermore the population was strongly opposed to the use of force in seeking to preserve the Union.

This work is carefully argued and certainly represents an accurate account of the polls it discusses. However, it perhaps reflects the dangers inherent in basing one's conclusions on a small number of polls – only one for each of the points he makes. Given that the only evidence offered about whether Russians wanted an end to the Union is a 1989 survey, how is it possible to argue that there was a transformation of attitudes over the period 1989–91? In fact looking at a greater amount of evidence will suggest roughly similar conclusions, but not identical ones.

By September 1989 demonstrations in favour of independence had occurred in most of the republics. Indeed that August around one million inhabitants of the Baltic states had gathered to mark the fiftieth anniversary of the Nazi–Soviet Pact. Popular fronts had existed in Latvia, Lithuania and Estonia for some time, were also operating in Moldavia and had just been founded in Armenia and Ukraine. Gorbachev had found it necessary to go on national television that July to warn about the consequences of nationalist unrest.

Table 6.1 gives us some impression of where public opinion stood on the issue at this time. It represents the results of a VTsIOM poll in several parts of the USSR. Respondents were allowed to choose more than one answer. Small sample size should make us slightly wary of the results, but they are nevertheless suggestive.

As can be seen, the data suggest that in his attitudes to the rising tide of nationalism, Gorbachev to a considerable degree spoke for ordinary Russians at this time. Only a minority chose those alternatives that implied giving republics more autonomy or even full indepen-

Table 6.1 Views about the future of the Soviet Union, 1989

With which of the following do you most agree? Those who desire the good of their people should above all ――	Armenia (%)	Baltics (%)	RSFSR (%)	Ukraine (%)
be concerned about the unity and cohesion of the Union	11	10	63	31
strive for a strong centre and strong republics	5	10	19	17
concentrate all forces on the preservation of national language and culture	53	26	9	21
struggle for the economic independence of republics	26	44	15	32
struggle for the full political independence of republics, not excluding secession from the Union	17	47	10	20

Note: Respondents were allowed to choose more than one answer.

Source: Obshchestvennoe mnenie v tsifrakh, 2 (1989). Poll of 104 in Armenia, 315 in Baltics, 387 in RSFSR and 205 in Ukraine.

dence as being best 'for the good of their people'. Almost two thirds wanted the authorities to seek to preserve the Union. However, the General Secretary's attitude was wholly unrepresentative of areas outside the Russian republic. Ukraine even as early as 1989 was deeply divided on the issue, Armenians appeared to put great emphasis on cultural autonomy from Russia with sizeable minorities in favour of decentralising important decisions or even full independence, whereas inhabitants of the Baltic states appeared to be evenly split between decentralisation and secession.

These conclusions are elaborated on by other questions asked in the same survey, which are shown in Table 6.2.

These data suggest that, although nationalist movements had begun in both Ukraine and Armenia, the people of these republics were a long way from desiring full independence, but rather wanted changes in the way the Union operated. It was only in the Baltics that full independence was already the goal. This is certainly a reflection of the state of the independence movements in each republic. Sajudis and the Estonian and Latvian popular fronts had been operating effectively for long enough for the populations to become aware of them and see

Table 6.2 Desirable forms of federation, 1989

Are changes required in the relationship between the Union and autonomous republics, autonomous areas and regions?	Armenia (%)	Baltics (%)	RSFSR (%)	Ukraine (%)
Changes are not needed and I am in favour of preserving existing relations	3	6	21	12
It is necessary to strengthen the centre's concern for the needs of union republics and minority peoples	6	14	27	27
All nations' educational rights should not be dependent on borders and geographical position, equal political rights and status within the USSR are necessary	83	30	34	39
It is necessary to transfer the basic functions of state power to republican organs	8	52	7	22

Source: As Table 6.1

them as alternative governments, whereas the Karabakh committee in Armenia and Rukh in Ukraine were too new and unfamiliar for that.

As regards the Russians, it is noticeable that a substantial majority were unhappy with existing arrangements and wanted the Union structures to show a greater concern for the wishes of minorities. Perhaps then Gorbachev, who had claimed the existence of a 'full equality of nations' in his book *Perestroika* and flirted with the idea of making Russian the official state language, was more out of line with public opinion on the issue than might be supposed, even within the Russian republic?

The period from Autumn 1989 to Spring 1990 saw a considerable straining of relations between some nationalities. December saw the Lithuanian Communist Party secede from the all-union CPSU, with Lithuania and Estonia declaring themselves independent in March and Latvia that May. Gorbachev responded with a show of force and with an economic blockade of Lithuania. January 1990 also saw Soviet tanks on the streets of Baku, the Azerbaijani capital, as relations between Azeris and Armenians deteriorated. Furthermore the elections to republican Supreme Soviets of March to May saw pro-independence forces victorious in several republics and radicals (as they then seemed) winning enough seats in elections to a new Russian Parliament for Boris Yeltsin to become elected as its chairman.

Public opinion had moved along with these developments. Thus as early as December 1989 an all-Union survey by VTsIOM had found 35 per cent fully supporting and another 19 per cent partly supporting demands by union republics for economic and political independence. Just 20 per cent were opposed. Also, only 11 per cent fully and 13 per cent partly supported the slogans of Interfront, the movement in favour of the Union in the three Baltic republics; 49 per cent throughout the entire Soviet Union were opposed to its slogans.[7]

This is confirmation that even Russians by this time, influenced perhaps by Yeltsin's election campaign with its stress on Russia's rebirth, were increasingly amenable to the prospect of *some* republics leaving the Union. There was even a feeling that it might be beneficial to Russia, as reflected in the 50 per cent in the RSFSR who in May 1990 responded affirmatively to the question 'Do you think the Russian people will live better overall if a number of republics leave the USSR?' Only 29 per cent disagreed (19 per cent partly, 10 per cent completely).[8]

It is also clear that by this time a decentralisation of power away from the discredited central institutions to republican ones was desired by substantially more people within Russia than had been the case the previous September, reflecting the greater degree of public confidence republican institutions now had. The May 1990 VTsIOM study asked Russians a series of questions about the desirable degree of decentralisation. Results are shown in Table 6.3a, b.

As is shown, many Russians by now appeared to accept Yeltsin's position of greatly increased powers to Russian institutions, if not full independence. Only 18 per cent came out in favour of the Gorbachevian position of a status quo. This represented a dramatic change since the September 1989 poll. As was shown in Chapter 3, this precise period was when central institutions were losing their legitimacy relative to republican ones. What appears to be occurring here is a process whereby identification with a different set of political institutions led to adoption of the values associated with those institutions (although this was naturally not wholly a one-way process).

The views of Russians about the various 'autonomies' within the Russian Federation are also revealing. Once again it appears that Yeltsin's position on the issue was in accord with that of the majority in the sense that neither he nor most Russians were in favour of a right of secession for Russia's republics, although some one in four in fact were.

Table 6.3 Views about centre–periphery relations, 1990

(a) How in your opinion should future relations between the Russian Federation and the Soviet Union as a whole be shaped?	%
They should be kept the same as now	18
Russia's economic and political rights should be widened but the last word on all questions should remain with the centre	35
Russia should receive political and economic independence (up to and including leaving the USSR)	42

(b) How in your opinion should future relations between the Russian Federation and its autonomous units be shaped?	May 1990 (%)	July 1990 (%)
The power of autonomous regions in the RSFSR should remain the same as at present	20	19
Economic and political rights of autonomous regions should be broadened but the last word on all questions should remain with the RSFSR as a whole	57	47
Autonomous regions should receive political and economic independence (up to and including leaving the RSFSR)	20	27

Sources: *Argumenty i fakty*, 21 (1990) and 34 (1990). Polls by VTsIOM of 1517 and 1489 adults respectively in the RSFSR.

That the divisions which existed in Russian public opinion by May 1990 were maintained over the next few months is suggested by a survey in the RSFSR which asked very similar questions that September, by which time the Russian Federation, Ukraine, Belarus, Uzbekistan and Turkmenistan had all declared their state sovereignty, and Karelia, closely followed by Komi and Tatarstan had become the first of Russia's republics to declare their sovereignty. Table 6.4a–c illustrates this.

It is clear from these data that over the Summer of 1990 there had been only limited movement in public opinion in respect to Russia's position within the Soviet Union. Russians were in virtually identical proportions – around two to one – still in favour of the predominant decision-making power lying with republican authorities. Yeltsin's campaign theme of central corruption and incompetence had a strong resonance. However, there are differences with respect to the internal structure of the Russian Federation. While similar numbers thought that Russian authorities should have authority over those in the auton-

Table 6.4 Views about the desirable distribution of power, Russia, September 1990

(a) Should the organs of the Soviet Union have the right to revoke or halt the decisions of the Russian Federation?	%
They should have the right	23
They should not have the right	53
(b) Should the organs of the Russian Federation have the right to revoke or halt the decisions of the Soviet Union?	%
They should have the right	48
They should not have the right	22
(c) Which way of organising the Russian Federation seems preferable to you?	%
One historically formed state with special rights for the national-territorial formations	29
A federation in which the national-territorial formations, regions and oblasts enjoy full rights	48
(d) On their own territory the laws of the autonomous formations should take precedence over the laws of the Russian federation	%
Agree	2
Disagree	47
(e) The autonomous formations should have the right to leave the Russian Federation if a majority of their population favours it	%
Agree	56
Disagree	28

Source: *Moskovskie novosti*, no. 40 (1990). Poll by VTsIOM, n = 1458.

omous provinces, 56 per cent were now prepared to grant to the autonomous formations the right to secede from Russia by majority vote.

There had also, in the period from Autumn 1989 to the Summer of 1990, been important shifts in the attitude of a number of groups towards the possibility of some non-Russian republics leaving the Soviet Union. This is illustrated in Figure 6.1, which illustrates responses to a Vox Populi survey conducted in July and August 1990.

Comparison of these data with the previous survey suggests that views had been shifting away from the maintenance of the Union. By this time, 43 per cent of Russians were prepared fully to agree that secession was acceptable and another 17 per cent partly to agree. Only 21 per cent disagreed to some degree. This compared with 63 per cent concerned with preserving the integrity of the Union only one year previously.

Figure 6.1 Views about secession by union republics, 1990

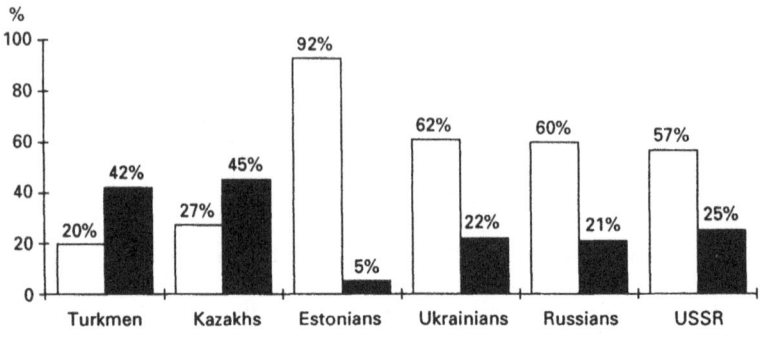

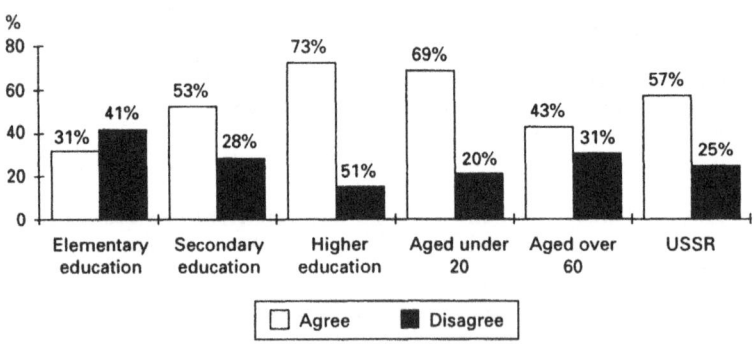

Source: *Mir mnenii i mneniya o mire*, 2 (1991). Survey by Vox Populi, n = 2504.

Among non-Russians too the situation appeared to have changed. Estonians were now over 90 per cent in favour of the right of full secession (only stressed by one in two Balts the previous September). Ukrainians, previously evenly split, had now moved three to one in favour of the possibility of republics leaving the Union. It was only among the Central Asian peoples that there was opposition to secession. This might reflect a number of factors: the feeling that this part of the world had benefited in various ways from being part of the Soviet Union and that a collapse of the Union would be highly damaging; also, crucially, the absence in Kazakhstan and Turkmenistan of nationalist elites arguing for independence and critical of all-Union administrative structures.

The demographic breakdown of these views is worth noting too. It is clear from the charts that age and education were significant intervening variables determining support for the potential break-up of the Union. As indeed was sex, with a substantial gender gap in existence, with 46 per cent of men compared to only 35 per cent of women strongly in favour of the proposition. This distribution of views is consistent with the patterns outlined elsewhere regarding democratic values, support for a market economy and so forth. The young, well-educated male was most likely to accept the proposition, the older, less well-educated female the least likely.

Clearly though, by the middle of 1990 Soviet citizens representing all demographic groups, with the exception of inhabitants of Central Asia, were prepared to concede the principle of self-determination. Most importantly, this now included Russians. Yeltsin's actions as Russian President – making bilateral treaties with other republics, supporting the Baltic republics' independence drives – were more in tune with public opinion in this respect than Gorbachev's threats to republics who wanted greater autonomy. And Yeltsin's actions, in combination with the sovereignty declarations by a number of republics, made the formation of a new union structure by the central authorities an urgent priority. This was also reflected in public opinion: in one national poll, taken that October and November, fully 80 per cent considered it to be necessary, 32 per cent immediately, and 48 per cent after a consultation period. Only 10 per cent said that they didn't think that there should be a new treaty.

However, acceptance of a right of secession, which had after all been guaranteed by the 1977 Soviet Constitution, and was therefore a well-established principle at this time, did not necessarily mean that secession was seen as desirable. This is illustrated by the last-mentioned survey, which found that fully 73 per cent said that efforts should be made to preserve the existing borders of the Soviet Union, while just 16 per cent disagreed. It also gave information about precisely how citizens thought that a reformed Union ought to be structured, through asking where competence ought to lie in a number of questions. The results are shown in Table 6.5.

As can be seen, while the survey confirms that overwhelming majorities favoured decentralisation of economic decision making, law and order and cultural issues – several of the most important questions of internal policy to republican authorities – it also suggests that overwhelming majorities wanted at this time to see defence and foreign policy activities run by all-Union authorities.

Table 6.5 Attitudes to secession, 1990

Who in your opinion ought to have the final say about the following problems?	Centre (%)	Republics (%)
Defence	84	10
State security	72	20
Foreign policy	70	23
Questions of economic development	28	67
Strengthening social order	25	69
Environmental protection	22	72
Development of culture	14	79

Sources: Dialog, 1 (1991), p. 3; Politicheskaya sotsiologiya informatsionn'yi byulleten', 2 (1991), p. 83. Survey by the Academy of Social Sciences, n = 4355, November 1990.

This finding reflected a number of factors. The Soviet public had by this time already witnessed the outbreak of virtual civil wars between Armenia and Azerbaijan and between Georgia and several of its constituent ethnic groups. Many Russians living outside the RSFSR, previously a privileged section of the community, had felt compelled to leave their homes and return to Russia. The consequences of a reduction in central military power were obvious. It also reflected a lingering great power mentality. The USSR's one achievement had been superpower status and the consequent respect of the world. One way of ensuring the loss of this would be to break up the armed forces.

January 1991 was a watershed in the sequence of events that led up to the dissolution of the Soviet Union. Most important was the attempted seizure by Soviet troops of the radio and television stations in Vilnius, Lithuania's capital, during which 14 Lithuanians died. Gorbachev claimed that he had not ordered the action, but was widely disbelieved, and in any case was held responsible for appointing the officials who did issue the orders. And there is no doubt that Russians strongly opposed the action of the Soviet troops. The more liberal Russian newspapers were by now using public opinion as a weapon against the authorities by commissioning instantaneous polls from various organisations. Komsomolskaya pravda reported a survey of Russian cities by VTsIOM three days after the killings which found that 55 per cent opposed the actions of the troops, although 29 per cent approved.[9] Moskovskie novosti the same day reported only 15 per cent support and 74 per cent oppo-

Figure 6.2 Support for use of force in Lithuania, Leningrad, 1989–91

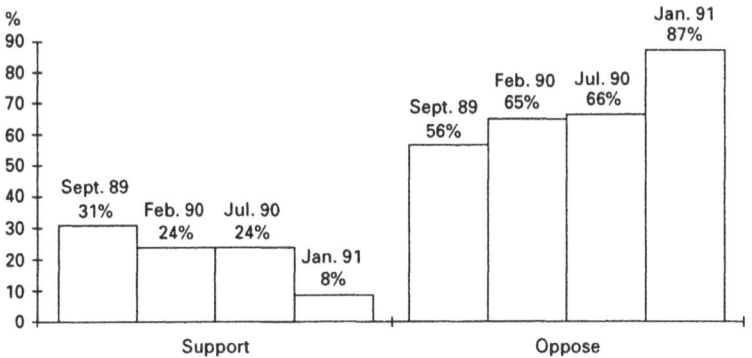

Source: Moskovskie novosti, 3 February 1991.

sition in the capital.[10] These findings helped to crystallise the growing feeling at that time that the actions of the central Government were hopelessly out of tune with what people wanted.

Just how influential the events in Vilnius were in affecting Russian determination to defend their empire can be seen through a series of polls carried out in Leningrad over the course of 1989–91. These are illustrated in the time series in Figure 6.2.

As can be seen, while at all points a large majority was opposed to the use of force to resolve the issue, over one in four were prepared to see the tanks sent in until January 1991, when the numbers fell to below 10 per cent. The only social demographic or opinion groups who were in favour in any greater numbers were the military (19 per cent in January 1991) and supporters of President Gorbachev (also 19 per cent), also, incidentally, showing the extent to which the Soviet President's support had become much more hardline than had been the case only two years previously. Of course Leningrad (as it then was) is no more representative of Russia as a whole than Moscow, but the trend, indicating the impact of the Vilnius events, is notable.

The period from January to August 1991 was one where there was an increasing polarisation of Soviet politics, with Gorbachev's Union authorities becoming very much more conservative and opposed to decentralising moves by the republics. The culmination of this was the August coup, which appears to have been timed by conservatives to prevent the signing of a new decentralising union treaty. The period also saw large majorities support independence in referendums held in

Table 6.6 Russian views about secession, 1991

Would you allow ——— to leave the Soviet Union?	Yes (%)	No (%)
Lithuania	40	41
Latvia	37	43
Estonia	37	42
Armenia	35	44
Georgia	34	45
Ukraine	22	59

Source: Mir mnenii i mneniya o mire, no. 7 (September 1991). Survey details: Poll by Vox Populi in Russian Federation, n = 1989, February 1991.

the Baltic republics in February and March, although a correspondingly large majority in those republics that held it voted 'yes' to the question 'Do you consider it necessary to preserve the Union of Soviet Socialist Republics as a renewed federation of equal sovereign republics in which human rights and freedoms for all nationalities will be fully guaranteed?' in the national referendum of 17 March 1991. In those republics where the referendum was held (the three Slavic and six Moslem republics) overall 76 per cent voted yes on an 80 per cent turnout.

Surveys from the first half of 1991 paint a picture of public opinion which had not changed much since the end of 1990. Large majorities for or against independence in the various republics still existed, and inhabitants of Russia, while split on whether to allow particular republics to leave, opposed the use of force to prevent them, and envisioned Russia's place to be at the centre of a reformed union. This can be seen in responses to a number of different survey organisations, illustrated in Table 6.6 and Figure 6.3.

The data in Table 6.6 are intriguing in that they show up a contradiction in Russian public opinion. While the principle of allowing republics to secede had by this point been conceded, when it came to applying this principle to particular places, the situation was very much more ambiguous. Thus pluralities within Russia in all cases opposed the secession of each of the republics asked about, this during the month when Lithuanians voted nine to one in favour of independence.

Figure 6.3 Russian views about secession, 1991

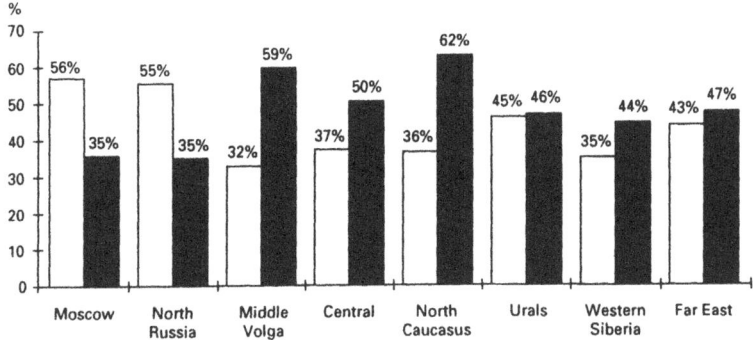

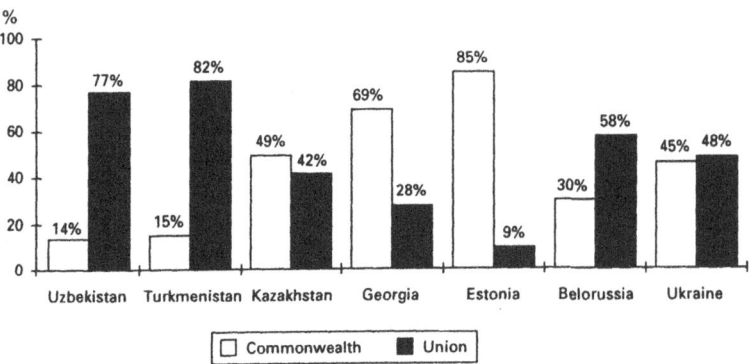

Source: *Mir mnenii i mneniya o mire*, 7 (1991). Poll of 2500 by Vox Populi, April 1991.

And while opinion was almost evenly divided in the case of the Baltics, Russians were certainly opposed to the departure of the Transcaucasian republics, and enormously so in the case of Ukraine, opposed by three in four. Somehow it was impossible to reconcile belief in the principle of self-determination with the desire to preserve the Union, and concern about the fate of the Russian Diaspora.

Vox Populi conducted a detailed survey on the future of the USSR three months after this, in April. They were interested in how people felt about the choice between a unitary state and substantial decentralisation. Results are shown in Figure 6.3. These suggest some important points. In the first instance, they confirmed the results of the March referendum, asking as they did a much clearer question. Clearly none of the events of 1991 had changed the mind of Russians about the desirability of preserving the USSR.

The regional dimension of the Russian results is notable, in that the two regions that were most in favour of the Union were also the two regions with the highest concentration of ethnic minorities within the republic: the Middle Volga and North Caucasus. These regions, unlike all of the former Union republics, have majority Russian populations. Perhaps the variation therefore reflected the fear among Russians living alongside non-Russians of a domino effect whereby the departure of the Union republics would lead to similar demands from lower-level national formations. Such a process also evokes the fear of conflicts between ethnic groups who favour or oppose staying part of Russia.

As regards the situation outside the Russian Federation, this appears from the data to have been broadly similar to a few months previously: Estonians against the Union, Ukrainians split, Central Asians largely in favour of the Union. The result that stands out, however, is that for Kazakhstan, which none of the previous surveys had identified separately. It appears that more people favoured than opposed an end to the Union, although the difference is within the margin of error for the size of the sample. In the preceding few months after Nursultan Nazarbaev had become Kazakh President in April 1990, the republic had seen passage of a bill on sovereignty which, while describing Kazakhs as first among the republic's ethnic groups, nevertheless stressed the political and legal rights of non-Kazakhs, creating a situation where the danger of conflict between nationalities was somewhat reduced.

Further confirmation that Russians – at least in the European part – remained around this time in favour of the Union on a reformed basis is gained from the results of the Times–Mirror survey of mid-1991. Asked 'What would be your first choice for the future?' 11 per cent chose the option 'Russia remains part of the Soviet Union and the central government is further strengthened', 64 per cent 'Russia remains a member of the Soviet Union but with much more independence and authority', and just 19 per cent 'Russia leaves the Soviet Union to become an independent country'.[11]

August 1991 of course saw the attempt to put the first of these options into practice. But contrary to the intentions of the plotters, the end result was the opposite. The total discrediting of the central authorities – which Chapter 4 demonstrated had already occurred in public opinion – gave the new republican elites the opportunity to take for themselves far more power than had been on offer in the 'nine plus one' agreement which had led to the draft Union treaty. Hence the Belovezhsky Woods agreement between the leaders of the three Slavic republics on the creation of a Commonwealth of Independent States on a voluntary basis, excluding those republics that wanted to become independent of Russia.

The relationship between the events of August to December 1991 and Russian and non-Russian public opinion is a complex one. It was not just the reaction of the people of Moscow and St Petersburg that defeated the coup. What the putschists stood for was out of tune with a public opinion impatient with gradualism and looking for ways to end communist power. The coup plotters were yesterday's men in a number of senses: the way they spoke, the way they dressed, their attitudes to the West and to reforming the system. But that is not to say that all their positions were disliked. Their concerns about the increasing powerlessness of the state, rising crime and also the break-up of the Union were widely shared. This does not imply that Russians approved of their 'solutions' to these problems.

That this was the case is evident from a number of sources. For example a VTsIOM survey three months after the coup asked 'Would you support the slogans of the GKChP [State Committee for the Emergency Position] about preserving the integrity of the Union, restoring order in the country etc.?' Those who responded affirmatively or negatively were exactly equal at 41 per cent, with the remainder unable to respond.[12] Similarly, an investigation in a number of cities by the Russian Academy of Sciences Institute of Social Research that October once again found huge majorities in favour of preserving the Union. Overall the Soviet urban population who had opinions on the issue were divided into four approximately equal groups: one in four who were opposed to any kind of union, and three quarters of city dwellers who wanted to preserve it, these in turn being approximately evenly divided into those who wanted only an economic union between the former republics, those who foresaw an economic and political union, and those who wanted the terms to include also military affairs (the latter being the largest single group).[13]

However, although most appeared to want some kind of union to be preserved even as late as October, there are two important qualifications. The first is that, as well as the six republics that had already decided to leave the USSR, the period towards the end of 1991 saw the build-up of a sentiment in favour of independence in Ukraine culminating in a massive vote – 90 per cent on an 84 per cent turnout –

in its favour that December. So to reconstitute any kind of union that involved Ukrainian participation would have implied the use of coercion.

Secondly, the discussions among the leaders of the former Soviet republics appear dramatically to have affected public opinion. Yeltsin, Ukrainian President Leonid Kravchuk and the leaders of the other republics themselves decided to abandon Union structures and replace them with a loose commonwealth, barely even a weak confederation. This decision was itself strongly supported by citizens throughout the USSR, *despite* their support for maintaining a union. Thus, for example, a survey of 14 Russian cities by VTsIOM in December found 64 per cent welcoming the signing of the treaty that created the Commonwealth of Independent States, and only 11 per cent disapproving.[14] Other surveys achieved similar results.[15]

These events therefore appear significantly, if temporarily, to have affected Russian attitudes. Thus a poll from the very end of 1991 asked people how they envisaged the future organisation of the country. The results are shown in Table 6.7.

These are quite remarkable data. It appears that the process of negotiating an end to the Soviet Union transformed Russian public opinion. Now three people wanted an end to the Union for every two who didn't. Among young people it was closer to 2:1 and it was only among the oldest that there was resistance. Why did the remainder of the population change their minds so rapidly? We can only speculate that views on the issue were being shaped to a high degree by identification with Boris Yeltsin, who at this time was getting poll approval ratings of 70–80 per cent. It was when Yeltsin decided to dismantle the Union that attitudes changed.

Evidence that this particular survey was not a statistical freak is given by data from another organisation, Vox Populi, in January 1992. They found that 72 per cent of Russians supported the idea of turning the USSR into a Union of Sovereign States, and only 12 per cent were opposed.[16]

The mystery deepens when one looks at attitudes after January 1992. For these strongly suggest that support for an end to the USSR was only temporary. Thus, for example, the weekly survey of Muscovites by the Institute for the Sociology of Parliamentarism has on several occasions asked people for their feelings about the USSR's break up. Results are shown in Figure 6.4.

As can be seen from the graph, throughout 1992 around two thirds said that they were sorry the Union had split up. Of course this is not the same as opposing the split or wanting to reverse it. Indeed the 23 April survey found that only 27 per cent in Moscow favoured not

Table 6.7 How Russians envisage the future organisation of the country, 1991

What would you like this country to be?	Russian (%)	Age of respondent		
		Under 30 (%)	30–59 (%)	60+ (%)
USSR as it formerly was	19	13	15	36
United but reformed Soviet Union with strong republics	22	21	23	21
Russia an equal with other republics in Commonwealth of Independent States	19	19	22	13
United Independent Russia with strong government in Moscow	24	27	24	18
Russian Federation with strong autonomous republics and territories	15	19	15	9

Source: 'Russians Between State and Market: The generations compared', University of Strathclyde, Studies in Public Policy, 205 (1993).

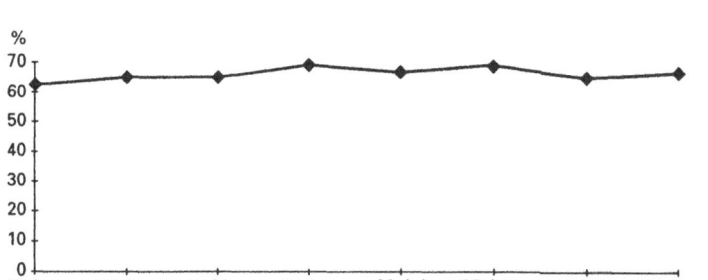

Figure 6.4 Percentage regretting the break-up of the USSR, Moscow, 1992

Source: Izvestiya, on the dates shown

recognising the legal break-up of the country, while 39 per cent accepted it. Fully 34 per cent couldn't determine their position.[17] Contradictory views seem a likely explanation of this uncertainty.

Other 1992 studies suggested more strongly that there had been a shift back towards a pro-empire mentality. Thus, for example, VTsIOM polling in May asked 'Which best fits your conception of Russia's future, the idea of ———?' and found that while only 15 per cent said 'a Russian Soviet Socialist Republic', just 31 per cent said 'a democratic

Russian state', compared to 40 per cent who named a Greater Russia as their preferred outcome.[18] Likewise the same month 57 per cent of Russians said that they would support the slogan 'USSR yes, CIS no', and only 39 per cent would not.[19] Evidently the economic dislocations caused by the split, concern over Russians outside the Russian Federation, and disputes over nationalistic issues such as that between Russia and Ukraine over the future of the Black Sea fleet had disturbed many Russians and caused significantly more to want to turn the clock back.

The collapse of the Union raised a number of issues which public opinion might influence within a newly shrunken Russia. Two in particular have got attention: the status of the autonomous formations within the Russian Federation, and what should be done about the Russian Diaspora, the many Russians who live outside the Russian Federation.

As regards the first of these, it was shown earlier how for most Russians the principle of increasing the autonomy of Union republics and even allowing some to secede appeared by the end of 1990 to have been extended to lower-level autonomous foundations. But just after the coup, in September 1991, according to a study by the centre 'Rossika', opinion had swung back towards not allowing this. The data in Table 6.8 illustrate the point.

These data give a familiar picture of Moscow being the most liberal in attitudes, rural areas the least. But even in the capital, more people were strongly against than strongly in favour.

However, there was no symmetry of attitudes when it came to questions about Russian-dominated parts of other former Soviet republics. Table 6.9 shows how many Russians, as of September 1991, thought it reasonable that these territories should in fact be returned to Russia, although a small plurality opposed such changes.

What then of attitudes after the final break-up of the country? Information from the end of 1992 allows us to assess whether the mood had changed, and also to distinguish between views about the various secessionist movements that have emerged. Results are shown in Figure 6.5 and Table 6.10.

As can be seen, overall some 45 per cent had a positive and 27 per cent a negative attitude to the right of nations to self-determination. The slogan at least seemed to have become established by this time. Differences on the issue appeared, unsurprisingly, to be linked to ideological position, as well as to age and education. Those people who had a positive attitude to the democratic cause, a negative attitude to the communist cause, or had voted for Yeltsin in the 1991 Russian presidential election were more likely to assert a general right to self-

Table 6.8 Acceptability of secession, 1991

Should one allow republics which belong to the RSFSR to leave?	Moscow	Large cities	Small towns, rural areas
Yes / mostly yes	46	32	24
Mostly no / no	46	60	69
Difference	0	−28	−45

Source: *Nezavisimaya gazeta*, 25 September 1991. Poll of 1500 in Russia.

Table 6.9 Attitudes to return of Russian irredenta, 1991

Should territories of adjacent republics which have overwhelmingly Russian populations (Crimea, Donbas, Northern Kazakhstan) be returned [sic] to Russia?

Response	Moscow	Large cities	Small towns, rural areas
Yes	36	43	44
No	41	47	44
Difference	−5	−4	0

Source: *Nezavisimaya gazeta*, 25 September 1991.

determination, whereas those who had a positive attitude to the communist cause, and voters for the unambiguously communist Nikolai Ryzhkov were much more likely to oppose it. Interestingly 'national patriots' took up an intervening position. A desire for a Russian, not a Soviet, state and pride in empire implied perhaps opposite answers to this question.

Overall though, substantially more supported the general principle of self-determination than opposed it. What though of specific cases? How did Russians feel about the most serious independence movements within their own country: Tatarstan and Chechenya? And how did they feel about parts of other countries: Trans-Dniestria, Abkhazia, South Ossetia, many of whose inhabitants wished to be part of Russia? The same survey gave an impression of opinions about this, shown in Table 6.10.

So it appears that there is no great hostility to allowing secession from or to Russia, in these specific cases. Even in the case of Tatarstan,

Figure 6.5 Views about self-determination, December 1992

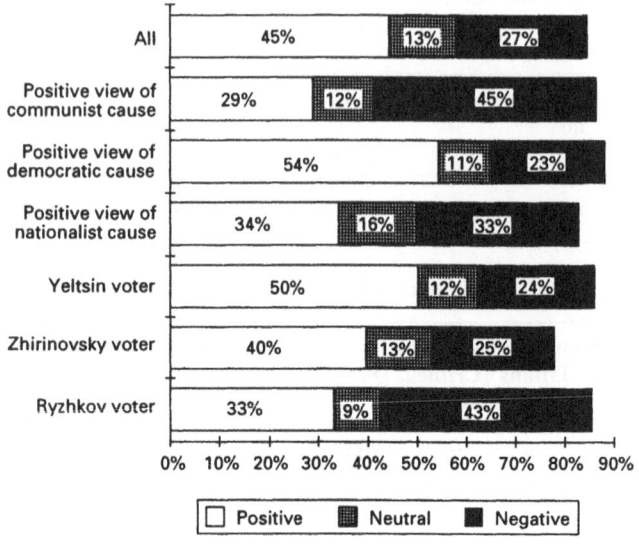

Source: Unpublished survey of Russian cities by the Institute of Applied Politics, n = 1509.

Table 6.10 Attitudes to secessionist movements, 1992

Several republics want their independence. Should they be allowed?

Republic	Allowed unconditionally (%)	Allowed on certain conditions (%)	Prevented (%)	Can't Say (%)
Tatarstan	23	33	25	19
Chechenia	33	32	16	19
Ossetia	30	32	16	22
Trans-Dniestria	29	31	19	21
Abkhazia	31	33	15	21

Source: Unpublished survey by the Institute of Applied Politics, n = 1509.

only one in four ruled out independence. By a very small margin, the region people were most happy to see gain independence was Chechenya: the renowned Chechen links with organised crime throughout Russia evidently meant that many considered it to be more trouble than it was worth. Overall, most Russians were willing to accept the breakup of their country or other countries if this was the choice of the people concerned. There does appear to have been a change from the pre-1992 position in that the principle of allowing secession to take place had by now been extended to the specific places where it was an issue.

It is important in this, however, to distinguish between the choice of the people and territorial claims by other governments. In the latter case, Russian opinion is overwhelmingly hostile. Thus in April and May 1992, according to research by the Institute for Social and Political Investigation of the Russian Academy of Sciences, three quarters thought that all territorial claims against Russia should be rejected.[20] Similarly surveys have consistently found overwhelming hostility to returning the Kurile Islands, seized at the end of the Second World War, to Japan.[21] This is hardly surprising: it is difficult to imagine a situation anywhere today where a nation would voluntarily surrender territory in the way, for example, Tsarist Russia once did with Alaska.

What then of the problem of the 25 million Russians living outside the Russian Federation as of the 1989 census? How do the Russian population feel in relation to these? Is it legitimate for Russia to act as 'policeman' on all the territory of the former USSR, as has been suggested by some prominent members of the Russian Government, or do such problems have to be resolved through negotiation with other governments?[22] It would appear that, despite the desire for some redrawing of borders, the strong preference among most Russians for peaceful solutions has remained. Thus, for example, only 19 per cent thought that military means were an acceptable response to 'the serious conflicts in South Ossetia, Trans-Dniestria and Crimea which directly affect Russia's interests' according to Vox Populi in mid-1992. Other surveys achieved similar results.[23]

There are a number of other issues of importance in understanding the attitudes of Russians to the other former Soviet republics. In particular, what actually counts as Russia to the ordinary Russian? Does his concept take in Russia within its present boundaries? Should there be a slightly expanded Russia, taking in Belarus, Eastern Ukraine and Northern Kazakhstan, as proposed by Alexander Solzhenitsyn?[24] Should the former Soviet Union be restored? Or should boundaries take in the whole of the former Tsarist empire, including even Alaska and Finland, as proposed by extreme nationalist Vladimir Zhirinovsky? Also, whatever the legal boundaries, how should relations between former Soviet republics be conducted? Is there any future for the institutions of the Commonwealth of Independent States? Should policy be coordinated, or imposed from Moscow? All of these are vitally important issues, but survey evidence up to 1993 has shed little light on them.

CONCLUSIONS

So what remained consistent over the period 1989–93, and what changed in relation to attitudes of former Soviet citizens to the Soviet Union and its collapse? And what is the significance of Russian attitudes for contemporary Russian politics?

The earliest surveys of public opinion discussed, from 1989, gave us a picture of Russian opinion which seemed to assume that everything would carry on as before. Russians and non-Russians alike would continue to live in a centralised union. And at that point, none of the other peoples for whom data are available were in favour of full independence, although there certainly existed a desire for more decentralisation among many of them.

The situation changed rapidly over 1990–91. It was a period when, among many non-Russians, a desire for a reformed Union rapidly became a desire for full independence. Russian public opinion at this time represents a corresponding process of coming to terms with this, shown by the growing number who supported decentralisation, and the increased willingness to concede the principle of self-determination, although by no means at this point a desire to see the Union fall apart.

The chapter began by referring to John Dunlop's contention that there had been a 'deimperialisation of the Russian psyche'. Is this an accurate description of the process? In some respects, yes. Empires, if they desire to remain such, must be willing to hold on to their colonies by force if necessary, as with, for example, events in Eastern Europe in 1956 and 1968, and Vilnius 1991. One obvious difference between the two former and the latter was the role of public opinion. The hugely hostile reaction to the use of troops to settle differences is very much a 'deimperialisation'.

So Russians appeared to have lost the will to defend their 'inner empire' by force after abandoning their 'outer empire' in Eastern Europe in 1989. But only at one very specific time – the end of 1991 – did this go as far as accepting the break-up of the Soviet Union itself. And following the end of the Union a significant proportion of Russians certainly still harbour aspirations for the creation of a greater Russia. It would therefore be overstating the case to suggest that an empire mentality has entirely vanished from collective consciousness. There is still a responsive constituency for politicians who would like to see a reformed USSR, mostly among older people and the more poorly educated. While this might not imply dramatic acts on the part of the Russian Government to create such a state of affairs, it creates an environment in which acts aiming to gradually re-forge some of the links broken on 1 January 1992 would be popular. However, as of 1993, this constituency remained relatively small. Furthermore, for such actions to succeed without bloodshed, there would need to be a willingness on the part of the peoples of other former republics, which the (pre-1992) evidence presented here suggests does not exist.

Views about the Russian Diaspora, however, imply different conclusions. The opinion that Russia should take action to defend the rights of Russians who live outside the boundaries of the Russian Federation is widespread. Therefore while there seems only limited support for a USSR Mark II, there may be considerable support for a more coercive relationship with some of the other former Soviet republics.

Also important for contemporary politics is public opinion about independence movements within the Russian Federation itself. Here it seems that views are similar to those about independence movements within the Soviet Union in 1988–91. While most Russians do not want to see any further shrinking of their country, if it becomes clear that a particular group chooses to leave, then most Russians do not think that action should be taken to prevent them. Secessionist movements within Russia itself do not, therefore, imply reactions such as those that have emerged within the former Yugoslavia. However, these remain very much theoretical questions. If real independence movements did emerge, and these threatened the rights of Russian nationals, the mood might well change, as appears to have been the case with Russian attitudes towards the newly independent former republics.

7 Attitudes to the Market Economy

The institution of the planned economy was a central feature of the Soviet regime. Virtual elimination of the private sector enabled the regime to claim that it had abolished the exploitation of man by man and created a qualitatively new way of organising production and distribution. History would prove the planned economy superior to capitalism. Such claims were vital components of the whole system of legitimisation.

Of course reality never matched the regime's grandiose claims. Relations of domination and subordination within work remained, rises in output were much more strongly linked to extensive factors such as urban population growth than they were to the organisation of the economy, and distribution was by no means according to need or work contribution, and remained quite inegalitarian. However, from the viewpoint of the ordinary Soviet citizen, the planned economy, particularly in its settled form of the 1970s, certainly had its good points. Full employment meant a high level of job security, indeed overmanning made the working life of many easy. The welfare system provided near universal free education, and extensive health care coverage, as well as services which were rare in many market economies such as child-care facilities. Furthermore, the policy of 'socialism with a consumerist face' meant that for the first time many Soviet citizens had access to consumer goods such as private cars and colour televisions.

However, the planned economy proved to be unsustainable in the long term. This was because from the start there were systemic flaws in the way it operated. These were – speaking in the most general terms – the problem that planners had insufficient information to design good plans, and the impossibility of creating an effective system of incentives, in particular incentives for innovation and incentives to avoid environmental devastation on a mass scale.[1] These problems, although present throughout the Soviet period, grew more acute as the economy developed. By the time Gorbachev achieved power it was no longer possible to compensate for them through, for example, extensive growth, computerisation, or a limited reform that would preserve the essential features of the economic system. As the new General Secretary put it, there was 'no growth left', and most economists agreed that there was no alternative to marketisation. The first two or three years of Gorbachev's rule were a period of coming to terms with the extent of economic crisis and a gradual acknowledgement that market mechanisms had become necessary. Once this psychological barrier had been crossed, the political problems inherent in radical economic reform became increasingly apparent. Most obviously these involved resistance from a number of important institutional interests, such as a party–state apparatus jealous of its status and privileges, die-hard communists ideologically hostile to the very ideas of private ownership and free markets, and the vast military–industrial complex, which could not hope to maintain its position of eminence under market conditions.

Just as important as institutional resistance was the problem of resistance on the part of a society that had liked aspects of the planned system. Marketisation of the economy had to involve changes in popular values, attitudes and expectations. In particular, it required acknowledgement that individual enterprise and creativity is indivisibly linked with self-interest; that the institution of private property is not the exploitation of man by man, but a natural human impulse; that, in Nozick's phrase, 'capitalist acts between consenting adults' are in the general interest;[2] that the state's role in the economy should be somewhat more limited than had been the case in the past, with individuals taking correspondingly greater responsibility for the well-being of themselves and their families.

This chapter explores these themes. It seeks to find out the extent and depth of support for attempts to introduce a market economy in the Soviet Union and its successors. In particular, what is the relationship between support for markets in general and particular components of a marketisation strategy: privatisation, free prices, free labour and capital markets, increasing inequality? And what have been the trends over time during the period, 1989–94, when the market economy ceased being an abstract point for discussion among scholars and politicians and became a reality affecting every Russian's life? Has support grown with increasing familiarity, or have the devastating effects of transition policies led to increasing hostility to the changes?

SUPPORT FOR TRANSITION TO THE MARKET

Soviet survey research began to investigate attitudes to the market economy in the early part of 1990. In the period before the attempt to

Figure 7.1 Support for transition to a market economy, 1990–93

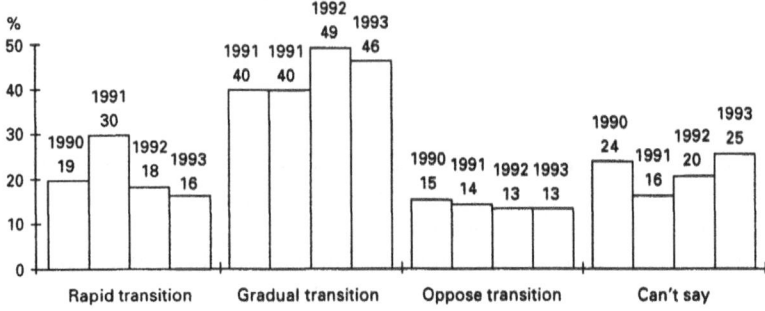

Sources: *Ekonomicheskie i sotsial'nye peremeny: monitoring obshchestvennogo mneniya*, 3 (1994), p. 14; surveys were of respectively 1020, 3002, 1877 and 1598 respondents.

introduce a market economy at the start of 1992, polls consistently found that an overall majority thought that there should be such a transition, as shown in Figure 7.1, which illustrates VTsIOM's time series data on the issue. Support was surprisingly little affected by the attempts at rapid change introduced at the end of 1991. Figure 7.1 presents time series data for VTsIOM's poll on the question from mid-1990 to mid-1993.

These data imply some significant conclusions. The first is that support for transition to a market economy remained strong among Russians over the three-year period in question. It reached its peak at the end of 1991, which was when a serious attempt at reform was first begun. Evidently there was a genuine social consensus for market reforms at that time, with around seven in ten supporting some kind of change, and just 14 per cent opposed. The number of supporters of a rapid transition to a market economy had increased significantly since 1990.

Also evident from the data is that up to 1993 the number of opponents to the creation of a market economy in Russia remained virtually unchanged, representing only a small section of Russian society. It seems that the severe consequences of marketisation – rapid inflation, increasing inequality and poverty, the threat of unemployment – did not lead to rising opposition to marketisation. Only a small hard core of opponents remained. This in part reflected the fact that almost no Russian politician, with the exception of a few Stalinists, now opposed the market. Even the reformed Russian Communist Party accepted that there was no alternative.

However, despite the consistency of support for transition to a market, it appears that there were considerable shifts in opinion about the desirable *rate* at which change should take place. The earliest of the surveys, from early 1990, found just 18 per cent wanting a quick change, compared to 34 per cent who felt that movement should be gradual. The situation at that time was nicely described by one survey respondent: 'We are familiar with real socialism and would like to get rid of it, but we don't clearly know what contemporary capitalism is and are rather afraid.'[3] After years of being told that markets were the exploitation of man by man and that capitalism meant mass poverty and mass unemployment, it was hardly surprising that Soviet citizens were hesitant about rushing change. In this, Gorbachev was still in tune with public opinion, since legislation passed by that time had gone no further than limited increases in enterprise autonomy, limited ownership changes via the introduction of co-operatives and individual labour activity, and a price 'reform' which did not go so far as allowing rational pricing. As Chapter 3 established, Gorbachev's popularity at this time still remained quite high, with 40–50 per cent saying that they fully trusted the President.

Late 1990 and 1991, however, saw the debate about marketisation move on, while Gorbachev and new Prime Minister, Valentin Pavlov, remained in the same position. It became increasingly evident that half measures in economic policy were merely disrupting the old system without putting anything in its place. Professional economists in the Soviet Union, influenced by the experiences of those East European countries that had already begun transition, became convinced that a much more rapid change which dealt simultaneously with the issues of demonopolisation, ownership, prices and the budget deficit had become necessary. This was reflected in a series of plans, the best known of which was that put forward by the team headed by Stanislav Shatalin and rejected by Gorbachev in October 1990.

Public opinion at this time, however, did not reflect political developments. The number of supporters of a rapid transition had barely risen from May to November, although the number of opponents of change had fallen. Evidently the technical details of the debate – won convincingly by the free marketeers – remained opaque to most Russians. Even by the end of 1991, only three in ten Russians wanted a rapid transition, with 40 per cent favouring a gradual one. Politically speaking, this is a striking finding. It shows that although there clearly was a social consensus for market reforms by the end of 1991, Yeltsin's decision to adopt a 'big bang' approach was by no means the preferred option. In this respect, the Yeltsin–Gaidar programme had many similarities to Thatcherism in the United Kingdom in that it attempted to shape popular economic attitudes rather than simply to reflect them. This represented a considerable risk, since it created a danger of being seen as out of touch with popular aspirations.

What of views about transition after the introduction of the reforms? Two features in particular stand out. First the increased proportion of respondents who found it difficult to reply to the question, as many as 31 per cent by March 1993, compared to just 15 per cent at the end of 1991.[4] The harshness of the effects of change, particularly disappointing in comparison with the promises of future prosperity that accompanied its introduction, clearly disillusioned a significant minority with the market. But these people had no available alternative, having also rejected a socialist economy. The result was rising levels of confusion and disorientation.

Also striking was the shift in the proportions favouring a gradual transformation above a rapid one, up from 4 : 3 to almost 3 : 1 among those who support transition. There emerged a growing sense of unease with the actual effects of economic policies, and a desire for less disruption and more sense that the Government had control over what was going on. This did not transfer itself into opposition to moves towards the market, but it weakened support for the Government as a whole.

Another interesting aspect of support for moves to establish a market economy is the question of which demographic groups favour and oppose change, and whether there have been changes in this over time. Figures 7.2 and 7.3 consider this.

As can be seen, the social groups shown in Figure 7.2 differed in their support for the market quite substantially, as of the end of 1990. In detail, support was from men more than women; the young more than the old; the more educated rather than the less educated; and urban rather than rural inhabitants. While the differences are sometimes not great, they are statistically significant.

The most obvious explanation for the differences is that those in favour at this time, when transition remained largely hypothetical, were the groups who expected to benefit, at least in the long run, from any transition to the market. The end result of transition would, its supporters argued, be that skills were appropriately rewarded, unlike in

Figure 7.2   Views about transition to the market, December 1990

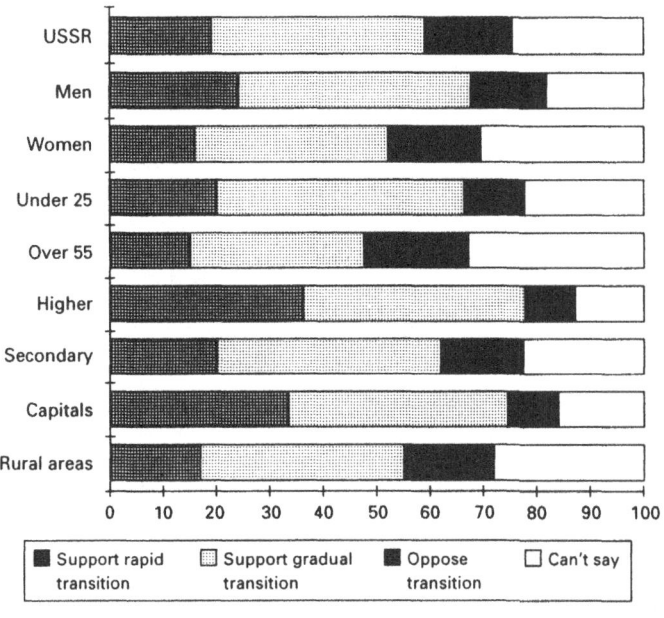

Source: *Obshchestvennoe mnenie v tsifrakh*, 11 (1991). N = 3399.

the planned economy, and these were the groups most likely to benefit. Similarly, opponents of the market were those who were likely to lose out: older people for the most part dependent on state support, women who feared that they would be the first to lose their jobs under the emerging market conditions, and the unskilled who benefited very much from the planned system in terms of wage levels and job security. The elderly had also been exposed to dogma about capitalist exploitation for a longer period.

Another striking feature of the data is the way in which many of those who did not actively support transition felt unable to respond, rather than saying that they opposed change. This can be interpreted as suggesting that there existed very little social base at this time for the politicians who felt that marketisation was a betrayal. Because most of the media and many politicians had suddenly begun to regard the market economy as a panacea that would cure all the country's economic problems, opponents were rather reluctant to admit their views to pollsters.

Figure 7.3 Support for transition to a market economy, March 1993

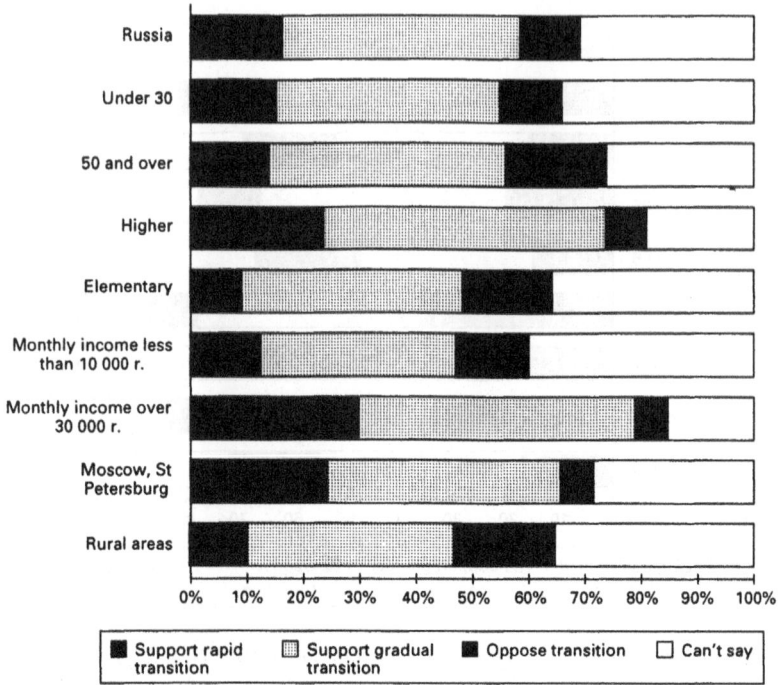

Source: *Ekonomicheskie i sotsial'nye peremeny: monitoring obshchestvennogo mneniya*, 1 (1993), p. 53 and p. 74 (n = 1999).

What, then, of changes in the attitudes of social groups during the period when transition ceased to be an abstraction and began to affect everyone? These are shown in Figure 7.3.

As can be seen, the patterns remained broadly similar in many respects. People with higher education and those who lived in the largest cities were most in favour of transition, while opposition was strongest among the elderly, rural inhabitants and the less educated. One change from 1990 would appear to be relating to age, however, since it also appears that no more people aged under 30 now supported the transition than those over 50. The reduction in opportunities that economic crisis caused led to an increased disillusion with the policy. This did not manifest itself in rising opposition, but in a greater proportion not offering an opinion.

The best predictor of attitudes to the transition, according to these data, was income. If the 1990 data were best explained by expected gains in transition to a market, then the 1993 responses were correspondingly associated with actual gains. The obvious implication is that the change can only become consolidated when there are enough people who have clearly benefited from the introduction of a market economy.

Before considering other aspects of attitudes to markets, it is necessary to comment briefly on some of the research that has been carried out by some other organisations. This is the case because on many occasions it has led to rather different conclusions about support for the market to those of this chapter, several of which are, in the view of this author, misleading.

In this, the two most suspect studies are that associated with the American Times–Mirror organisation, which took place in European Russia in May 1991, and that carried out on behalf of the European Commission, again in the European part of Russia in December 1991 and December 1992.[5] The first of these found that 'a solid third explicitly disapproved of the effort [to create a market economy]', whereas only 39 per cent approved.[6] This is out of line with other findings, but can be explained by the difference in emphasis contained in the question, which refers to approval of *efforts to establish* a market economy, rather than the issue of whether or not to have a market economy as such. Some responses therefore express hostility to Gorbachev's policies, not to the concept of the market.

As regards the *Eurobarometer* question, this reads 'Do you personally feel that the creation of a free market economy, one that is largely free from state control, is right or wrong for Russia's future?' On the basis of answers to this, the authors write 'The pain of Russia's economic reform programme is evident as anger against the free market mounts ... with more now opposing than supporting' as of the end of 1992.[7] This is not the case, or at least it is not what is shown. Answers to this question merely prove that Russians do not want a free market economy that is largely free from state control. What many want is a market economy that involves a considerable degree of state control.

COSTS AND BENEFITS OF TRANSITION

The section above demonstrated that survey evidence has shown consistent support for the transition to a market economy from the first

Figure 7.4 Views about prospects for economic improvement

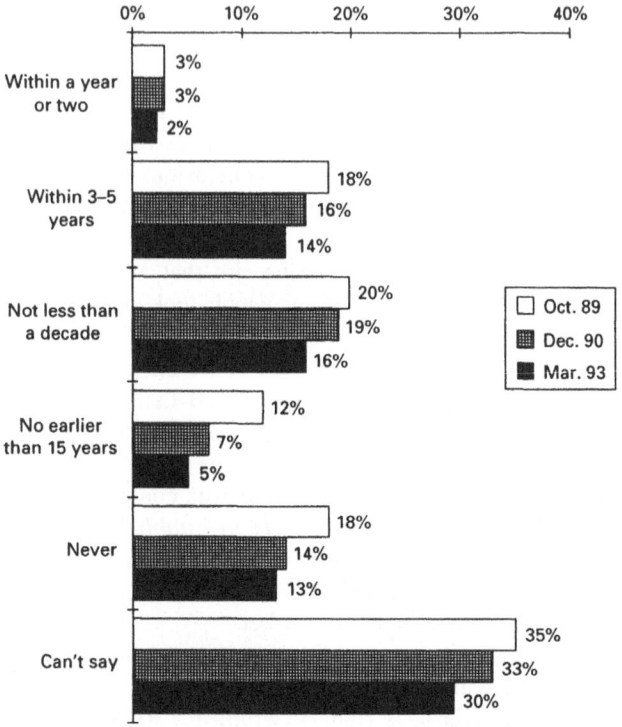

Sources: V. Rutgaiser, L. Khakhulina, S. Shpil'ko, V. Kosmarskii and A. Grazhdankin, 'Otnoshenie naseleniya k radikal'noi ekonomicheskoi reforme', *Voprosy ekonomiki*, 4 (1989), all-Union poll, n = 1148; *Obshchestvennoe mnenie v tsifrakh*, 11 (1991), all-Union poll, n = 2294; *Ekonomicheskie i sotsial'nye peremeny: monitoring obshchestvennogo mneniya*, 2 (1993), p. 59, poll of Russians, n = 1999.

studies onward. So what are the reasons underlying popular support for transition to the market? Do they reflect the arguments of ideologists of market economics about incentives, rewards for talent and so forth? Are they based much more on considerations of self-interest? Or is support for a market economy only the result of opposition to the plan, with its permanent shortages and permanent subordination of society to the planners?

What can be ruled out immediately is support based on expectations of immediate material gain, notwithstanding extravagant promises of rapid improvement given by the political leadership. Chapter 3 demonstrated that personal material expectations for the immediate future were gloomy. Twice as many people supported transition as expected their family personally to benefit from it. A similar situation exists with respect to expectations for general economic recovery. One of VTsIOM's regular social barometer questions has been 'When, in your opinion, will economic reform give positive results for the majority of people?' Figure 7.5 summarises the results.

As shown in the histogram, throughout the period in question, almost nobody thought that the economy would improve in the short term. The most common response was uncertainty, which is reasonable given the inherently uncertain nature of these matters. But only around one in five in each of the surveys were hoping for improvements within five years.[8] One must therefore conclude that any support based on material factors is only in hope of gains in the long term.

So what underlay such pessimism? Studies have approached this issue through the use of unstructured questions asking people what they see as the advantages and disadvantages of transition. This is a useful approach, since it gives a sense of some of the factors that are most important in determining people's attitudes. However, the disadvantages are first that answer codes often do not include factors that might well be significant; and secondly, there is an underlying assumption to such questions that attitudes are determined by rational factors, rather than vague emotional responses, identifications with particular politicians and the like. Table 7.1 shows some responses.

The Russian population, then, saw both costs and benefits, but the former rather outweighed the latter at this time. Thus, the dominant responses in both studies were connected with rising inflation, the threat of unemployment, and increasing inequality. However, many also mentioned the better rewarding of skills, an end to shortages, and the prospect of economic recovery.

Overall, though, it would appear that the evident support for a market economy was without enthusiasm. While survey after survey found that many more support than oppose the idea, markets have been consistently associated with many unpleasant outcomes, both for the respondent and the country in general. The conclusion must be that such support is of the 'there is no alternative' variety.

Table 7.1 Costs and benefits of economic transition, 1990-91

(a) With which of the following do you above all connect the market economy?

	(%)
With the revival of the economy	20
With free entrepreneurship	14
With raising living standards	17
With inflation	55
With reducing living standards	26
With stratification into rich and poor	36
With unemployment	22
With shops full of goods	18
With private property	14
With competition	11
With capitalism	4

Source: Obshchestvennoe mnenie v tsifrakh, 11 (1991). VTsIOM poll of Russia, December 1990, n = 2298.

(b) Cost and benefits of transition to the market, March 1991

	(%)
Price rises	47
I might lose my job	44
Rewarding skills	43
Overcoming levelling	29
Overcoming shortages of goods and services	25
Widening freedom of choice in job	25

Source: Dialog, 8 (1991), p. 3: all-Union poll by Institute of Sociology, AN SSSR, n = 2928.

ATTITUDES TO OWNERSHIP CHANGES

So there is support for a transition to the market, although much concern about the consequences. But what of the various features without which a market economy cannot operate, such as private property, free prices, unemployment? In other words, what is the depth of support for a market? And is it possible to identify any significant trends over time? This section considers attitudes to ownership changes, and sections below discuss prices and unemployment.

Let us look first at the concept of private property. A boast of the socialist system was that since it had eliminated private ownership, it had removed the conditions for 'the exploitation of man by man'. However, reality was that state ownership and control tended to imply no ownership, with nobody taking responsibility for property. This elimination of the link between self-interest and human creativity was one of the main causes of system failure.

Gorbachev's economic advisors were aware of the difficulties. They were the origin of the limited changes in ownership that occurred in 1987–89 with the legalisation of co-operatives and individual labour activity, as well as changes increasing the effective autonomy of state enterprises through the system of *khozrashchet*, or full cost accounting. However market-oriented economists argued that these changes didn't go far enough. A much more widespread privatisation was necessary in order to overcome the 'soft budget constraint', the fact that large enterprises were dependent on the state for their survival rather than on responding to market conditions.

So what was the stance of public opinion on the debates about ownership? Did a majority accept the various kinds of privatisation? Or did there remain a popular sentiment, encouraged by years of communist dogma, that private ownership meant exploitation of the workers and exploitation of the consumer through speculative prices for second-rate products?

Attitude to Co-operatives

The introduction of co-operatives is something that has been extensively studied in the literature, and considerable information already exists on the extent of public acceptance of them.[9] However, interpretations of the data might be questioned, since the common conclusion is that there was a gradual trend towards increasing social acceptance of them. Some data are shown in Figure 7.5a, b.

As shown, at the period where the political debate about co-operatives was at its most intense, the popular position was deeply ambivalent. While quite a few more thought that co-operatives ought to exist than thought they should be removed, nevertheless more people disapproved of them than approved. This contradictory attitude is understandable when one considers the views Russians had about the advantages and disadvantages of the new co-operatives. These were examined in the May 1990 VTsIOM study, some of the results of which are shown in Table 7.2.

On the positive side, the table shows the ways in which people felt co-operatives to be superior. That more attention was paid to using

Figure 7.5 Attitudes to co-operatives, 1989–90

(a) Would it be better to promote the development of co-operatives or to curtail them?

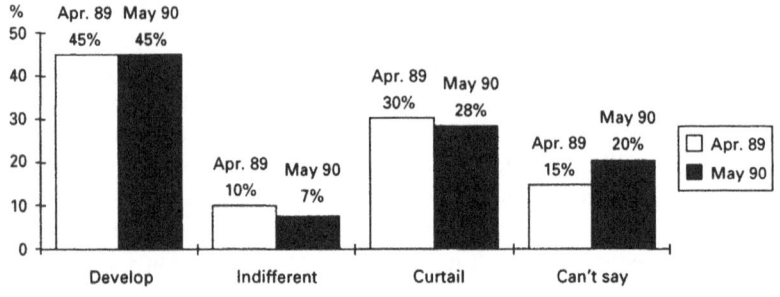

Sources: *Ogonyok*, 43 (1989), p. 5 and *Voprosy ekonomiki*, 4 (1991), VTsIOM polls. April 1989, n = 3000; May 1990, n = 2842.

(b) What is your response to the development of co-operatives?

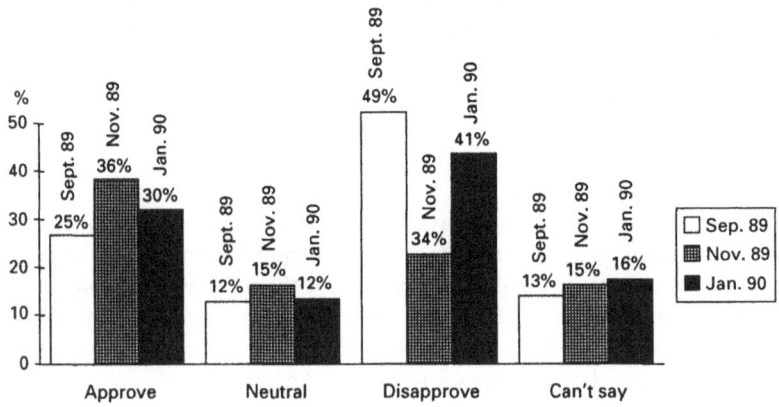

Sources: *Obshchestvennoe mnenie v tsifrakh*, 4 (1989), 7 (1989) and 4 (1990). VTsIOM polls of respectively n = 1148 (urban); n = 1073 and n = 2597.

material and human resources effectively, that wages were better. Surveys also found other advantages were seen to be the widened choice of goods and services available, and the way in which their introduction widened the choice of jobs available for people.[10] In short, people did perceive the new co-operatives as having many of the advantages that their supporters claimed. However, there is also little doubt that much of the population was appalled by the prices charged by many

Table 7.2 Advantages and disadvantages of co-operatives

Question	More often in co-operatives (%)	No difference (%)	More often in state enterprises (%)
Who is more businesslike and uses raw materials and energy resources better?	66	13	8
Where do people have more opportunity to display initiative and use their knowledge?	61	16	12
Where is work paid more justly?	52	10	21
Where do workers work more diligently?	51	23	14
Where does one more often encounter financial irregularities, speculation and graft?	46	35	10
The quality of whose goods, as a rule, is better?	13	33	44

Source: *Voprosy ekonomiki*, 4 (1991). VTsIOM study, n = 2842.

co-operatives, often disappointed with the quality of goods, resentful of the huge earnings made by some, at the way they often deprived the state sector of resources and skilled workers, and, perhaps most importantly, saw many as being linked with organised crime. Parts of the mass media that were hostile to marketisation fed these dislikes with many well-publicised cases of speculation or money laundering by co-operatives. Perhaps it is no surprise that public opinion was inclined to the view that they were unavoidable but unpleasant.

There is no evidence that attitudes to co-operatives had become more favourable by the end of 1991 in parallel with the rising support for markets that occurred during that period. A survey of 6000 Russians by the RSFSR Goskomstat in March, for example, found only one in three considered co-operative enterprises to be a good thing, while 42 per cent thought they were bad.[11] That autumn, Vox Populi found that only 11 per cent had a positive attitude to co-operatives whereas 85 per cent had a negative view.[12] There were more people (15 per cent) who felt that it was acceptable to burn down co-operatives where low-quality goods were sold at excessively high prices than there were with positive attitudes. There is no doubt that the social base for them was very narrow.

However, with the collapse of communism, co-operatives became much less of a political issue. Partly this was linked to increased familiarity and the reality that for many who were at first reluctant, using the services of co-ops had become unavoidable. More importantly, though, ideological shackles having been removed, the issue was now the acceptability of genuine private property (which many co-operatives were, under a different name, in any case). This is in many ways reflected in the absence of studies concerned with co-operatives in the period 1992–93.

Attitudes to Private Property

What then of the concept of private property? Was there the same degree of public hostility to this as clearly existed towards co-operatives in the period 1989–91? Are there distinctions to be made between various types of private ownership? And how did these attitudes change over the period? Figure 7.6 again illustrates VTsIOM time series data.

Here a clear trend towards the acceptance of private enterprises in the period up to the end of 1991 is shown; 55 per cent were prepared to accept their development by the time of the last study cited. The trend is, unsurprisingly, the same as that towards support for a market economy.

It is necessary, however, when looking at attitudes to private ownership, to make a clear distinction between ownership of small and of large enterprises, and also between ownership by Soviet / former Soviet citizens and foreign ownership. Figures 7.5a–d, 7.11a, b and 7.12, from VTsIOM and Vox Populi surveys, illustrate these issues very clearly indeed.

As is shown, there is a consistent trend in attitudes to private ownership. Over time Russians have become increasingly more committed to the idea, as they get more used to it. There is near unanimity that private ownership of small plots of land is acceptable. Of course this is something that has existed for many years in the Soviet Union. After trying to eliminate them and failing, even Stalin had to accept that confining food production to collective farms was politically impossible. In the less tense 1970s, the private plot became a major source of food for very large numbers of people. In this context, perhaps it is not the level of support for their existence that is surprising, but rather the fact that as many as 6 to 7 per cent opposed their existence.

It is also evident that there has been growing social acceptance of

Figure 7.6 Attitudes to private ownership, 1989-91

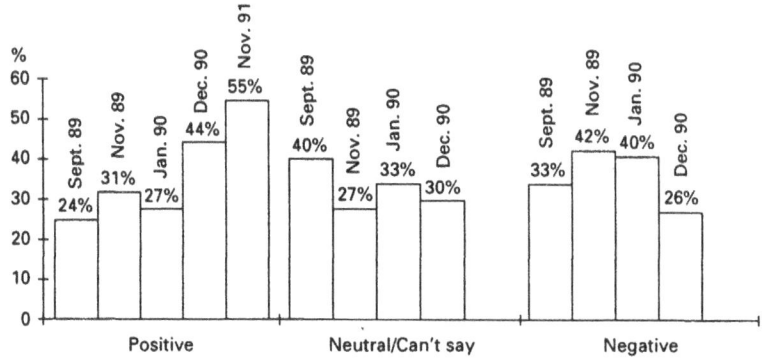

Sources: *Obshchestvennoe mnenie v tsifrakh*, 4 (1989), 7 (1989), 4 (1990) and 10 (1991); *Voprosy ekonomiki*, 4 (1991). VTsIOM all-Union polls, n = 1148 (urban), n = 1073, n = 2597, n = 3399.

privately owned small businesses, which almost seven in ten approved of by the end of 1992. Again this represents social acceptance of something which has been the *de facto* situation for some time. The extent of moonlighting and black-market activities during the 1970s and early 1980s perhaps made this change easier to accept. A significant minority of just over one in five, however, has remained opposed. An element of Russian society, it appears, does not wish to allow anyone to work for themselves and profit from it.

As regards private ownership of heavy industry, the VTsIOM data indicate a consistent proportion of around a half opposed to it over the period 1990-93, with barely one in four in favour of it. Vox Populi, in a similar question, found a clear rise in hostility from 1991 to 1993.

What might explain such hostility? One obvious reason would be the legacy of past stereotypes. The rapacious capitalist mill-owner ruthlessly exploiting the workers was an image that the communist regime was eager to repeat. Of course such Victorian stereotypes bear no relation at all to the reality of modern corporate ownership, divided as it is by its nature between many individual and institutional shareholders, and often with divided ownership and control. However, to understand these matters is something that even people familiar with the operation of market economies find elusive. It is unsurprising that past stereotypes appear to exert a continuing influence on collective attitudes.

Figure 7.7 Attitudes to private ownership

What would be your attitude to private citizens owning _____ in our country?

(a) small enterprises, cafes and shops

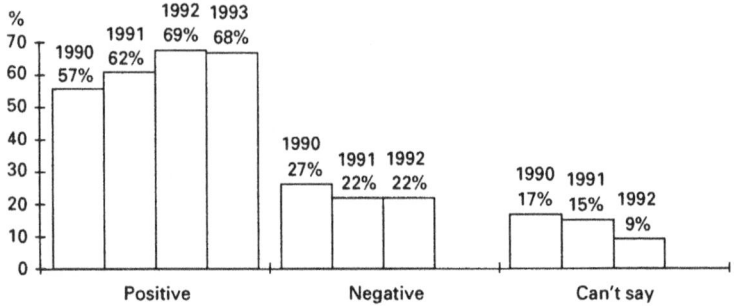

(b) small plots of land

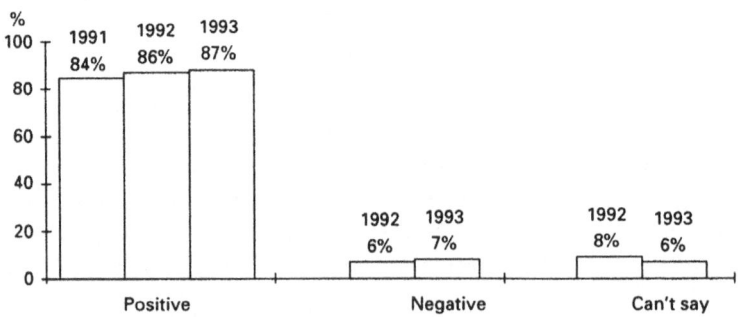

(c) large factories and mills

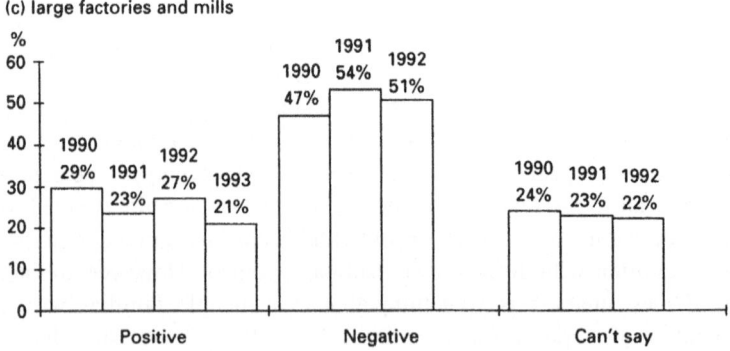

Attitudes to the Market Economy 191

(d) huge tracts of land

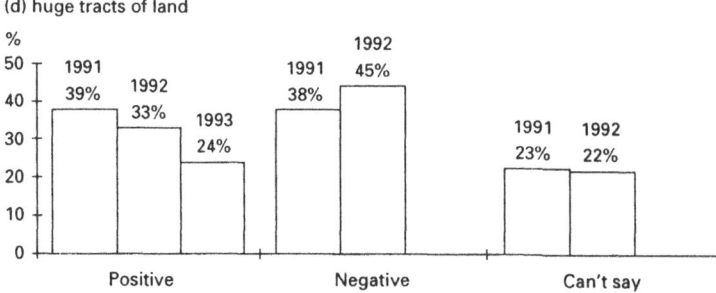

Figure 7.8 Attitudes to foreign ownership

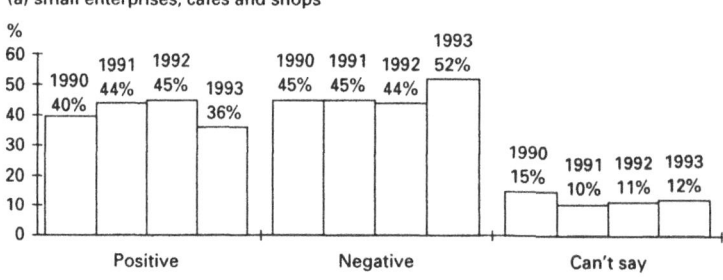

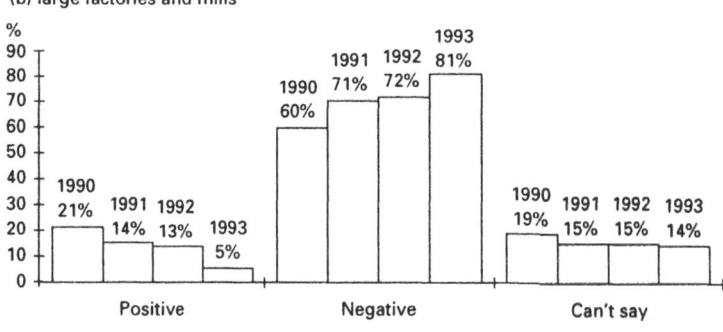

Sources: *Ekonomicheskie i sotsial'nye peremeny: monitoring obshchestvennogo mneniya*, 1 (1993), p. 21 and 3 (1994), pp. 14–15; and *Obshchestvennoe mnenie v tsifrakh*, 4 (1990).

192 *Public Opinion in Postcommunist Russia*

Figure 7.9 Attitudes to private ownership, 1991–93

Do you believe that private ownership of large enterprises should be introduced in this country?

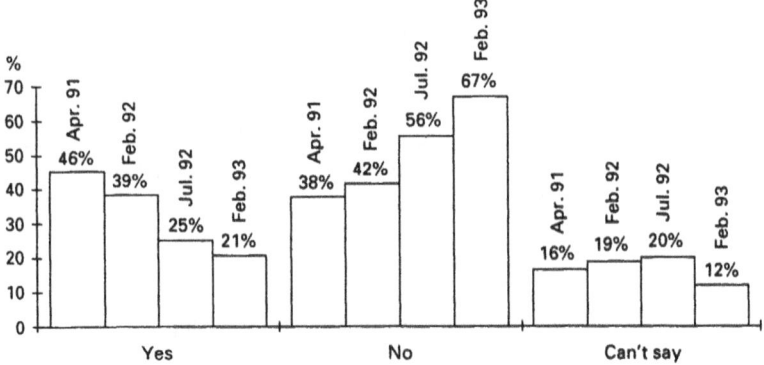

Source: *Mir mnenii i mneniya o mire*, 5 (1993). Vox Populi polls, n = 1285, n = 1985, n = 1990 and n = 1996 respectively.

Why, though, might resistance to private ownership of large enterprises have risen so greatly since the start of 1992, despite the Russian Government's efforts with the privatisation voucher and constant propagandising to encourage 'popular capitalism'? One answer lies in the particular circumstances of attempts to privatise in Russia. The reality of the situation is that very few people have sufficient resources to invest, and very few of those who do have achieved their wealth through legitimate channels. Furthermore, sources of institutional investment – in particular pension funds – simply do not exist. It is understandable that popular concerns about the implications of privatisation for social justice remain considerable.

One qualification should be made to the above, however. It must be stressed that the same opprobrium does not attach itself to the idea of transferring state enterprises to the ownership of their workforces. The argument that this is in accordance with Russia's 'collectivist traditions' is often made. Thus, for example, VTsIOM in mid-1990 found only 16 per cent of Russians saying that this form of privatisation, or rather 'collectivisation' was unacceptable.[13] The Russian Academy of Sciences Institute of Sociology's polling branch, SotsioEkspress, consistently over 1992–93 found that around six or seven in every ten Russians agreed that 'All enterprises should be transferred to the ownership of those people who are working in them.'[14] This has no doubt contributed to the situation where the majority of newly privatised enterprises have been transferred to the ownership of existing workforces or management. It hardly needs to be said that the case for the efficiency of such an ownership form is tenuous, since workers are far more likely to be concerned about job security than restructuring.

There is even greater social hostility to foreign ownership than there is to private ownership of large enterprises. The Russian population is evenly split about allowing foreigners to own even small enterprises, and an overwhelming majority – 81 per cent by the end of 1993 – is against it in the case of larger factories.

Once again, the legacy of the old regime may be evident. Constant propaganda about attempts by Western countries to undermine the Soviet Union, with reference to specific circumstances from the Civil War to Korea, and incessant reference to the pernicious nature of modern international capitalism may affect the views of some. But more convincing types of explanations are based on conceptions of national pride, and the legacy of autarchy in economic thinking. Russia has abundant natural resources, enough to be self-sufficient in many cases. Liberal ideologies that stress the economic and other benefits of trade are unfamiliar, as is recent experience of being integrated into the world economy. It is again understandable that there remains a desire to prevent the profits gained by the labour of Russians and from Russian resources to be exported.

Overall, then, willingness to allow private property by no means extends to all possible forms of ownership, and there remains a group within Russian society that is hostile to the idea altogether. So just who are the people who are antagonistic to private property? A January 1993 survey by the institute of Applied Politics, illustrated in Table 7.5, enables some conclusions to be drawn about this.[15]

As shown, the demographic groups inclined to support private property are, naturally, the same as those who favour the free market: the younger and more highly educated sections of the population. However, it is worth stressing that much better predictors of attitudes to these matters are political identifications. Voters for Boris Yeltsin in the 1991 Russian presidential election and those who were most in favour of democracy were also the strongest supporters of private property. Voters for Nikolai Ryzhkov, those who thought that democracy does more harm than good, and those who supported the 1991 coup attempt (and also those with a positive attitude to communism and the role of the CPSU in the history of the country, not shown) were the most strongly against. It is a commonplace of Western survey research

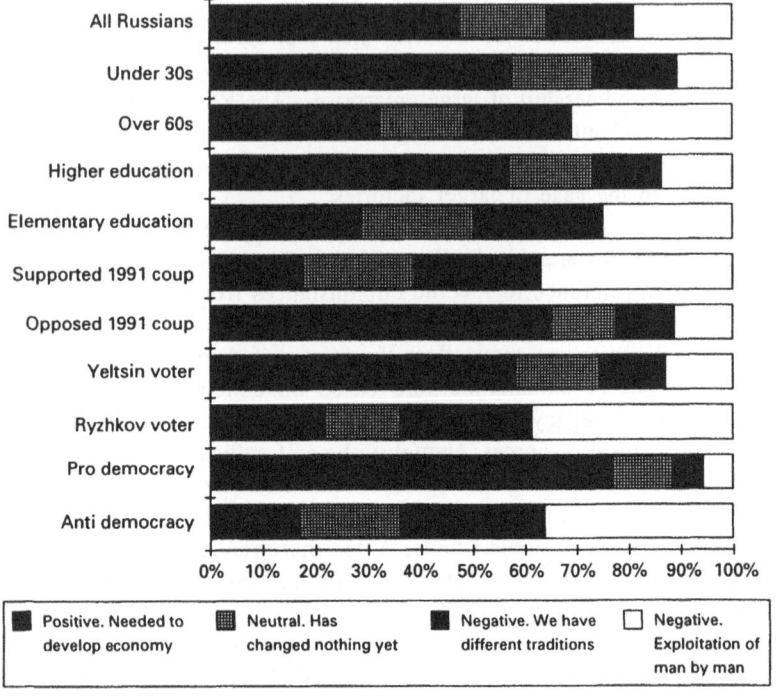

Figure 7.10 Attitudes to private property, January 1993

Source: Unpublished survey, Institute of Applied Politics. N = 1500.

that most voters are not strongly interested politically, and tend to adopt views as a result of identification with particular political parties.[16] A comparable process appears to be occurring in Russia, based on identification with political movements and certain individuals. Hence the clear grouping around support for or opposition to democracy and the free market.

THE PRIVATISATION PROGRAMME

From the middle of 1992 the Russian Government has been engaged in transferring large sections of the Russian economy into private hands – either by sale or competitive tender to the highest bidder or by sale

Attitudes to the Market Economy 195

Figure 7.11 Desirability of privatisation, 1993-94

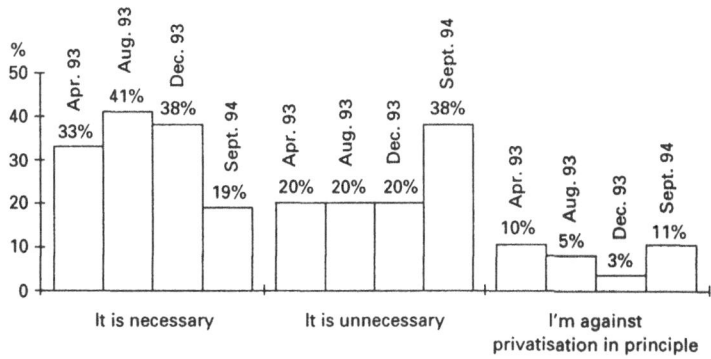

Sources: *Ekonomicheskie i sotsial'nye peremeny: monitoring obshchestvennogo mneniya*, 3 (1994), p. 24 and 6 (1994), p. 69.

to management or workforce. The economic motivation for this was to put control of enterprises into the hands of people who would be motivated to turn them into profit-making organisations. The political imperative of creating a class of property owners with a stake in supporting marketisation was also a major consideration.

So how have the Russian people perceived the privatisation programme? How effective has it been, have Russians benefited personally, do they perceive general benefits, and to what extent do they support the policy? VTsIOM have been investigating these issues since the privatisation began, in their regular surveys of the labour force.[17] Figure 7.11 illustrates views about how necessary people thought the policy was.

In the early stages of the privatisation programme, there was evidently widespread willingness at least to give it the benefit of the doubt. Around twice as many people thought that it was necessary as thought it was unnecessary, and principled objections to privatisation were only held by tiny numbers. During 1994, however, the mood changed, and by the end of that year more than twice as many thought that privatisation was unnecessary as supported it for their enterprises.

Do workers think that privatisation has any benefits or any major drawbacks? Asked in January 1994 whether privatisation would improve the economic position of the enterprise where they worked, 26 per cent thought it would help, the same proportion that it would

Figure 7.12   Views about effects of privatisation

Have you personally gained or lost from privatisation of your enterprise? (Per cent of those whose enterprise has already been privatised or is going to be in the near future.)

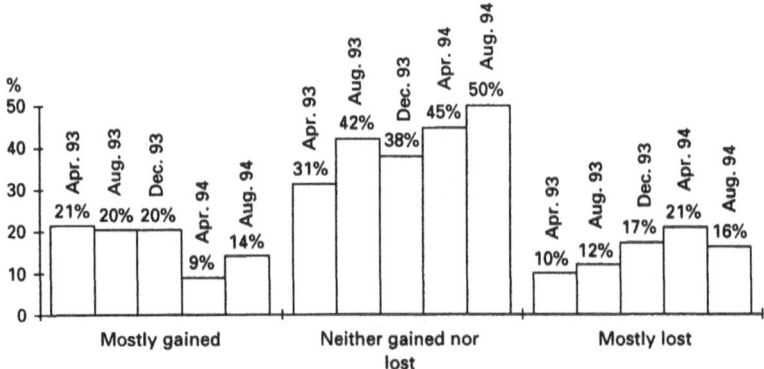

Sources: *Ekonomicheskie i sotsial'nye peremeny: monitoring obshchestvennogo mneniya*, 3 (1994), p. 24; 4 (1994), p. 64 and 6 (1994), p. 69.

make no difference, and a mere 8 per cent that it would make matters worse.[18] However, when asked whether privatisation had actually had any positive effects later the same year only 12 per cent said that it had, while 41 per cent said that it had made no difference and 23 per cent that it had made matters worse.[19]

Did workers gain or lose from ownership change? Figure 7.12 shows feelings about this question. As shown, the numbers of Russians who felt that they had personally gained remained quite low, and by 1994 was significantly outweighed by the number who believed that they had lost out, but by far the greatest proportion simply felt that there had been no effect on them.

What were the most important benefits of change and what were the major problems for workers? Those who felt they had gained were most likely to mention as reasons for this the opportunity to earn significantly more and job security. Those who felt they had lost out said precisely the opposite: lower wages and increased job insecurity were their main concerns.

Once again, then, the policy of privatisation has been viewed without enthusiasm by public opinion. The policy of issuing a privatisation voucher to every citizen has done little to ease this. A majority of Russians throughout 1993–94 believed that the privatisation voucher had made no difference to people, only around one in ten thought that it had provided material support, and no more than 20 per cent believed that it was helping people to become property owners. Undoubtedly people were concerned much more with issues relating to the social justice of privatisation.

SUPPORT FOR PRICE REFORM

Under the plan, prices were kept low and stable. They were rarely changed largely because of the political risks implicit in such an action. This was certainly one of the few features of the socialist system that was unambiguously beneficial for the Soviet citizen, or at least for the Soviet citizen who did not connect low prices with shortages. Indeed it is common to argue that this was one of the factors underlying regime stability in the Brezhnev era, just as it had been one of the factors undermining Khrushchev.[20]

However, the long term effect of fixed prices was to create a situation where the cost of resources bore no relation to their value. The example of farmers feeding chickens with bread rather than grain because it was cheaper was the textbook case. Huge subsidies became necessary to keep down the prices of basic goods, and this eventually led to the virtual bankruptcy of the state. So from a purely practical point of view, price reform had become imperative by the mid-1980s. More importantly, free prices determined by the interaction of supply and demand are the way in which a market economy allocates resources. Reform is impossible without deregulation of prices.

What, then, of public opinion on the question of free pricing? Had years of low and stable prices created the expectation that this would always be the case? Or were reformers able to win the argument that without free pricing there would never be an end to shortages, let alone any effective economic reform?

Before any significant change of retail prices took place, the polls suggested that the Soviet people were willing to accept some kind of price reform, or at least not to oppose it. Thus VTsIOM, among the urban population of six republics, found that 37 per cent considered it necessary that price reform should be carried out, compared to 10 per cent who said that it wasn't particularly necessary, and 17 per cent who said that it should not happen. The remainder could not say.[21]

However, it is clear from surveys carried out in 1990–91 that the actual experience of inflation reversed the position. Huge majorities in most Soviet republics were clearly opposed to free market prices. The most detailed source of information is a survey of 16 000 in every republic except Lithuania, which was carried out by *Goskomstat*; the State Statistics Committee, in June 1990.[22] This found that in Russia 48 per cent said that there was no need to change food prices, 47 per cent that it was necessary to change prices only for some products, and just 4 per cent that prices should be changed for the majority of products. As a general principle, only 4 per cent thought that the market should determine prices for all products, 31 per cent believed that the state should continue to set prices for a range of things, and fully 45 per cent that the state should continue to set prices for all products. Similarly, in December 1990, VTsIOM found that 44 per cent of Russians thought that the state should continue to fix prices for the majority of products, 38 per cent that it should continue to fix prices for a small number of important goods, and just 6 per cent that it should 'in general interfere as little as possible in the fixing of prices'.[23]

However, this perhaps overstates the extent of resistance to changes in this area. It is not surprising that a population used to low prices does not like its first experiences of rapid inflation. It is also not surprising that the initial popular reaction should be in favour of price controls. In the Soviet context, this was in many ways a more rational response than mindless application of free market principles: the economy remained predominantly monopolistic, and in shortage conditions, the opportunities for speculative profits were vast. Preventing this was just as much a concern for Russians as it was, for example, for the Progressives in the United States in the early part of the century.

Furthermore, resistance to price reform that was carried out for good reasons and adopted by reasonable means was much less strong. Surveys at this time consistently found that when the question was posed as a trade off where higher prices also imply fewer shortages then people would accept higher prices.[24] Thus, for example, the Times–Mirror survey of May 1991 asked 'Some people feel that prices should be allowed to rise so that products will be available, even if everyone can't afford them. Others feel that prices should be kept low, even if it means that products are sometimes not available. Which opinion generally comes closer to your point of view?' In Russia, 59 per cent said 'let prices increase' and just 31 per cent said 'keep prices low'.[25]

After 1991 although there appears to have been rising acceptance of free prices, more remained opposed than in favour. Thus, for example, VTsIOM found that a system of free prices and assistance for the less well off had gained in support over the period from the end of 1991 to the end of 1992, whereas support for rationing had fallen, although the proportions remained 44 per cent to 36 per cent in favour of the latter.[26] Russians – just about – preferred the familiarity of a rationing system. Similarly, research by the Institute of Social and Political Investigation of the Russian Academy of Sciences found just one in seven saying that they thought that price rises were essential if the reform strategy was to succeed in ending economic crisis in Russia, while 67 per cent said that they did not make this connection.[27]

It appeared then that reformers remained a long way from victory in their argument that free prices are an absolutely fundamental feature of the attempt to create a market economy.

ATTITUDES TO UNEMPLOYMENT

Another inescapable feature of a transition to the market is unemployment. The removal of state subsidies implies the closure of many of the huge number of technically obsolete factories that exist today in the former Soviet Union. Again unemployment is something with which there is little familiarity among the Russian public. Another achievement – at major costs in terms of efficiency – of the planned economy was full employment.

So first, what does public opinion understand by the term unemployment? This is a significant question, since it very much determines the kind of policy options available. Table 7.3 provides an interesting view on this.

As can be seen, the popular conception of unemployment was rather confused. The term was so unfamiliar that from one in five to one in six felt unable to give a judgement about the question, and a further 25 per cent thought that even not being able to find a job anywhere, or not being able to find a job after graduating do not count as unemployment.

The data also suggest that the judgements of many about unemployment were somewhat harsh. If people cannot find a job where they live, it appears that the view was that they should look elsewhere. A clear majority think that people who lose their job might have to learn new skills or professions.

That said, there is no doubt that there existed in public opinion, in the period under investigation, a considerable, if declining, amount of hostility to allowing unemployment. This is shown in Figure 7.13.[28]

The first point to emerge from the data is that on every occasion the most popular response has been that unemployment is unacceptable.

Table 7.3 Meaning of unemployment

A typical idea of unemployment is as follows: a factory closes and people are put out onto the street. Would you describe the following cases where people are dismissed as unemployment?	Yes, this is unemployment (%)	No, this is not unemployment (%)
Unable to find any job anywhere	61	25
Unable to find job in own city (district)	36	45
Unable to find work in area of specialisation (or corresponding to skill level)	24	56
Unable to find work with previous level of pay	9	73
If a person cannot find work after finishing school, technical college, vocational school or institute	51	29

Source: *Rabochii klass i sovremennyi mir*, 3 (1990), pp. 35–48. VTsIOM poll, n = 1148 (urban).

This response should not be dismissed as reactionary. There exist clear links in other countries between unemployment, crime, declining physical and mental health, urban decay and other undesirable outcomes.[29] The wish to have a society that tries to look after everyone, and dismisses nobody as functionless is an admirable one.

However, the question is whether this is possible today in many of the most economically developed countries, let alone in Russia, where much industry, particularly in the defence sector, is simply useless. And in addition to arguing that it is impossible to avoid, reformers further claim that unemployment is in some ways desirable. This relates to the question of how to free up the labour market – that is to get people allocated to the most 'useful' jobs (that is, those jobs for which there is a demand).

It emerges from the histogram that such arguments were taking an increasing hold over the period 1988–93. By the end of the latter year over half of respondents were prepared to accept one or other of the arguments offered for the existence of unemployment. This represents a remarkable change in the Russian collective consciousness. Stereotypes of a 'collectivist' mentality are contradicted by such a finding.

However, one should again not overstate the case. There remained (at least as of November 1991) a widespread view that the state should

Figure 7.13 Attitudes to unemployment, 1988–93

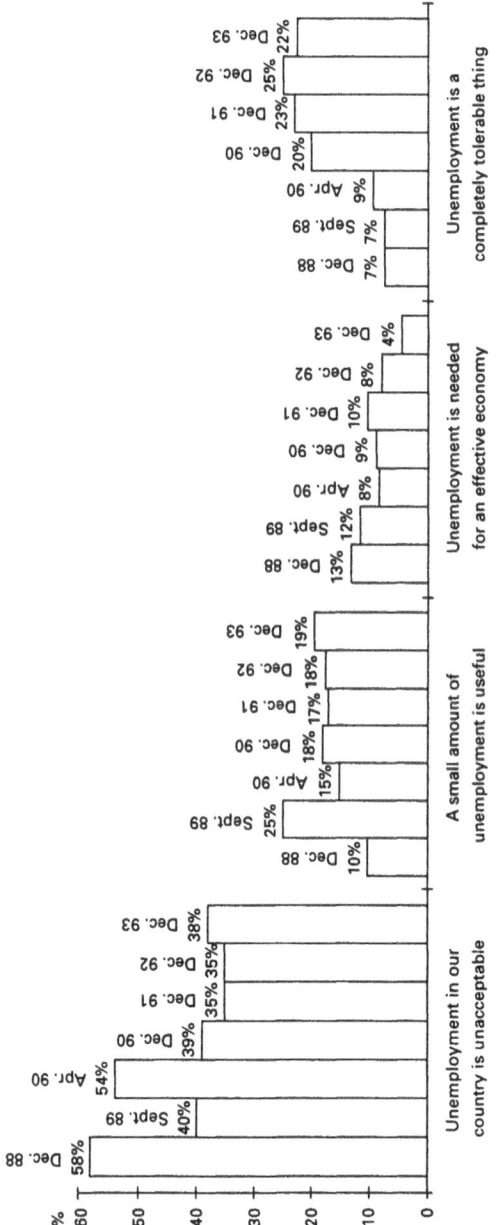

Sources: Obshchestvennoe mnenie v tsifrakh, 4 (1989), 7 (1989), 4 (1990), 12 (1990) and 10 (1991), also *Voprosy ekonomiki*, 4 (1991); *Ekonomicheskie i sotsial'nye peremeny: monitoring obshchestvennogo mneniya*, 1 (1993), p. 22 and 3 (1994), p. 15.

have a responsibility to provide a job for everyone who wants one. According to VTsIOM fully 90 per cent of Russians thought this.[30] Expectations about what the state should provide have clearly not wholly shifted. Public opinion on the issue of unemployment, then, remains contradictory.

ATTITUDES TO THE DISTRIBUTION OF INCOME AND WEALTH

During the seven decades of Soviet power, patterns of income and wealth distribution changed frequently.[31] The rhetoric of the regime remained that of the communist utopia where distribution would be according to the principle 'from each according to his ability, to each according to his needs', but the reality was that income remained strongly linked to work and status. This was emphasised in the Stalin period when movements such as Stakhanovism explicitly linked work performance with pay and privileges, and a network of perks emerged for officials. After the uncertainties of the Khrushchev period, in Brezhnev's Soviet Union, Party and state officials were able to consolidate their hold over a network of special privileges: their own hospitals, schools, dachas, curtained limousines and so forth. This was particularly inegalitarian since privileges were not related to merit but position, and usually extended to family members of officials too. In this respect the system is correctly described as corrupt and nepotistic. However, outside bureaucratic structures wages became increasingly egalitarian, with ordinary workers sometimes better paid than many professionals such as teachers and doctors. Thus the distribution of income contained elements both of equality and extreme inequality.

So what did the public make of the system that Gorbachev inherited when he came to power? Polls from 1989–90 before anything much had changed, give us some picture.[32] Overall there is no question that public opinion perceived income distribution as unfair. Thus, for example, a widely reported VTsIOM survey of the urban population of six republics in September and October 1989 found only 2 per cent of the population agreeing that the distribution of income in Soviet society was just; 45 per cent thought that it wasn't totally just, and 53 per cent that it was not at all just.[33]

What precisely did offend people's sense of justice? This can be looked at in relation to the system of official privileges, and the principles on which wages were paid.

Attitudes to the Market Economy 203

One reason why there was a general sense of injustice was clearly the privileged status of Soviet officialdom. When Gorbachev took over, there is no doubt that the Soviet system was grossly corrupt. Party bosses such as Vladimir Sherbitsky in Ukraine, Dinmukhamed Kunaev in Kazakhstan and Grigory Romanov in Moscow shamelessly exploited their positions of absolute power in their fiefdoms to achieve lifestyles that were outrageously decadent.[34]

An attack on this system – which was at the same time an attack on his conservative opponents – was very much part of the agenda in the early Gorbachev period, and a source of his popular support. However, as a product of the communist system himself, Gorbachev could never entirely escape accusations that he himself was implicated in such abuses of power. There were persistent rumours of presents from the Stavropol region to Leonid Brezhnev at the time when Gorbachev had been Party boss there. Raisa Gorbachev's fondness for shopping trips to Paris caused a national outcry. This was an issue that was fundamental in undermining the Soviet leader's popular standing. Particularly devastating was a passage in Boris Yeltsin's autobiography, *Against the Grain*, in which he accused Gorbachev of being too fond of his expensive lifestyle. Yeltsin himself made a point of publicly renouncing his official privileges.[35]

So what was the position of the public on such matters? Opinion polls at the time showed clearly that the system of privileges was despised, and the public was in favour of its complete abolition. A VTsIOM study carried out in April 1990 – allowing multiple responses – found just 12 per cent agreeing that 'There should be a list of privileges and a list of the positions which they apply to defined in law'; 24 per cent thought that 'privileges should be given to outstanding individuals for their special services to society or outstanding achievements (labour, military, etc.)'; fully 69 per cent thought that 'there should be no privileges, but concessions [*l'goty*] are necessary for those in need (invalids, large families, etc.)' and 27 per cent said that 'There should be no privileges: financial remuneration is all that is needed to encourage people'.[36] A system where rewards were allocated in a more open, predictable way, through wages and appropriate social welfare, was then overwhelmingly what Russians preferred. The same study confirmed that while people did not oppose certain perks, such as the provision of transport and the payment of telephone bills, which would assist in performing official duties, there was considerable public opposition to the allocation of housing, and a near-universal feeling that free medical services, holidays, and in particular supplies of consumer goods were unacceptable.

What then of attitudes to wages? Studies also revealed several concerns here. For example a study of the urban population in mid-1989, while finding that most complaints centred around wages not matching price rises and about taxes being too high, also found that there was concern about 'levelling', that is to say the failure of wages to relate to the usefulness or effectiveness of the work performed.[37]

What then of attitudes to the sort of changes in income distribution that were likely to be the result of attempts at transition to a market economy? This is a topic that other studies have attempted to consider. Unfortunately these are in general uninterpretable due to poor question design. For example the New Soviet Citizen study chose to use as their measure the statement 'Those who work harder and better should be paid more'. It is not surprising that 95 per cent of Russians, 96 per cent of Ukrainians and 97 per cent of Lithuanians agreed that, indeed, this was reasonable.[38] Similarly, VTsIOM's measure has asked people to choose between the statement 'Without great differences in wages nobody will be interested in work' and 'It is unjust when one person receives too much and another too little'. The second sentence is of course tautologous – by definition receiving 'too much' or 'too little' is unjust.[39] It is impossible therefore to conclude anything about attitudes to changing patterns of income distribution from these sources.

It is possible though to consider two related issues: attitudes towards the *nouveaux riches*, that is to those people who are succeeding in making themselves rich as a result of changes; and attitudes towards the increasingly visible disparities in wealth and living standards between these people and the rest of the population. Once again it is useful to ask whether there is evidence of these attitudes changing over the course of 1988–93.

Let us first consider the emergence of millionaires in the Soviet Union. While there is little doubt that the elite of the Brezhnev era had lifestyles that paralleled the very richest in Western society, their prosperity was carefully hidden from the rest of the population. It thus came as something of a shock to Soviet society when it was announced that there existed a number of rouble millionaires. As economic reform gathered pace, many were able to take advantage of a monopolistic, shortage-ridden, unregulated and highly corrupt economy to become very rich. The privatisation programme gave further opportunities for making vast profits, and as ideological constraints were removed conspicuous consumption by these new rich became increasingly visible.

The first point to be made is that majority opinion does not appear to be hostile to wealth as such. A Vox Populi survey in September

1991 asked 'Is it a good or bad thing if some people become rich, as long as they earn their wealth in an honest way?' Three quarters thought it was good, 8 per cent had mixed feelings, and only 13 per cent said it was bad.[40] Evidently, 70 years of a system that was hostile to money and to the rich had by no means led to a majority acceptance of the ideological view that wealth was unacceptable.

However, an absence of hostility to wealth in the abstract by no means implies that the new rich have been accepted. As one writer put it, 'the point is not so much to be or not to be rich, but how and at what price to become it'.[41] This is because there existed in the public mind a clear link between wealth and dishonesty. This is illustrated by a number of questions taken from VTsIOM surveys from 1989–90 and a survey of the urban Russian population from early 1993. VTsIOM asked respondents in 1990 'What is your attitude to the emergence in our country of millionaires?' 11 per cent had nothing against it, and another 38 per cent said that their attitude was positive as long as the money was earned honestly; 40 per cent were opposed because they felt that it was impossible to earn that much money in an honest way, but only 7 per cent were against it in principle, even if the money was earned honestly.[42] Similarly in 1991, responding to the question 'Why are some people a lot wealthier than others?' 18 per cent said that it was 'Because the majority of them are a lot more able, talented, goal-oriented and able to achieve'; 24 per cent said that wealth was inherited ('Because the majority of them have rich parents or relatives'); 16 per cent mentioned entrepreneurship ('Because the majority of them have a grasp of business') and 10 per cent ascribed it to hard work ('Because the majority of them are able and diligent workers'); but the most popular answers were 'Because the majority of them have made their money dishonestly', mentioned by 69 per cent, and a fatalistic 'Income in our society is in general unjustly distributed', the view of 33 per cent.[43] An environment in which the richest are dismissed as criminals was not one where the pursuit of profit would easily become socially accepted.

What then of changes after the collapse of communism, during the period when the Russian Government was attempting to introduce a market economy and encouraging entrepreneurship as an essential part of the change? As can be seen in Table 7.4, by January 1993, Russian urban dwellers appeared to be no more willing to accept the rich than previously. Only around 15 per cent expressed positive attitudes towards them, while one third were negative and another one in eight thought they should be jailed. One change would appear to be that slightly

Table 7.4 Views about the new rich, 1993

What is your opinion about the new rich?	(%)
I admire them	2
I view them positively	13
Indifferent	25
Negative	34
I consider it necessary to jail them	13
Who are the new millionaires?	**(%)**
All of them are honest, hard-working people	1
It varies. There are honest people and swindlers among them	58
They are all speculators and swindlers	34

Source: Unpublished survey of ten Russian cities by the Institute of Applied Politics, Jan. 1993, n = 1509.

more respondents were willing to accept that there now existed millionaires who had made their money legitimately, but again this is only really a reflection of reality.

Which social groups were more inclined to accept the new rich, and which were most likely to want to lock them up? Figure 7.14 gives us a sense of this.

The data are striking. While, overall, slightly more are hostile to the new rich, among young people, those with higher education and those who had a negative attitude to the communist cause significant majorities are willing to accept them. The same is also true of people who support a market economy and private property. The categories are of course heavily overlapping. When one considers the views of the elderly, the uneducated or the communist voter or supporter one finds almost no positive opinions about the new rich. Not one single person over the age of 60 who was interviewed said that they admired the wealthy. One in three communists and one in three of those who did not finish secondary education thought that they should be jailed.

While Figure 7.14 exaggerates the differences in that it omits the intervening groups – those aged between 30 and 60, those with an intermediate level of education, those who are neutral about communism – it does show how there exist sections of the Russian population with completely different or even irreconcilable views on the issue. Russia appears to be two nations: one section of society accepting the change as inevitable or even a good thing, the other unwilling or unable to change its views. In historical perspective, this is reminiscent of the historical divide between more individualistic Westernisers and more collectivist Slavophiles.

Figure 7.14 Attitudes to the new rich by demographic group and voting behaviour

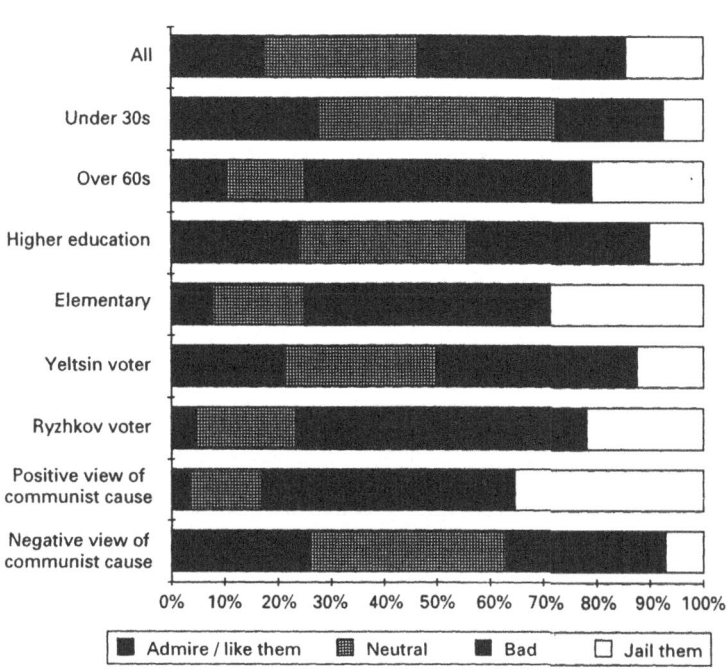

Source: As Table 7.4.

Clearly, then, there remains a widespread concern about the way in which introducing a market is allowing many undeserving people to gain. The equation of wealth with dishonesty which it has long been argued is a feature of Russian culture does not appear to have been altered to any great degree by recent changes. However, the fact that the younger generation is significantly more willing to accept disparities of wealth suggests that a gradual process of attitude transformation may be underway.

So much for attitudes to the new rich. What then of attitudes to the poor in society: most particularly those people dependent on state benefits for their livelihood, such as pensioners and the disabled? To what extent does there remain an expectation that the state should continue to look after these people?

Here, it is clear that before the introduction of economic reform there was a virtually universal feeling that the state did indeed have a responsibility for providing a subsistence minimum income. Two questions from the Times–Mirror Survey of May 1991 illustrated this clearly. The first put to respondents the proposition 'It is the responsibility of the state to take care of very poor people who can't take care of themselves.' Fully 93 per cent of Russians completely or mostly agreed with the proposition. The second statement was 'The state should guarantee every citizen basic food and shelter.' Here 81 per cent fully or partly agreed and 15 per cent fully or partly disagreed.[44]

It is furthermore clear that, before the changes, the popular conception of what actually counted as being poor remained significantly different to that which exists in other industrialised countries. There appeared to be a relative not an absolute conception of poverty. That is to say, poverty was not considered only to be an absence of the most basic necessities: enough to eat, a roof over one's head and so forth. It was also having a great deal less than those surrounding one. This can be illustrated through a detailed VTsIOM study from July 1990. It asked about general principles and specific instances of what counts as poverty. In general it found that 89 per cent agreed that not having the means to buy basic necessities counted as poverty. For comparison, the British Social Attitudes Survey of 1987 found 95 per cent agreeing with this statement.[45] However, the contrast arrives when respondents are asked whether being unable to live in the way those surrounding one do counts as poverty. In the USSR, two thirds of respondents agreed with this, compared to only 25 per cent in the UK.

The point is confirmed by responses to another question from the same survey. It asked what people actually meant by a subsistence minimum. Here just 16 per cent said that it should just cover basic food and clothing, and another 25 per cent moderate food and clothing, while fully 50 per cent felt that it meant an income that allowed one to live no worse than the majority of one's neighbours.

Table 7.5 gives further details as to what was seen as being poor. As can be seen, conceptions do seem to extend a long way past what many might expect. Thus, for example, not being able to entertain guests, not being able to afford good quality or fashionable clothes, even (for a bare plurality) not owning a colour television set or a suite of furniture, all these were taken to count as poverty. A large majority felt that not owning items which in the past would certainly have been considered luxuries but are now increasingly widespread, such as a black and white television or a refrigerator, should be considered poverty.

Popular conceptions about poverty, then, appeared to be extremely

Attitudes to the Market Economy

Table 7.5 Conceptions of poverty, 1991

Would we consider a family poor where ——?	Yes (%)	No (%)
I. Nourishment		
income was barely sufficient for even poor nourishment	89	5
income was enough for only modest nourishment (without fruit, vegetables, etc.)	85	9
income was enough to feed the family but not enough to have guests	72	17
II. Clothing		
unable to buy new clothes, had to wear same clothes for days, mend and alter them	87	8
unable to buy good and fashionable clothes, but only cheap cut price ones	79	11
only rarely afford good quality or fashionable clothes	46	38
III. Consumer durables		
unable to afford basic domestic appliances	90	5
had enough money to get such articles as a fridge, sewing machine, black and white television	56	29
unable to afford a colour television, suite of furniture etc.	44	42

Source: L. Zubova, N. Kovaleva and L. Khakhulina, 'Bednost' v SSSR: tochka zreniya naseleniya', *Voprosy ekonomiki*, 6 (1991), pp. 60–7; some data also in *Obshchestvennoe mnenie v tsifrakh*, 16 (1990).

radical, if this evidence is to be believed. Just as society was reluctant to accept extremes of wealth, so it remained reluctant to accept even relative poverty. In brief, egalitarian social attitudes remained, as of mid-1990.

But what of the period after the introduction of economic reform in January 1992? The reform had the effect of greatly increasing the number of people who were living below the subsistence minimum – that is, in absolute, not just relative, poverty. Was this resisted by public opinion, or was there growing acceptance that it was unavoidable if unacceptable? Did conceptions remain relative, or become more absolute? Evidence comes from a series of VTsIOM polls from 1992–94. Respondents were asked in these to choose between two definitions of the subsistence minimum: 'that level of income which ensures the person only physical survival' (an absolute conception), and 'that level of income which ensures the person a modest, but more or less decent existence' (a relative one). Figure 7.15 illustrates the data.

Figure 7.15 Conceptions of poverty, 1992–94

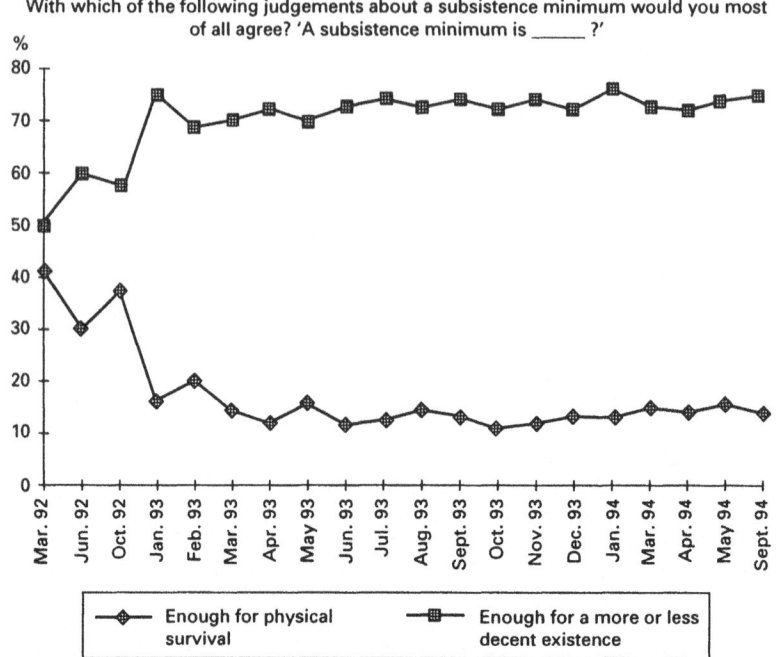

Source: *Ekonomicheskie i sotsial'nye peremeny: monitoring obshchestvennogo mnenya*, 1 (1993), p. 38, 4 (1994), p. 44 and 6 (1994), p. 51.

Again, these results are both interesting and perhaps counterintuitive. The earlier part of the chapter showed how Russians had become more willing to accept many aspects of the market economy, notably unemployment and private businesses. But this table suggests that views about poverty have actually moved in the other direction. As poverty has increased, people have become more, not less, convinced that a subsistence minimum should provide people with a respectable standard of living. The *laissez-faire* ethic that the state has no role beyond preventing starvation and providing shelter for its citizens and that beyond this it is up to the individual appears to have been flirted with briefly around the time when markets were introduced and then dismissed as unacceptable.

Overall, then, in attitudes to rising income differentiation, Russians appeared to be far from reconciled to allowing the market to act unrestrained by state intervention. The only source of comfort for extreme marketisers is that the system of wealth distribution under the old system was equally unpopular.

CONCLUSION: PUBLIC OPINION AND ECONOMIC REFORM

It is clear from public opinion poll data that there is majority support for a market economy, and that this support has remained remarkably consistent over time, at least according to more reliable indicators. However, it is equally clear that there are significant limitations to this support. More people want a gradual transition. Such gradualism is reflected in opposition to certain kinds of property, in particular private ownership of the largest enterprises and foreign ownership of anything at all; in a feeling that the state should continue to fix prices and guarantee people a reasonable standard of living; and in a general feeling that unemployment was unacceptable. If anything, these feelings have strengthened rather than weakened over time.

Such reactions should not surprise us. The fact is that privatisation of the Russian economy does encounter genuine problems of social justice in that very few of those who can afford to buy property have acquired their wealth legitimately. Furthermore, allowing unemployment is indeed bad for society in many ways. There is no doubt that many social problems in the West – crime, delinquency, drug abuse, health problems – are related to the existence of a large underclass of permanently unemployed. Similarly long historical experience of an egalitarian society makes it more difficult to adjust to an unequal one, with its reduced sense of social cohesion and increased insecurity. In this respect Russian society remains significantly different from many Western ones. One is reminded of Daniel Bell's argument that recent decades in Western societies have represented a change from the culture of production to the culture of selling and consumption.[46] Russian attitudes remain distinctly less individualistic and more production oriented than elsewhere.

Such reactions may not be surprising, but are they significant for the course of Russian economic reform, and Russian politics as a whole?

In some respects, the answer must be that they are not. Economic reform logically cannot take them into account. Opinion about private and foreign ownership of large enterprises provides an example. A market economy without the modern corporation – the prime source of innovation as well as jobs in many sectors of the economy – is impossible to conceive. Similarly free pricing is in general (although not in every case – defence and agriculture for example are in most countries not organised in this way) essential for rational allocation of resources. V.O. Key famously described public opinion as those elements of what people think that their leaders choose to pay attention to. The argument is that it would be irresponsible for leaders to pay sole attention to a public opinion that is ill-informed.[47]

Such is the economic reality. However, the political reality is utterly different. Price controls, no unemployment, confiscation from the wealthy and hostility to private business provide a clear and simple populist platform on which to campaign. There is substantial popular support for all these things, in some cases majority support. This has a two-fold effect. In the first instance it creates great pressure on the Government to water down some of its more severe economic policies, in particular the attempt to control the budget deficit through cutting subsidies. In a wider political context the sense that Government policy is out of line with social preferences undermines the legitimacy of the Government itself, making tough policies still more difficult to adhere to. The political conclusion must be that a much more convincing effort is necessary to persuade the Russian public of the virtues of change if there is not to be a still more significant backlash against reform.[48]

8 One Nation?

Up to now, this study has concentrated on trends in public opinion. Although from time to time reference has been made to the views of different groups within Russia, the stress has been on similarity of attitudes rather than difference. Yet this is a country of great variation: across 5000 miles and 11 time zones; between more than a hundred different ethnic groups; between generations with wholly different life experiences; between people's lives in rural areas and in Russia's biggest cities; between the privileged and the deprived. So what sense is it possible to make of the differences in attitude that exist in Russian society?

This is of course a topic that has attracted a great deal of attention from analysts, both in the Soviet period and more recently. The literature on the Soviet period was rewarding.[1] Clear hypotheses emerged: for example about how rising educational levels weakened support for the values of the communist regime; about the differences in the world view between generations, with younger people, for example, being more individualistic and less likely to favour state control; and about the links between material satisfaction and regime support. It was possible to draw clear conclusions about possible directions of change from these findings: for example that regime stability was linked with continued economic growth, and that there were secular trends that were weakening support irrespective of regime performance.

Recent work is perhaps more disappointing. Despite the profusion of survey evidence, the debate about the attitudes of various groups has moved little since the pre-Gorbachev era, despite the huge changes that have taken place. Many studies simply replicate, by means of sophisticated multiple regressions or factor analyses, intimidating to the statistically challenged, the findings that support for whichever dependent variable they are trying to explain – in terms of attitudes to politics, economic reform, or foreign policy – is most strongly linked with age and education.[2] The better studies have attempted to look at the effect of factors such as income, former Communist Party membership, urban–rural residence, gender, and life satisfaction.[3] Yet, because the starting point for most analyses is the attitude they are trying to explain, rather than the demographic or opinion group, few studies provide a convincing picture of how attitudes between groups differ across a range of topics, or why.[4] This chapter therefore seeks to present some evidence to contribute to an understanding of these questions. The picture is incomplete, since the surveys used have rarely paid much attention to measures of class, social status and such matters appropriate for Russia. Nevertheless some interesting findings, and some clear areas for future investigation, emerge.

The chapter is largely based on an unpublished survey of 1500 Russians conducted at the end of 1992 and the start of 1993 by the Institute of Applied Politics. Where appropriate, reference is made to the findings of other Russian survey organisations.

THE EFFECTS OF AGE AND GENDER

The concept of political generation is a familiar one for analysts of the Soviet Union. In brief, the arguments include the huge difference in life experiences between those whose formative years occurred under Stalin's rule and under each of his successors. For older generations, industrialisation, victory in the 'Great Patriotic War', the attainment of superpower status, and continuing economic growth contributed to an acceptance for the majority of the legitimacy of the socialist system. However, for younger people, formative experiences were of economic stagnation, open corruption and bureaucratisation, and growing social tension. These led to a willingness for many to support alternatives, leading up to a change of system itself.

Experiences of economic change in the recent period in many ways reinforced these divisions, since inflation and declining production and welfare spending tended to affect the old, for the most part dependent on state support for their livelihoods, disproportionately. In addition few elderly people were in a position to take advantage of new opportunities created by economic and political liberalisation.

However, in other respects recent changes might be expected to work in contradictory directions. Disillusionment with reformers leaves younger people with no obvious cause with which to identify. Growing political alienation rather than support for the opponents of the old system may be the result.

Data from the January 1993 survey – consistent with the findings of other organisations – show that such generalisations have considerable explanatory power. The political and economic attitudes of old and young people are hugely different. Figure 8.1 illustrates differences by age and gender in political interest, and Figure 8.2 looks at views about the historical role of the Communist Party.

Figure 8.1 Political interest by age and gender

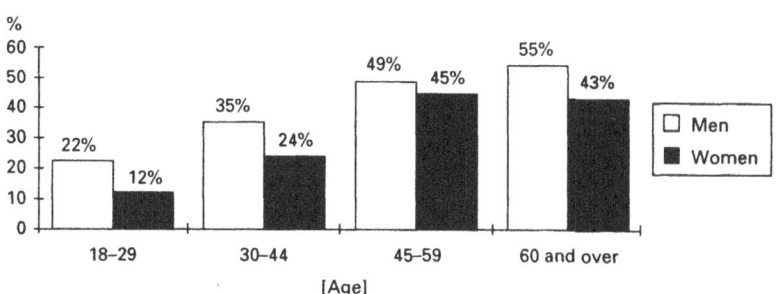

Note: Respondents said they were rather strongly or very strongly interested in politics (on a 5-point scale).

Figure 8.2 Views about the Communist Party by age

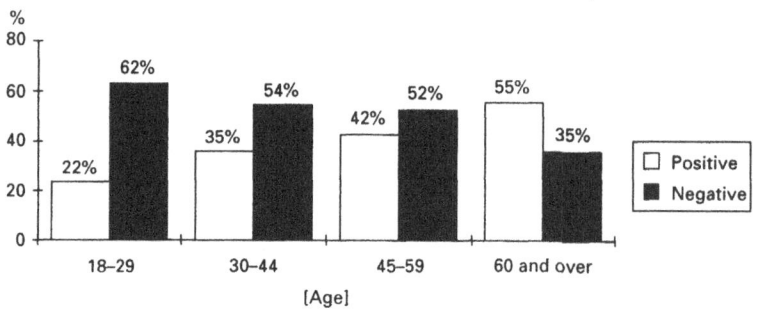

Note: Positive – responded either 'In general positive' or 'Positive but it made some mistakes'.
Negative – responded either 'Negative, although there were some good points' or 'Overall, negative'.

As can be seen, people whose formative political experiences were during the Khrushchev era and earlier tended both to be much more interested in politics than their younger Russian counterparts, as of early 1993, and much more positive towards the Soviet period. This is in many ways a surprising finding. Based on the politics of early 1993 one might expect those who were supportive of communism to be more disillusioned and alienated, but the reverse is the case.

How can these data be explained? In the Stalin and Khrushchev periods, the childhood of the older generation, politics was clearly able to make a difference – things changed in the country as the result of the decisions of leaders. The country was industrialised, people were exterminated, on the word of Stalin. Furthermore, in some respects, such as continuing growth, communist rule appeared to be a success during these years. One thinks of the launching of the first Sputnik, and of Khrushchev's boasts on numerous occasions that the country would soon be the world's leading power.

However, for people whose earliest political experiences were during the Brezhnev era or later, the situation continued to deteriorate regardless of the words of politicians. The gap between promises and reality was only too obvious. This led to support for change in general, and thus initial enthusiasm for anti-establishment politicians, which both Gorbachev and Yeltsin were when they first came to power. However, a general desire for change did not transfer to support for specific incremental changes, particularly when these changes appeared to make little difference to many areas of life. Young people now, therefore, appear to be highly alienated from politics.

The data also demonstrate a clear gender gap in terms of political interest. In each age group, men were significantly more likely to be interested in politics. The finding is a familiar one in comparative perspective. Since Russian politics remains dominated by men, women are more likely to perceive it as closed and remote. In some respects this is more so in the recent period as the state has ceased to provide many of the welfare facilities that women tend to benefit more from, such as child-care. Furthermore, with the still high level of female participation in the labour force, the 'double burden' of responsibilities in the home and at work gives little spare time for political activity.

When looking at matters such as interest in politics, analysis often suggests that the effect of education is highly significant. Increased access to information, and ability to comprehend and articulate views not only makes politics more interesting, but also increases the individual's ability to take part. However, in the case of Russia in early 1993 there did not appear to be a strong relationship once age effects are taken into account, as is illustrated in Figure 8.3.

The exception is among older people, where the more educated appeared significantly more interested in politics. Positive feelings about the regime – or at least their public expression – were an important prerequisite for getting higher education in the earlier periods of Soviet history.

Let us turn to differences in attitudes towards economic issues between the demographic groups under consideration. Figures 8.3 and 8.4 il-

Figure 8.3 Political interest by age and education

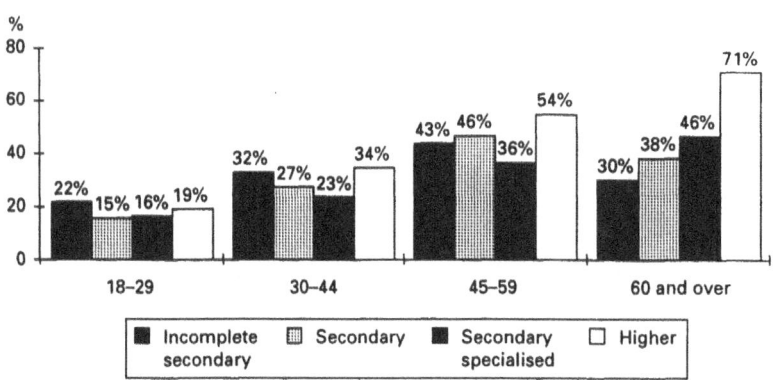

Figure 8.4 Attitudes to inequality by age and gender

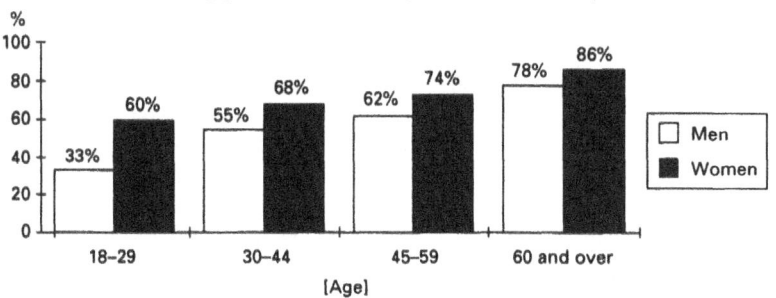

lustrate support for the creation of private property in Russia, and feelings about the acceptability of rising inequality in society.

Once again clear differences by age and gender are revealed. It is evident that young people in general find private property acceptable, and young men in particular see nothing bad in rising social inequality. The economic problems of the 1970s and 1980s were often linked by Western analysts with rising materialism and concern for personal economic well-being among the young, and in this respect Russia is no different.

However, the old appear to see the world in wholly different terms. The political line of the Soviet regime was always that private ownership

Figure 8.5 Support for private property by age and gender

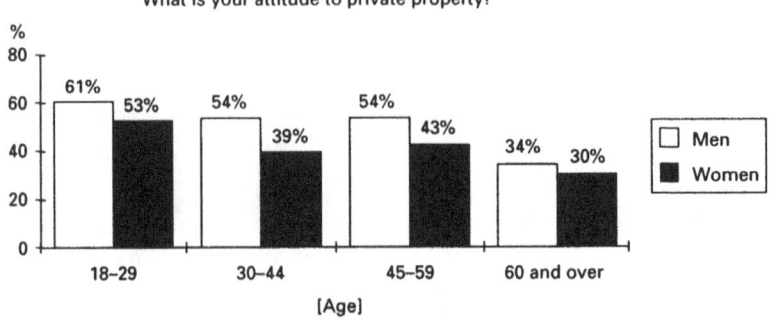

Note: Support indicates that the respondent chose the answer 'Positive. I think that without private property the economy will not be able to develop normally.' The other available alternatives were: 'Neutral. Private property may exist, but nothing is changing for the better.' 'Private property may be good for other countries, but not for us: we have different traditions'; and 'Negative: private property means the exploitation of man by man.'

and the use of hired labour represented the exploitation of man by man. Images of grasping capitalists and appalling factory conditions are evoked. But it is not just a question of propaganda. A society where conspicuous inequalities in incomes and standards of living are absent is an appealing vision for many. To be sure the Soviet Union was never such a society, but its ideology aspired to egalitarianism, and objections to the current situation where many are becoming rich by dishonest means are wholly understandable.

Again a difference in attitudes between the sexes is apparent, with women significantly more hostile to the direction of economic change than men. In terms of personal self-interest, significant restructuring of the economy and rising unemployment may be expected to affect women more than men. Explanations might also consider wider world views and socialisation, with women more often brought up to place a value on concern and care for other people rather than the importance of individual achievement.

What of differences between the generations in terms of attitudes to political pluralism and democracy? Figure 8.6 is illustrative.

As was the case with respect to opposition to a market economy, hostility to democracy appears to increase with age, and at all ages to be much greater among women than men. Older people are evidently more nostalgic for a simpler kind of politics, divided into right and

Figure 8.6   Attitudes to democracy by age and gender

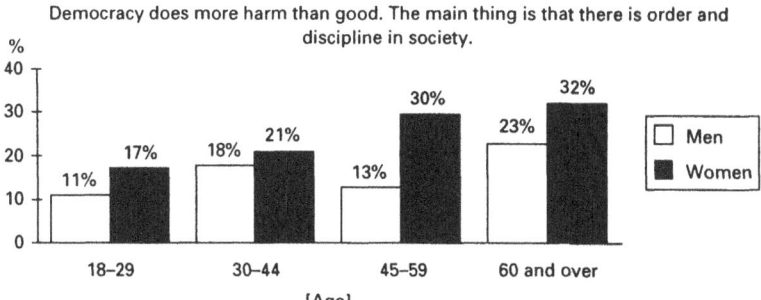

Note: Respondents were asked their opinion of democracy. The other choices available were 'No normal society can exist without democracy, and the more democracy is developed the better' and 'In the final analysis it is impossible to manage without democracy, but there ought to be limits to it, since too much democracy is harmful to society.'

wrong views, whereas the young are more supportive of a system where the people have some degree of restraint over their leaders and there is free discussion of alternatives.

The gender gap with respect to support for democracy is intriguing. It is common to argue that women tend to be more tolerant and 'dovish' in their attitudes than men. However, this does not appear to be the case. Women are a great deal more likely than men to favour 'order and discipline' above democratic politics. This may well represent a hostility to the extremism of the economic programme of Russia's 'democrats'.

THE EFFECT OF EDUCATION

It was suggested above that political interest tends to be more strongly related to political generation than to educational level or any other demographic characteristic. Different age groups also have strongly different attitudes to economic change and its consequences. But does education have any significant effect within generations?

The conventional view of the effects of rising education on attitudes in Russia is that it tends to increase support for individualistic change and for political tolerance.[5] Figure 8.7 illustrates the situation with respect to support for private property.

Figure 8.7 Support for private property by age, income and education

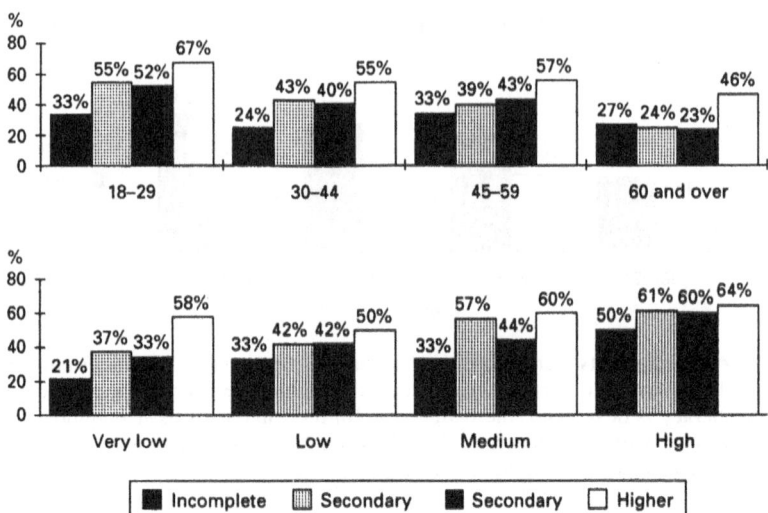

Note: Very low indicates a monthly income below 3000 roubles (one third of the sample); low indicates income between 3000 and 4999 roubles, medium indicates an income from 5000–8999, and high are those with monthly income higher than 9000 roubles.

Clearly within each age group, higher levels of education appear related to support for economic change. They also increase the likelihood that the respondent will find growing social inequalities acceptable. There are perhaps a number of aspects to this. More education increases ability to think in abstract theoretical terms, rather than simply responding to what happens or forming views on the basis of personal or political identifications. By 1993 there was little coherent theoretical alternative to marketisation. However, it could also be argued that there is an element of self-interest in that moves towards a merit-based system will benefit the more skilled in society. Therefore it is worth examining the interaction of education and income. This demonstrates that, while there is clearly an income effect on support, the higher the level of education the greater the support for private property, independent of personal income. Similar patterns apply in support for other elements of economic change.

What then of support for political pluralism and democracy? Figure 8.8 shows some data on this.

Figure 8.8 Hostility to democracy by education and age

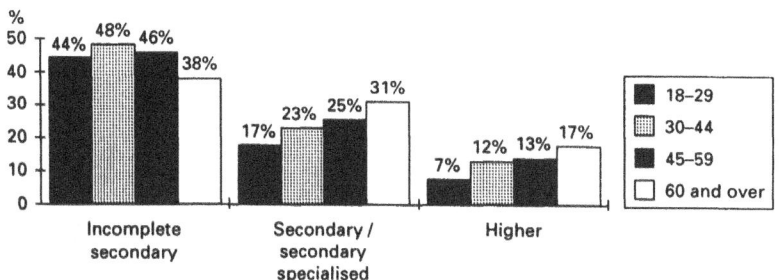

Note: Those hostile to democracy chose the option 'Democracy does more harm than good. The main thing is that there is order and discipline in society.'

It is usual to argue that increased educational levels increase receptivity to alternative points of view and to the need for a system of government that is more able to limit abuses of power by leaders. The less well educated tend to be more willing to accept simplistic solutions and imposed policies rather than respecting alternatives. As shown, this appears to be the case to a very great extent among the Russian urban population. In fact, levels of education appear to have a much more significant effect on attitudes to democracy than they do to views about economic change, or levels of political interest. Education does seem to lead to individuals regarding discussion of alternatives as a good in itself, although it does not imply any particular world view.

ECONOMIC SECTOR

One of the most significant social changes that has occurred in Russia in the recent period is clearly the rapid expansion of the private sector of the economy, both through privatisation of existing state property and through the legalisation of private entrepreneurial activities. So does the sector in which an individual is employed affect his or her attitudes?

As shown in Figure 8.9, there appears to be some link between the level of support for a market economy and employment sector, although support for planning does not differ greatly between the groups (with the exception of entrepreneurs). The degree of support for a market may be supposed to be a function of personal self-interest. One would not expect workers in the private sector to oppose its continuing expansion,

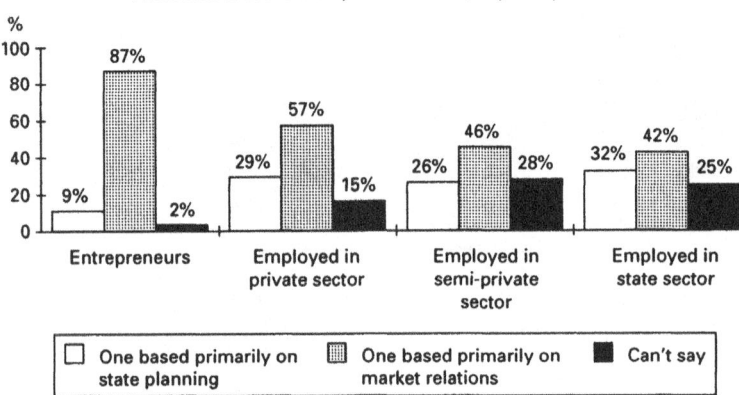

Figure 8.9 Views about the market by employment sector

Source: *Ekonomicheskie i sotsial'nye peremeny: monitoring obshchestvennogo mneniya*, 4 (1993), p. 51. N = 1346.

whereas this process is a threat to many who are working in inefficient heavily subsidised state industry or agriculture.

However, it is impossible to tell from these data whether the variation can be explained by differences in age, education, gender, income and so forth between those who remain in state employment and those now working under newer forms of ownership. For example, those employed in the private sector do tend on average to be younger and often better paid than those who still work in state enterprises. This relationship for now remains provisional, therefore.

CLASS AND EMPLOYMENT STATUS

Early studies of public opinion in Western democracies suggested that a dominant factor explaining differences in attitudes and behaviour was social class. This was defined in various ways, but the central feature was the status of the job carried out by the individual. Those with higher status employment, in general linked with higher income, tended to be more conservative. More recent work suggests that there has been a process of 'class dealignment'. Many in higher status jobs, particularly among the 'humanitarian intelligentsia', that is workers in education, health and so forth, were becoming more radical, whereas among the working class there were substantial divisions according to, for example, home ownership or membership of a trade union.

Figure 8.10 Desirable economic and political systems by occupation

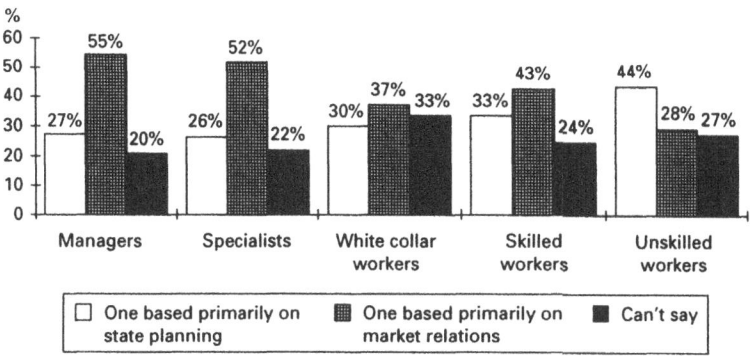

(a) What kind of economic system is better, in your opinion?

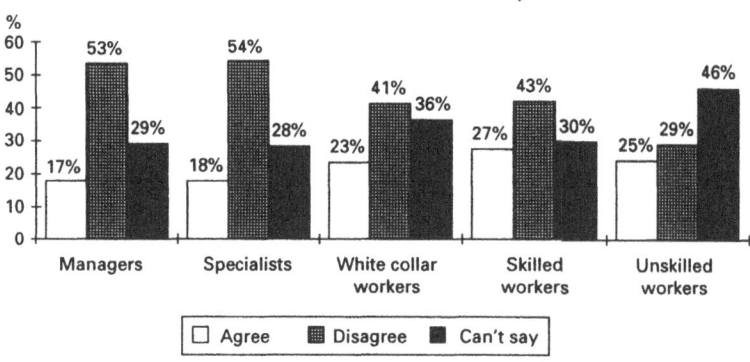

(b) Do you agree that the only way out of the situation in which the country finds itself is the establishment of harsh dictatorship?

Source: *Ekonomicheskie i sotsial'nye peremeny: monitoring obshchestvennogo mneniya*, 4 (1993), pp. 51, 55.

How does employment status appear to relate to attitudes in Russia? As Figure 8.10 demonstrates, as of mid-1993 there appeared to be some differences between the views of the different groups in terms of attitudes to a market economy and the desirable form of political system. Those with higher status jobs, managers and specialists, were rather more in favour of a market economy, and considerably more likely to oppose the establishment of political dictatorship in Russia. Unskilled workers, by contrast, supported the retention of a predominantly planned economy in large numbers, while only one in four were opposed to dictatorship as a solution for Russia's problems.

These findings can be interpreted in terms of the world experiences and personal self-interest of the groups in question. A functioning market economy is – to some degree at least – merit-based, rewarding ability. However, the emergence of mass unemployment illustrates the difficulty market economies have in integrating the least skilled. By contrast, one of the few achievements of economic planning was full employment, and increasing egalitarianism in wages in the 1970s and early 1980s may evoke nostalgia among the unskilled working class.

As regards the political views of the different classes, one sees some evidence of a greater degree of working-class authoritarianism. The work experience of the unskilled tends to be a hierarchical one, with relationships of domination and subordination in the workplace. By contrast, higher status jobs involve a much greater degree of flexibility, compromise and personal initiative. The analogy with appropriate forms of political rule is clear.

As with state–private employment, however, there must be some caution in interpreting the data. Clearly the various social classes differ considerably in terms of income and educational level, and it may be factors such as these, rather than experiences of work itself, that are more significant.

RURAL–URBAN RESIDENCE

There is a substantial body of literature detailing differences in attitudes between rural and urban dwellers. Those who live in predominantly agricultural areas are held to have much more traditional and authoritarian attitudes, and indeed to be somewhat hostile to cities and urban life in general, as being hotbeds of sin, corruption and democracy. This is often held to be based in the supposed greater simplicity of rural life. Peasant egalitarianism, dating back to past communal traditions, is sometimes cited as an influence.

In the Russian case, the organisation of agriculture is a further reason why rural inhabitants may have more favourable attitudes to the old system, and be more hostile to change. Proposals to improve the agricultural sector involve the break-up of state and collective farms, and the transfer of land to private individuals. For those people who have no wish to change their traditional way of life, this represents a considerable threat. There are also major implications for social justice involved in the transfer of state or collective property into private

Figure 8.11 Desirable economic system by rurality

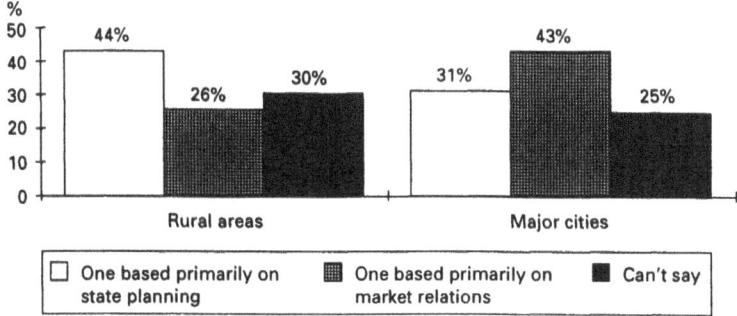

Source: *Ekonomicheskie i sotsial'nye peremeny: monitoring obshchestvennogo mneniya*, 4 (1993), p. 38.

Note: Major cities are those over 300 000 population, excluding Moscow and St Petersburg.

hands. By no means a majority of rural dwellers are in a position to take advantage of any reformed system.

As shown in Figure 8.11, in terms of attitudes to economic change, rural and urban Russia are indeed different worlds. Only around one in four rural inhabitants favoured a market economy as of mid-1993, whereas almost one half favoured retaining planning. In Russia's cities, by contrast, significantly more were in favour of markets, and this is still more the case in Moscow and St Petersburg than elsewhere.

There is also some evidence that the inhabitants of rural areas indeed tend to be more politically authoritarian than is the case in cities, as shown in Figure 8.12. While more people opposed than supported the establishment of dictatorship, the difference was not great, whereas in Russia's biggest cities, respondents disagreed that dictatorship would be a solution by a proportion of three to one.

Of course some of the differences in both economic and political attitudes can be explained by differential educational levels between urban and rural inhabitants. It has also been suggested that there is a differential access to information of the kind that might lead people to support change.[6] One must also consider a 'contagion effect': the same process that leads, for example, to the working class in the south of England being more conservative than its northern counterpart. All groups in rural Russia tend to resist economic reform more strongly than is the case in cities.

Figure 8.12 Attitudes to the imposition of dictatorship by rurality

Do you agree that the only way out of the situation in which the country finds itself is the establishment of harsh dictatorship?

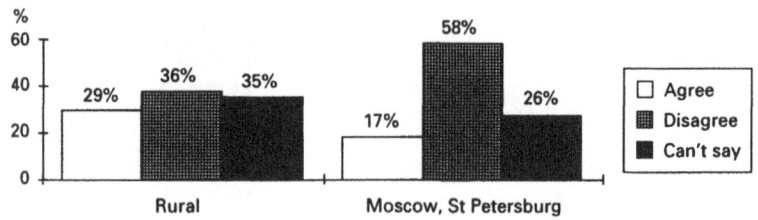

Source: *Ekonomicheskie i sotsial'nye peremeny: monitoring obshchestvennogo mneniya*, 4 (1993), p. 40.

RELIGION

Western studies of the influence of religion on political attitudes come to a variety of conclusions. Broadly, those who belong to the established religion in any particular country – for example Catholics in Southern Germany or Austria, the Church of England, American Protestant Churches – tend to be more politically conservative, while religious minorities – of whatever denomination – often have more non-conformist attitudes.

How might Russian Orthodox beliefs affect political attitudes? Orthodoxy is not a religion that concerns itself much with being a moral example. The main thing is simply the performance of ritual and fasting. It is not concerned with earthly behaviour beyond preaching obedience to the authorities, and has therefore often been accused of serving as a justification for personal and state tyranny. Furthermore, theologically there remain strong elements of anti-Semitism and isolationism in its doctrine. On the other hand, however, the fact that religious believers were persecuted by the communist regime might suggest a resistance to state abuse of power.

Surprisingly, the impact of belief in Orthodoxy on individual attitudes has not been much considered by analysts of Russian survey data. In part this is because the number of practising believers remains quite small. Figure 8.13 explores the issue.

As shown, it is not possible to identify differences in attitude between those who believe in God and those who do not. This is hardly surprising, and quite consistent with Western poll evidence, since believing in God is not a particularly strong statement of religious belief.

Figure 8.13 Political and economic views by religiosity

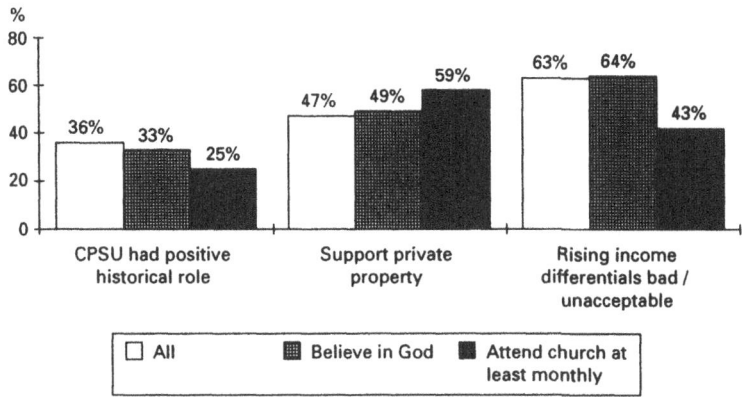

Notes: 'CPSU had positive role' indicates those responding to the question 'How would you appraise the CPSU's historical role, either "In general positive" or "Positive, although it made some mistakes"' (on 4-point scale).
  'Support private property' indicates those responding to the question 'What is your attitude to private property?' with the option 'Positive. I think that without private property the economy will not be able to develop normally' (on 3-point scale).

Source: Institute for Applied Politics survey, January 1993, n = 1509.

However, when one considers the views of those who attend church on a reasonably regular basis, one finds significant differences with the rest of the population. Church-goers were, as of the start of 1993, both more hostile to communism and considerably more in favour of economic change and accepting of its social consequences than the population as a whole. This despite the fact that those who attend church regularly are predominantly older, more female (by a factor of three to one), significantly less educated and poorer than the population as a whole, all of which would lead one to expect less support for change. Explanations for this phenomenon are not obvious. Perhaps what it illustrates is simply the tendency for practising Orthodox believers to identify more strongly with the government of the day and its policies? In this respect, then, the Orthodox can be compared with members of the dominant religion in many other parts of the world.

UNFINISHED BUSINESS: POLITICAL GEOGRAPHY, BRANCH OF ECONOMY, ETHNICITY

Analysis of Western survey data as a rule considers factors such as regional differences, differences between the attitudes of people working in different sectors of the economy, or not working at all, and the influence of factors such as membership of a minority or majority ethnic group. Unfortunately, however, published Russian research only gives limited possibilities for generalising about the importance of these factors, for a number of reasons.

Most importantly, often one is talking about small numbers of people, or groups that are difficult to sample. This is particularly the case when talking about ethnic minorities. The 1989 census identified well over 100 different groups, the largest of which, the Tatars, only numbered some 5 million people. Representative national surveys will therefore not interview minorities in significant numbers unless special efforts are made to oversample a particular group. Technical problems such as translation are here formidable. Such research has, therefore, been a rarity, which is unfortunate, since differences between Russians and other groups over matters such as the appropriate distribution of power between centre and republics, and indeed on matters such as minority rights, are highly intriguing.

As regards political geography, there is evidence from polls that support for change is stronger in the Urals, Northern Russia and parts of Siberia and the Far East than it is in the southern and central parts of European Russia. This is confirmed much more strongly by election results.[7]

However, published poll data do not as a rule give sufficiently detailed breakdowns to be able to analyse these findings adequately. Categories such as 'Central Russia' cover hugely different areas, from Moscow to the country's agricultural heartland. It is therefore impossible as yet to analyse the extent to which regional differences can be explained by other demographic differences, such as in economic structure or the number of rural inhabitants, and the extent to which they are based on genuine cultural and attitudinal differences between areas, such as for example that between the northern and southern United States. This is a hugely promising area for future research.

As regards branches of the economy, this is also a feature that is likely to have a considerable amount of explanatory power. Russia's industrialisation represented a vast but defective modernisation. Its industries, predominantly created in the thirties, forties and fifties, have changed very little since, thanks to the technological adversity of the planned economy. Many areas of the country are thus dominated by massive, loss-making heavy industrial enterprises, particularly in the defence sector. Economic reform applied to these sectors of the economy is just another name for plant-closure. So how are workers in threatened industries, and working at threatened factories, responding to change? Given the amount of Russian industry that is outdated and unprofitable, what are the potential implications of this? Again, understanding the answers to these questions is vital for comprehending the directions that Russian politics are likely to take.

CONCLUSIONS

It has become almost commonplace for commentators to argue that one of the features of postcommunist Russia is that it is a mutating society without any clear social base for change or resistance to change. As this brief discussion of the importance of various social categories has demonstrated, such an argument is misconceived. It is possible to identify very many 'fault lines'. There are clear constituencies for political and economic change: among the young, better-educated, wealthier and urban dwellers; and clear groups opposed to change and highly disgruntled: the old, rural inhabitants, the unskilled working class.

These findings have clear implications in terms of the likely development of a party system in Russia. They enable us to see which social constituencies parties are likely to attempt to appeal to, and to estimate the likely degree of support for reformist and anti-reform groups.

However, Russia is a rapidly changing society. The data reported here only represent snap-shots during the first half of 1993, and the relative sizes of these various groups are in a state of flux. The recent period, for example, saw a large increase in the size of the private sector of the economy, and also a considerable rise in the number of people living below the officially defined poverty line. From the data cited here, the effects of these particular changes might be expected to be contradictory. What is clear, however, is that understanding the social bases behind attitudes in Russia will improve our ability to identify likely directions of change.

9 Public Opinion and Post-Soviet Politics

What were the main features of Russian public opinion in the recent period? To what extent does one observe continuity, and are there major discontinuities in mass attitudes? What has been the impact of public opinion on post-Soviet politics? And do the findings raise any general theoretical points about the role of public opinion in the transition from communism in Russia?

MAIN FEATURES

Chapter 2 was concerned with general indicators of public mood: overall levels of happiness, feelings about the way matters had changed in the recent past, the greatest problems facing the country, expectations for the future. It showed how the emergence of a reformist leader in Mikhail Gorbachev raised popular expectations about the way that people's lives would change, and how these hopes were soon disappointed. The overwhelming majority by the end of the Gorbachev period saw their standard of living and the country's economy as deteriorating, and few expected things to improve in the near future. The change of leadership in 1992 did little to improve the popular mood, which by 1993–94 could be described as one of disillusionment and profound pessimism.

Another conclusion to emerge out of the chapter related to public priorities. When serious polling began, researchers consistently found that the most serious problems were considered to be the shortages and poor quality of goods. Economic reform has made this much less of a problem, but new concerns have emerged: overwhelming numbers of Russians feel that price levels and rising crime are the most serious social problems facing Russia, and unemployment has emerged as a new worry.

The next two chapters considered feelings about political institutions. Looking at the Gorbachev period, it was found that the institutions of the Soviet state, and even the Communist Party itself retained some trust until 1989, but after that time there occurred what can only be described as a legitimacy crisis for the ruling institutions, a crisis which was of course simultaneous with the growing disillusionment identified earlier. Other important causes were revelations about corruption and abuse of power. The dramatic falls in public confidence were also directly related to the emergence of new institutions that were able to act as an alternative focus of loyalty and identification for Russians and the other Soviet nationalities.

Public perceptions of Russia's new rulers from January 1992 were never as favourable as they had been for the Gorbachev leadership in its early days. The boost in popularity achieved by the Yeltsin Government as a result of its strong resistance to the attempted putsch of August 1991 proved temporary, and was more than outweighed by distress at the effects of the big bang economic reform of the following January. The Gorbachev period, with its revelations about the malfeasance of past and present politicians, had got many people out of the habit of trusting their leaders. As the effects of economic reform became more severe, trust in political institutions deteriorated still further. In the absence of alternative institutions, however, the situation was one of rising alienation, a kind of low grade legitimacy crisis, which weakened state authority without undermining it completely.

Data from the whole period 1989–93 reveal, however, a consistent pattern of greater trust in two institutions in particular: the armed forces and the Russian Orthodox Church. The general pattern of disillusionment did not extend to these. It was suggested that these institutions represented symbols of Russia's pre-Revolutionary culture which had remained substantially untainted by the Soviet period: spirituality and military strength.

It also appears that over this period – after the initial novelty of the First Congress of Soviet People's Deputies in 1989 had worn off – there was a consistently greater degree of popular trust in executive structures than there was in parliaments. The internal divisions within legislatures, lack of a sense of collective responsibility, and consequent poor quality of legislative output contributed to public mistrust. There arose, therefore, some degree of pressure for a presidential form of government, which was a concern to those who wished to see the consolidation of a form of representative democracy in Russia.

Chapter 5 presented evidence about issues related to Russian political culture. It found that in some respects, mass attitudes did not conform to stereotypes of an 'authoritarian' or 'subject' political culture. There were substantial degrees of support for the principle that the people should indeed choose their leaders. Majorities also appeared to favour the protection of a range of human rights: in particular freedom of movement, of speech and the press, and also freedom of association. There also appeared to be a higher degree of interest in politics than one might have imagined, although this seemed to have declined over time.

However, together with these there coexisted a number of significant elements of continuity with the past. These included a low level of political efficacy, both in the sense that personal political actions could succeed, and in the sense that the state was responsive to social pressure. This was related to a low and declining level of political participation in the recent period. Significant levels of social intolerance, xenophobia, aggression and willingness to accept the abuse of minority rights were identified. Many were also willing to accept the suspension of democracy and the transfer of powers to a dictator. The absence of a tradition of political pluralism and acceptance of alternative points of view and the legitimacy of opposition, it was argued, have led to a situation where many Russians retain the tendency characteristic of Soviet communism to view politics in terms of right and wrong, wanting action rather than discussion, and blaming problems on evil external forces.

The book went on to consider views about two of the central issues of the recent period, the collapse of the USSR and the reform of the economy. Chapter 6 examined issues surrounding the supposed 'deimperialisation of the Russian psyche'. It suggested that in the Gorbachev period most Russians favoured a substantial decentralisation of political power, but that this stopped short of accepting that an end to the Union was desirable. It was not public support, but a combination of the self-interest of regional elites, rising distrust of the political centre and the unwillingness on the part of public opinion to countenance any use of force to preserve the country that contributed to the end of the USSR.

In the postcommunist period, evidence was cited which suggested that the overwhelming majority of Russians regretted the end of the Union, and a number wished for Russia's great power status to be restored. However, it was suggested that much smaller numbers were willing to countenance the use of force against other former Soviet republics in defence of Russian interests. Even so, the evidence was highly provisional: survey research has concentrated to a very great extent on questions of political and economic change, reflecting the views of the (Western and Russian) researchers who have been responsible for designing it, and has failed to explore critical issues in the post-imperial situation, such as Russian irredentist sentiments, feelings about what should be done about Russians living outside the Russian Federation, and desirable directions of development of the institutions of the Commonwealth of Independent States.

Attitudes to the development of a market economy could be discussed with a great deal more confidence. It was shown that, from the time at which it became a political issue, a consistent majority supported the idea of creating a market economy, while a smaller number, around one in four, consistently opposed it. Among the supporters of markets, however, there were great differences about the desirable pace of reform, with a relatively small social constituency in favour of rapid transition to a market economy.

It was clear that, despite substantial reservations, over time a number of important features of the market had become accepted: these included the development of co-operatives, private ownership of small businesses, free pricing (within limits), even by 1993 the acceptability of getting rich by honest means.

However, public opinion never accepted a number of aspects that were central to economic reform. These include private ownership of larger enterprises, and foreign ownership of anything. These remain linked with notions of exploitation of people and of the natural environment. Although there has been an increasing willingness to accept unemployment, a majority have remained consistently opposed. Similarly, there exists widespread social disquiet about the consequences of the transition for social justice. There is particular concern about the increasingly conspicuous inequalities between winners and losers, and the association of economic success with dishonesty. Russians clearly retain a relative conception of poverty where the state should act to retain a reasonable level of economic equality.

It was argued that these features of public opinion were understandable in Russian conditions. Means of state regulation to avoid the excesses of the free market are underdeveloped, and the fact that the economy remains predominantly monopolistic provides great opportunities for the unscrupulous to make excessive profits. Furthermore, the ethos of capitalism requires people to accept that many members of society – predominantly the unskilled and those working in outdated parts of the economy – have no place in the new order of things. Such atomistic conceptions of society – denying some people the right to belong – appear to be unacceptable to many. It is not surprising that there remains a desire for a large economic role for the state in order to mitigate the worst consequences of marketisation. The section concluded by raising the possible contradiction between the desirable and what is economically feasible.

Chapter 8 raised questions about differences between social groups in the new Russia. In terms of attitudes to political democracy and a market economy, it demonstrated vast differences between the generations and between urban and rural areas. Many other social characteristics appeared to have some effect on attitudes: gender, social status, income, education, religion, employment in the private or state sectors of the economy. These differences formed the basis for political movements in support of and opposed to reform.

CONTINUITY AND CHANGE

When looking at Russian public opinion over the period 1989–93 should we see the main feature as continuity or as change? Clearly, as Leo Bogart points out, when considering public opinion it is necessary to distinguish between short-run reactions to events, responses to major developments in politics, and broad secular trends.[1] Research on Russian attitudes in the recent period by Western scholars has, up to this point, tended to stress discontinuities with the past, and to argue that there has been acceptance of broadly Western values.[2]

In respect of short-term opinions, the evidence presented does indeed suggest extreme fluctuation: Gorbachev's popularity declining from over 90 per cent support in 1988 to under 10 per cent by the end of 1991; the Communist Party moving from a situation where polls showed majority trust to only 3 per cent trust after the coup of August 1991; assessments of the state of the economy and expectations for the future in precipitous decline.

In terms of more long-standing social values, to the extent that it is possible to distinguish them from opinions, survey research also suggests some significant changes. Many of the values of the communist system seem to have been abandoned. This is the case in terms of economic attitudes with respect to the acceptability of private ownership and of high levels of wealth earned legitimately. In the political sphere, ideas relating to human rights and self-government also appear to have become acceptable.

One should be cautious in taking this too much at face value, however. There are very significant elements of continuity in attitudes. Democracy and markets appear to be the new political orthodoxy, just as communism was earlier in the century. Most Russians wish in public to express support for these labels, but it does not follow that there is any comprehension among the majority of what they actually mean. This is demonstrated for example by the levels of political and social intolerance, and of hostility to non-Russians, politicians in general and to the new rich.

In this context, what is perhaps significant is not the extent of support for democracy and markets, but the depth of opposition. Depending on the precise issue under investigation, between a quarter and a third of the population expresses hostility to the changes. This hostility is heavily concentrated among those groups who are most threatened by economic reform, an understandable reaction to the feeling of one's life being under attack. This proportion outnumbers those who are consistently in favour of reform.

Besides the level of opposition to change, continuity from the Soviet period can also be seen in the number of people who simply do not have attitudes to the most central issues of the day. This disorientation is reflected in the many opinion surveys to which there are a high number of 'don't know' responses. As Bogart points out, it is impossible to tell whether 'don't know' as a response represents real lack of interest or agonised uncertainty.[3] But nevertheless private attitudes do not become part of public opinion unless they are expressed in public. Stereotypes of a passive political culture, of a section of the population that is fundamentally unaware about what is going on and that feels powerless to make a difference are evoked.

Overall, then, writing about Russian public opinion has tended to underplay the extent to which it retains elements of the past.

PUBLIC OPINION AND POST-SOVIET POLITICS

What has been the direct impact of public opinion on Russian politics in the recent period? And what does the nature of public opinion tell us about likely future trends?

The impact of public opinion on politics is of course a complex relationship. Opinions, as expressed in polls, and in other forms, such as via the media, or most importantly through election results, influence what political elites attempt to do, but equally the actions of elites themselves influence opinion.

Clearly in the Gorbachev period public opinion had a substantial impact on some of the most important decisions. It is said that Gorbachev refused to submit himself to popular election even as early as 1989 because he was concerned about poll findings that 20 to 30 per cent of the population might vote against him. In retrospect, failure to earn a popular mandate in this way was a great mistake. Years operating in a culture which pretended that popular support for the Party and its leader were unanimous appears to have made it difficult for him to adjust to the new environment.[4] Similarly, his hesitancy in conducting economic reform may well be linked to the clear evidence provided by polls – including those commissioned by his own Government – which showed public misgivings about many aspects of his proposals.

Ultimately, though, what strikes the analyst most about the Gorbachev period is the role played by public opinion in de-legitimising the communist system. Surveys by 1990–91 were clear in showing a rejection of the political and economic systems, and of the existing balance of power between centre and periphery. The absence of the public support that had been such a resource earlier in the *perestroika* period, added to resistance from a conservative bureaucracy and an incomplete vision of desirable change was central in undermining the Gorbachev leadership.

The years 1992–94 looked different, in the sense that public opinion was never in accord with Government policy. The Gaidar Government's project of shock economic therapy was unpopular from the outset. Radicals in the Government felt that it would be irresponsible not to undertake the project despite this: other alternatives would lead to still worse outcomes for people. The hope was that public opinion would follow behind the changes.

This was a risky political strategy. As the evidence presented throughout this book suggests, in the first two years of the Yeltsin administration there was little evidence of change in mass attitudes in the direction desired by reformists. The data rather suggest that the views of increasingly many Russians involved a mixture of disillusionment, alienation, pessimism and disorientation. Disillusionment in the failings of the leadership and in the failure of reform to deliver improvements in standards of living, a disillusionment worsened by the rising expectations that had preceded it. Alienation in that the most important institutions of the state were distrusted by overwhelming numbers of people, and there was a widespread belief that 'normal' democratic politics would have no effect, or was merely conflict for the sake of conflict. Pessimism that things would improve in the near future, if at all. Disorientation as a complete system of values collapsed and was not replaced by any other – certainly not yet by the values of the market and individualism. This section of the population is considerably greater in size than that which consistently supported current changes, or that which retained the values and orientations of the old regime.

What are the political implications of the fact that such a large section of the Russian population is disillusioned, disoriented and alienated? Disorientation clearly implies a highly volatile electorate, not aligned firmly with any of the political groupings that are emerging, making it hard for any government to establish authority. Political alienation is perhaps the more worrying phenomenon, though. What we see is a substantial section of society which, having rejected the values of the old regime and not adopted those of the new, is left disconnected from the rest of society, with a sense of meaninglessness, no longer feeling bound by society's rules. The social consequences in terms of rising crime and acts of senseless violence are evident.

Politically, such a process is leading, among many people, to a craving for order and protection, and for some new certainties. Many of the excluded begin to search for scapegoats for their own problems and anti-Semitism and ethnic conflicts rise. This is fertile ground for populist forms of politics, even fascism. This is true of many postcommunist countries, and emphatically true of Russia, since as well as appealing to the economically insecure and the psychologically alienated, the demagogic leader can manipulate a nostalgia for the days of empire, a lost feeling of pride in superpower status and in Russia's control over the destinies of many subordinate peoples, and a sense that Russia was somehow special and unique. The electoral success of the ultranationalist and anti-Semite Vladimir Zhirinovsky, who achieved 7 per cent of the vote in the Russian presidential election of June 1991, and whose Liberal Democratic Party was supported by fully 24 per cent in the parliamentary elections of December 1993, is the clearest manifestation of such a process.[5]

There are some grounds for a less pessimistic conclusions, however. There is little direct evidence that Russians have the desire for a more aggressive foreign policy. For example, survey evidence consistently finds that military solutions to disputes with other countries are ruled out by the overwhelming majority. There is also a sense that rather than military involvement, many would prefer Russian withdrawal from some of the most intractable post-Soviet conflicts, such as those in the North Caucasus or in Tadjikistan.

Furthermore, there clearly exist in Russia substantial groups who do accept the desirability of Russia's becoming a normal post-imperial country and of conducting politics in a civilised fashion. These attitudes are much more common among the young than the old. The simple processes of generational replacement would therefore lead one to expect a secular trend towards a more desirable outcome. However, the disjunctions between public opinion and Government policy have, as yet, had less dramatic implications than the emergence of fascism. Clearly it was possible to govern without popular support for many policies for a period of time, but the continuing pressure for a moderation of economic policy and for a somewhat more authoritarian form of political leadership was finally reflected in the changes to the composition of the Russian Government after the December 1993 elections.

CONCLUSION

There is still much to learn about the nature of public opinion in Russia, and about the ways in which it is moving in response to the changes that are taking place. However, our understanding has progressed immeasurably since the pre-Gorbachev period, when all that could be confidently asserted was a limited amount of survey evidence from émigré sources, supplemented by the claims of eminent dissidents about the attitudes of 'the Russian people'. And that we do know so much more is a tribute both to the work of the Russian sociological profession in establishing the infrastructure for studying public opinion, and to the extent to which Russian politics has changed. Now the unanimous will of the people is something that Russia's leaders can no longer pretend they represent.

Notes

1 THE DEVELOPMENT OF RUSSIAN PUBLIC OPINION

1. Matthew Wyman, Bill Miller, Stephen White and Paul Heywood, 'The Russian Elections of December 1993', *Electoral Studies*, 13 (1994), p. 263.
2. Quoted in Elisabeth Noelle-Neumann, *The Spiral of Silence: Public Opinion – Our Social Skin* (Chicago and London: Chicago University Press, 1984), p. 38.
3. For a profound discussion of the nature and causes of opinion inconsistency, see Leo Bogart, *Silent Politics: Polls and the Awareness of Public Opinion* (NY: John Wiley, 1972), pp. 129–39.
4. Bogart, *Silent Politics*, pp. 14–20.
5. Bogart, *Silent Politics*, p. 154.
6. Linda Lubrano, Wesley Fisher, Janet Schwartz and Kate Tomlinson, 'The Soviet Union', in William A. Welsh (ed.), *Survey Results and Public Attitudes in Eastern Europe and the Soviet Union* (NY: Pergamon, 1981); a detailed account of official attitudes to such research is Vladimir Shlapentokh, *The Politics of Sociology in the Soviet Union* (Boulder CO: Westview Press, 1987); the Taganrog research was carried out by Boris Grushin, who subsequently managed to publish some of the results – see B. Grushin and L. Onikov (eds), *Massovaya informatsiya v sovetskom promyshlennom gorode* (Moscow: Politizdat, 1980).
7. The 'classic' 1950s account is Alex Inkeles and Raymond Bauer, *The Soviet Citizen: Daily Life in a Totalitarian Society* (Cambridge MA: Harvard University Press, 1959); for 1970s research see Zvi Y. Gitelman, 'Soviet Political Culture: Insights from Jewish Émigrés', *Soviet Studies*, 29 (1977), pp. 543–64; James R. Millar (ed.), *Politics, Work and Daily Life in the USSR* (Cambridge: Cambridge University Press, 1987).
8. Czeslaw Milosz, *The Captive Mind* (London: Penguin, 1980), p. xiv.
9. For example, T.W. Adorno, E. Frenkel-Brunswick, D. Levinson and R. Sandford, *The Authoritarian Personality* (NY: Harper and Row, 1950); Zbigniew Brzezinski, *The Grand Failure: The Birth and Death of Communism in the Twentieth Century* (London: Macdonald, 1989), pp. 1–12.
10. Geoffrey Hosking, *The Awakening of the Soviet Union* (enlarged edition, Cambridge MA: Harvard University Press, 1991), esp. chapters 3 and 4.
11. Vladimir Shlapentokh, *The Public and Private Lives of Soviet Citizens: Changing Values in Post-Stalin Russia* (NY and Oxford: Oxford University Press, 1989).
12. *Pravda*, 6 February 1987.
13. See Hedrick Smith, *The New Russians* (updated edition, London: Vintage, 1991), p. 86.
14. For an example of the state of affairs by the end of 1988 see Yuri Levada (ed.), *Est' mnenie! itogi sotsiologicheskogo oprosa* (Moscow: Progress,

1990); for 1989 see *Obshchestvennoe mnenie v tsifrakh, passim*; also Yuri Levada *et al.* (eds), *Sovetskii prostoi chelovek* (Moscow: Nauka, 1993).
15. V.G. Britvin, S.V. Kolobanov and E.G. Meshkova, *Obshchestvennoe mnenie v usloviyakh perestroiki: problemy formirovaniya i funkstionirovaniya* (Moscow: Institut sotsiologii AN SSSR, 1990) in many ways documents the change in the focus of survey research in this institution.
16. *Moskovskie novosti*, 14 April 1991.
17. See, for example, 'Mnenie o proekte platformy TsK KPSS', *Partiinaya zhizn'* 7 (1990), p. 26; G. Smirnov, 'Otnoshenie k Leninu (itogi sotsiologicheskogo issledovaniya)', *Izvestiya TsK KPSS*, 2 (1991), pp. 50–1; *Politicheskaya sotsiologiya informatsionnyi byulleten'*, *passim*.
18. Tatyana Zaslavskaya, 'Sotsiologicheskii monitoring ekonomicheskikh i sotsial'nykh peremen v Rossii', *Ekonomicheskie i sotsial'nye peremeny: monitoring obshchestvennogo mneniya*, 1 (1993), pp. 3–9 constitutes a statement of the goals of VTsIOM's research.
19. Articles critical of Russian practice would include John P. Willerton and Lee Sigelman, 'Public Opinion Research in the USSR: Opportunities and Pitfalls', *Journal of Communist Studies*, 7 (1991), pp. 217–34; Jeffrey W. Hahn, 'Public Opinion Research in the Soviet Union: Problems and Possibilities', in Arthur H. Miller, William M. Reisinger and Vicki L. Hesli (eds), *Public Opinion and Regime Change: The New Politics of Post-Soviet Societies* (Boulder CO: Westview Press, 1993), pp. 37–50; Darrell Slider, 'Public Opinion and the Political Process', in Stephen White, Graeme Gill and Darrell Slider (eds), *The Politics of Transition: Shaping a Post-Soviet Future* (Cambridge: Cambridge University Press, 1993) and, from the Russian viewpoint, Vasilii Ovsyannikov, 'O nauchnosti oprosov obshchestvennogo mneniya', *Sotsiologicheskie issledovaniya*, 9 (1991), pp. 18–21; Vsevolod Vil'chek, 'Killery s anketoi v rukakh', *Moskovskie novosti*, 24 November 1993, p. 7. More constructive discussions include Elena I. Bashkirova and Vicki L. Hesli, 'Polling and *Perestroika*', in Miller *et al.* (eds), *Public Opinion and Regime Change*, pp. 17–37; Michael Swafford, 'Sociological Aspects of Survey Research in the Commonwealth of Independent States', *International Journal of Public Opinion Research*, 4 (1992), pp. 346–59; Boris Grushin, 'Pochemu nel'zya verit' bol'shinstvu oprosov, provodimykh v byvshem SSSR', *Nezavisimaya gazeta*, 28 October 1992; Brian D. Silver, 'Evaluating Survey Data from the Former Soviet Union', paper given to conference on 'Survey Research in the Successor States of the USSR', George Washington University, 17–18 September 1992.
20. The offending poll is in *Argumenty i fakty*, 40 (1989).
21. *Nezavisimaya gazeta*, 28 October 1992, p. 5.
22. Willerton and Sigelman, 'Public Opinion Research', p. 228.
23. Roger J. Stubbs and Peter F. Hutton, 'Yea-saying: Myth or Reality in Attitude Response?', paper presented to the Market Research Society Annual Conference, 1976, quoted in Robert M. Worcester, *British Public Opinion: A Guide to the History and Methodology of Political Opinion Polling* (Oxford: Blackwell, 1991), p. 138.
24. Noelle-Neumann, *The Spiral of Silence, passim*.
25. *Moskovskie novosti*, 10 June 1990.

26. Quoted in Smith, *The New Russians*, p. 88.
27. Miller *et al.* (eds), *Public Opinion and Regime Change*, p. 280.
28. S.P. Khaikin and E.P. Pavlov, 'Kak pomoch' interv'yueru', *Sotsiologicheskie issledovaniya*, 4 (1991), pp. 58–65.
29. *Nezavisimaya gazeta*, 28 October 1992. Of course these kinds of problem are not confined to survey research in Russia. For example, a classic study of the United States comments in its appendices that two of its interviewers were arrested in Alabama. See A. Campbell, P. Converse, W. Miller and D. Stokes, *The American Voter* (NY: Wiley, 1960).
30. Swafford, 'Sociological Aspects', p. 351.
31. *Ibid.*, p. 355.
32. Quoted in Worcester, *British Public Opinion*, p. 135. The categories for this section are largely drawn from the same source.
33. 'Zabastovki: prichiny i posledstviya', *Obshchestvennoe mnenie v tsifrakh*, 5 (1989).
34. See George Gallup, *The Sophisticated Poll Watcher's Guide* (Princeton: Princeton University Press, 1976).
35. Philip Converse, 'The Nature of Belief Systems in Mass Publics', in David E. Apter (ed.), *Ideology and Discontent* (NY: Free Press, 1964), pp. 206–61.
36. Swafford, 'Sociological Aspects', p. 355.
37. *Central and Eastern Eurobarometer*, passim.
38. Levada, *Est' mnenie!*, p. 281. The answers to this particular question are discussed in Chapter 3 below.
39. *Ibid.*, p. 8.
40. Vladimir Rukavishnikov, 'Pik napryazhennosti pod znakom belogo konya', *Sotsiologicheskie issledovaniya*, 10 (1990), pp. 12–13.
41. Timothy Heleniak, 'Glasnost and the Publication of Soviet Census Results', *Journal of Soviet Nationalities*, 2 (1991), pp. 139–60.
42. VTsIOM's weighting procedures are outlined in E.V. Kozerenko and S.G. Novikov, 'Vyborka monitoringa – aposteriornyi kontrol', *Ekonomicheskie i sotsial'nye peremeny: monitoring obshchestvennogo mneniya*, 4 (1993), pp. 8–10.
43. Swafford, 'Sociological Aspects', p. 350.
44. James L. Gibson and Raymond M. Duch, 'Attitudes Towards Jews and Soviet Political Culture', *Journal of Soviet Nationalities*, 2 (1991), pp. 110–11.
45. The data on telephones are from *Pravda*, 26 September 1985, quoted in Willerton and Sigelman, 'Public Opinion Research', p. 234.
46. See, for example, VTsIOM's *Ekonomicheskie i sotsial'nye peremeny: monitoring obshchestvennogo mneniya*, 1 (1993), pp. 9–10.
47. For the polls, see *Radio Free Europe / Radio Liberty Research Bulletin*, 15 January 1993; *Nezavisimaya gazeta*, 29 July 1992.
48. A.V. Dmitriev and Zh.T. Toshenko, 'Sotsiologicheskii opros i politika', *Sotsiologicheskie issledovaniya*, 5 (1994), pp. 42–51.
49. Wyman *et al.*, 'The Russian Elections', p. 262; *Ekonomicheskie i sotsial'nye peremeny: monitoring obshchestvennogo mneniya*, 2 (1994), p. 70.

2 THE MOOD OF THE NATION

1. Václav Havel, 'The Power of the Powerless', in his *Living In Truth* (London: Faber, 1986), pp. 36–122.
2. I.E. Ladygina, 'Mnenie naseleniya ob usloviyakh udovletvoreniya potrebnostei', in V.G. Britvin, S.V. Kolobanov and E.G. Meshkova (eds), *Obshchestvennoe mnenie v usloviyakh perestroiki: problemy formirovaniya i funktsionirovaniya* (Moscow: Institut sotsiologii AN SSSR, 1990), pp. 81–93.
3. A.I. Grazhdankin and B.V. Dubin, 'Tsennostie orientatsii lichnosti i uroven' zhizn'yu', *Obshchestvennoe mnenie v tsifrakh*, 3 (1990). N = 2696.
4. *Radikal*, 22 (1992), p. 15.
5. *Argumenty i fakty*, 18 (1992).
6. Alexei Levinson, 'VTsIOM sprashivaet: kakaya nastroeniya?', *Izvestiya*, 27 February 1993, p. 15.
7. *Ekonomicheskie i sotsial'nye peremeny: monitoring obshchestvennogo mneniya*, 3 (1994), pp. 39, 45 and 5 (1994), pp. 71, 78, 85.
8. *Eurobarometer*, 35 (1991), pp. 1–18.
9. Michael Ellman, 'The Increase in Death and Disease under *Katastroika*', *Cambridge Journal of Economics*, 6, 1994, pp. 619–34.
10. *Ekonomicheskie i sotsial'nye peremeny: monitoring obshchestvennogo mneniya*, 4 (1994), p. 54.
11. N.Ya. Kirichenko and V.M. Konstantinov, 'Pitanie naseleniya', *Obshchestvennoe mnenie v tsifrakh*, 3 (1989). N = 1611.
12. M. Krasil'novka and T. Avdeenko, 'Potrebitel'skoe povedenie naseleniya v krizisnykh situatsiyakh', *Voprosy ekonomiki*, 1 (1992), pp. 74–82.
13. *Ekonomicheskie i sotsial'nye peremeny: monitoring obshchestvennogo mneniya*, 1 (1993), p. 51. VTsIOM survey, n = 2465.
14. A more technical discussion of the point is Richard Rose and Ian McAllister, 'Is Money the Measure of Welfare in Russia?', *University of Strathclyde Studies in Public Policy*, 215 (1993).
15. For this evidence see for example the June 1990 Goskomstat survey, reported in *Mnenie naseleniya o tsennakh na tovary i uslugi* (Moscow: Goskomstat SSSR, 1991), p. 313; also *Obshchestvennoe mnenie v tsifrakh*, 10 (1991), pp. 8–9.
16. V. Rutgaiser, A. Grazhdankin, V. Kosmarskii, L. Khakhulina and S. Shpil'ko, 'Otnoshenie naseleniya k ekonomicheskoi reforme', *Voprosy ekonomiki*, 4 (1990). VTsIOM survey of the urban population of six republics, n = 1148.
17. *Dialog*, 9 June 1991, and *Nezavisimaya gazeta*, 7 November 1991.
18. *Ekonomicheskie i sotsial'nye peremeny: monitoring obshchestvennogo mneniya*, 3 (1994), p. 63.
19. Ellman, 'The Increase in Death and Disease', p. 336.
20. J.S. Flemming and R.C.O. Matthews, 'Economic Reform in Russia', *National Institute Economic Review*, 3 (1994), pp. 65–82.
21. A.M. Demidov, 'Obshchestvennoe mnenie i sotsial'no – politicheski voprosy perestroiki', in Britvin *et al.*, *Obshchestvennoe mnenie*.
22. See Vladimir Kosmarskii, 'Public Attitudes to the Transition', unpub-

lished paper given to international conference on the Soviet economy in crisis and transition, Stockholm, June 1991.
23. *Obshchestvennoe mnenie v tsifrakh*, 11 (1991).
24. Richard Rose and Christian Haerpfer, 'Adapting to Transformation in Eastern Europe', *University of Strathclyde Studies in Public Policy*, 212 (1992), pp. 42–5 gives East European parallels.
25. See, for example, Eric Jacobs and Robert Worcester, *Typically British?* (London: Bloomsbury, 1991), pp. 97–100.
26. Michael S. Lewis-Beck, *Economics and Elections* (Ann Arbor: University of Michigan Press, 1988), chapter 8.

3 PUBLIC OPINION AND SOVIET POLITICAL INSTITUTIONS

1. On the political role of the Soviet citizen under Brezhnev see Vladimir Shlapentokh, *The Public and Private Life of the Soviet Citizen* (Oxford: Oxford University Press, 1989), esp. chapter 3. For evidence of the level of compliance with officially sanctioned political activity, see Donna Bahry and Brian D. Silver, 'Soviet Citizen Participation on the Eve of Democratization', *American Political Science Review*, 84 (1990), pp. 821–47.
2. Mikhail Gorbachev, *Perestroika: New Thinking for our Country and the World* (London: Collins, 1987), p. 25.
3. All public opinion data in this chapter are based on samples of the whole USSR unless otherwise stated.
4. Conducted by the Academy of Sciences Institute of Sociology, reported in *The Economist*, 23 June 1990.
5. On the difficulties of the political reformer, see Samuel Huntington, *Political Order in Changing Societies* (New Haven and London: Yale University Press, 1968), chapter 6.
6. *Obshchestvennoe mnenie v tsifrakh*, 9 (1990).
7. *Obshchestvennoe mnenie v tsifrakh*, 10 (1990).
8. G. Smirnov, 'Otnoshenie k Leninu', *Izvestiya TsK KPSS*, 2 (1991), pp. 50–1. A more detailed account is to be found in the article 'Vashi otnosheniya k istorii', *Informatsionnii byulleten'*, *tsentr sotsiologicheskikh issledovanii akademii obshchestvennykh nauk pri TsK KPSS*, 1 (1991), pp. 90–113.
9. Tatyana Zaslavskaya, 'Sotsialism, perestroika i obshchestvennoe mnenie', *Sotsiologichiskie issledovaniya*, 8 (1991), pp. 3–21.
10. *Moskovskie novosti*, 28 July 1991.
11. Nikolai Pishchulin and Sergei Sokol, 'Za-Protiv', *Dialog*, 16 (1990), p. 3.
12. *Mir mnenii i mneniya o mire*, 1 (1991).
13. *Nezavisimaya gazeta*, 20 November 1991.
14. *Izvestiya*, 14 March 1992.
15. *Mir mnenii i mneniya o mire*, 1 (1991).
16. On this, see Matthew Wyman, 'The Economic Functions of the Intermediate Level Party Apparatus', unpublished thesis presented for the degree of M. Soc. Sci., Birmingham University, December 1989, parts 7 and 8.

17. *Moskovskie novosti*, 15 July 1990.
18. *Informatsionnii byulleten'*, tsentr sotsiologicheskikh issledovanii akademii obshchestvennykh nauk pri TsK KPSS, 1 (1991), p. 102.
19. On local politics, see Ronald J. Hill, *Soviet Political Elites* (London: Martin Robertson, 1977); William Taubman, *Governing Soviet Cities* (NY: Praeger, 1973).
20. Vladimir Rukavishnikov, 'Pik napryazhennosti pod znakom belogo konya', *Sotsiologichiskie issledovaniya*, 10 (1990), p. 23. The samples were of 2228 and 1790 respectively in postal surveys of the whole Union, which admit to having oversampled younger, more educated people. Evidently elementary weighting techniques remained unfamiliar at this point.
21. Elena Petrenko, 'Kul'turnyi sdvig ili religiosnii bum', *Moskovskie novosti*, 11 August 1991. The surveys were respectively: August 1989 in four republics, n = 1789; May 1990 in four republics, n = 2399; and June 1991 in an all-Union survey, n = 2966. See also *Moskovskie novosti*, 18 March 1990.
22. Yuri Levada *et al.* (eds), *Sovetskii prostoi chelovek: opyt sotsial'nogo portreta na rubezhe 90-kh* (Moscow: Nauka, 1993), p. 223.
23. *The Pulse of Europe: A Survey of Political and Social Values and Attitudes* (Washington DC: Times–Mirror Center for the People and the Press, 1991), p. 164.
24. Petrenko, 'Kul'turnyi sdvig', and Sergei Filatov and Dmitrii Firman, 'Religiya i politika v massovom soznanii', *Sotsiologichiskie issledovaniya*, 7 (1992), p. 3. The 1990 poll was taken from July to September in Moscow, Pskov, Khar'kov and Smolensk oblasts, n = 1855, and the 1991 poll was taken in 12 cities in Russia and Northern Kazakhstan, n = 2000.
25. Filatov and Firman, 'Religiya i politika', p. 4.
26. *The Economist*, 23 June 1990.
27. Some of the numbers are also discussed in Richard Dobson and Steven Grant, 'Public Opinion and the Transformation of the Soviet Union', *International Journal of Public Opinion Research*, 4, 4 (1992), pp. 312–13.
28. *Moskovskie novosti*, 14 April 1991; see also Dobson and Grant, 'Public Opinion', pp. 312–15.
29. Dobson and Grant, 'Public Opinion', p. 313.

4 PUBLIC OPINION AND POST-COMMUNIST POLITICAL INSTITUTIONS

1. *Mir mnenii i mneniya o mire*, 1 (1993).
2. *Mir mnenii i mneniya o mire*, 1 (1994).
3. For conformation see, for example, Amy Corning, 'The Russian Referendum: An Analysis of Exit Poll Results', *Radio Free Europe / Radio Liberty Research Report*, 7 May 1993, pp. 6–9; *Ekonomicheskie i sotsial'nye peremeny: monitoring obshchestvennogo mneniya*, 4 (1993), pp. 46 and 56.
4. *Nezavisimaya gazeta*, 29 July 1992; *Megalopolis ekspress*, 16 June 1992; *Radio Free Europe / Radio Liberty Research Bulletin*, 15 January 1993.

5. For example, *Ekonomicheskie i sotsial'nye peremeny: monitoring obshchestvennogo mneniya*, 4 (1993), p. 55.
6. Some of the arguments here are based on Geoffrey Hosking, 'Yeltsin's Long Revolution', in *The Independent*, 5 October 1993.
7. *Spisok narodnykh deputatov RSFSR* (Moscow: Izdanie verkhovnogo soveta RSFSR, 1991).
8. *Nezavisimaya gazeta*, 22 January 1992.
9. The March survey is in *Radikal*, 22 (1992), and the May data from *Nezavisimaya gazeta*, 30 May 1992.
10. See Vladimir Rukavishnikov, 'Sotsial'no-politicheskaya situatsiya i obshchestvennoe mnenie', *Sotsiologicheskie issledovaniya*, 11 (1992), p. 55.
11. See *Radio Free Europe / Radio Liberty Research Report*, 2, 3, 15 January 1993, p. 44.
12. *Ekonomicheskie i sotsial'nye peremeny: monitoring obshchestvennogo mneniya*, 5 (1993), p. 41.
13. Ruslan Khasbulatov, *The Struggle for Russia: Power and Change in the Democratic Revolution* (London: Routledge, 1993).
14. See Julia Wishnevsky, 'Media Still Far From Free', *Radio Free Europe / Radio Liberty Research Report*, 14 May 1993, pp. 86–91; Jamey Gambrell, 'The Front Page in Moscow', *New York Review of Books*, 8 October 1992, pp. 56–62.
15. Vladimir Nadein, 'V parlamente Rossii gotovitsya nastuplenie na svobodu slova', *Izvestiya*, 10 July 1992, quoted in Gambrell, 'The Front Page', p. 60.
16. *Ekonomicheskie i sotsial'nye peremeny: monitoring obshchestvennogo mneniya*, 5 (1994), p. 75. The 1990 data are from *Ekonomicheskie i sotsial'nye peremeny: monitoring obshchestvennogo mneniya*, 1 (1994), p. 20.
17. *Ekonomicheskie i sotsial'nye peremeny: monitoring obshchestvennogo mneniya*, 4 (1994), p. 52.
18. Mark Rhodes, 'Roundup: How Russians View Their Media', *Radio Free Europe / Radio Liberty Research Report*, 31 July 1992. Survey by Vox Populi, n = 2292.
19. See Anthony King, 'Nation's Morale Approaching a Crisis', *The Daily Telegraph*, 22 February 1993, p. 4.
20. *Izvestiya*, 17 February 1993.
21. Richard Sakwa, *Russian Politics and Society* (London: Routledge, 1993), p. 84.
22. This section is indebted to Wendy Slater, 'The Russian Orthodox Church', *Radio Free Europe / Radio Liberty Research Report*, 14 May 1993, pp. 92–5.
23. On this see Walter Lacquer, *Black Hundred: The Rise of the Extreme Right in Russia* (London: Harper Collins, 1993), chapter 14.
24. *Nezavisimaya gazeta*, 12 August 1993, p. 5. Survey was of 1655 Russians.

5 CONTINUITY AND CHANGE IN RUSSIAN POLITICAL CULTURE

1. Typically taken to represent this viewpoint are Richard Pipes, *Russia Under the Old Regime* (London: Peregrine, 1976); and Zbigniew Brzezinski, 'Soviet Politics: From the Future to the Past', in Paul Cocks, Robert V. Daniels and Nancy Whittier Heer (eds), *The Dynamics of Soviet Politics* (Cambridge MA: Harvard University Press, 1976), pp. 337–51. See also Andrei Amalrik, *Will the Soviet Union Survive Until 1984?* (London: Allen Lane, 1970).
2. A comprehensive discussion of these issues is Stephen Welch's review article, 'Issues in the Study of Political Culture – the Example of Communist Party States', *British Journal of Political Science*, 19, 2 (1987), pp. 479–500.
3. The classic 1950s account, based on interviews with Russians who had emigrated after the Second World War, is Alex Inkeles and Raymond Bauer, *The Soviet Citizen* (Cambridge MA: Harvard University Press, 1959). Representative of the 1970s data are Zvi Gitelman, 'Soviet Political Culture: Insights From Jewish Émigrés', *Soviet Studies*, 29, 4 (1977), pp. 543–64, and Brian D. Silver, 'Political Beliefs of the Soviet Citizen: Sources of Support for Regime Norms', in James R. Millar (ed.), *Politics, Work and Daily Life in the USSR* (Cambridge: Cambridge University Press, 1987), chapter 4.
4. A formidable statement of the hypothesis is Brian Barry, *Sociologists, Economists and Democracy* (London: Macmillan, 1970); also Mary McAuley, 'Political Culture and Communist Politics: One Step Forward, Two Steps Back', in Archie Brown (ed.), *Political Culture and Communist Studies* (London: Macmillan, 1984).
5. For example Welch, 'Issues', pp. 484–5.
6. Leo Bogart, *Silent Politics: Polls and the Awareness of Public Opinion* (NY: John Wiley, 1972), p. 15.
7. A highly readable outline of such problems is George Gallup, *The Sophisticated Poll Watcher's Guide* (Princeton: Princeton University Press, 1976).
8. Brzezinski, 'Soviet Politics', p. 347.
9. For a more detailed version of this argument see chapter 4 of Dennis Kavanagh's *Political Science and Political Behaviour* (London: Allen and Unwin, 1983).
10. See in particular Jeffrey W. Hahn, 'Continuity and Change in Russian Political Culture', *British Journal of Political Science*, 21, 4 (1991), pp. 393–421; James L. Gibson and Raymond M. Duch, 'Emerging Democratic Values in Soviet Political Culture', in Arthur H. Miller, William M. Reisinger and Vicki L. Hesli (eds), *Public Opinion and Regime Change: The New Politics of Post-Soviet Societies* (Boulder CO: Westview Press, 1993), chapter 4.
11. *The Pulse of Europe: A Survey of Political and Social Values and Attitudes* (Washington DC: Times–Mirror Center for People and the Press, 1991), q112q.
12. Unpublished survey, n = 1509 in a number of Russian cities. The author

wishes to thank Stephen White and Olga Kryshtanovskaya for the data.
13. See esp. Donna Bahry and Brian D. Silver, 'Soviet Citizen Participation on the Eve of Democratization', *American Political Science Review*, 84, 4 (1990), pp. 821–47.
14. See in particular Samuel H. Barnes and Max Kaase, *Political Action: Mass Participation in Five Western Democracies* (Beverley Hills: Sage, 1979).
15. See, for example, Arthur H. Miller, William M. Reisinger and Vicki L. Hesli, 'Public Support for New Political Institutions in Russia, the Ukraine and Lithuania', *Journal of Soviet Nationalities*, 1, 4 (1990–91), pp. 98–9; Cynthia S. Kaplan, 'New Forms of Political Participation', in Miller *et al.* (eds), *Public Opinion and Regime Change*, chapter 7.
16. See for example S.C. Craig and M.A. Magiotto, 'Measuring Political Efficacy', *Political Methodology*, 8, 1 (1984), pp. 85–110.
17. Gibson and Duch, 'Emerging Democratic Values', p. 81.
18. Hahn, 'Continuity and Change'; Robert J. Shiller, Maxim Boycko and Vladimir Korobov, 'Hunting for Homo Sovieticus: Situational versus Attitudinal Factors in Economic Behaviour', *Brookings Papers on Economic Activity*, 1 (1992), pp. 127–94.
19. *Obshchestvennoe mnenie v tsifrakh*, 7 (1990).
20. Gibson and Duch, 'Emerging Democratic Values', p. 81.
21. *Mir mnenii i mneniya o mire*, 6 (1991); *Ekonomicheskie i sotsial'nye peremeny: monitoring obshchestvennogo mneniya*, 4 (1993), p. 45.
22. Quoted in Jonathan Sachs, *The Persistence of Faith* (London: Weidenfeld and Nicolson, 1989).
23. Gibson and Duch, 'Emerging Democratic Values', pp. 77–9.
24. The quote is from Gibson and Duch, 'Emerging Democratic Values', p. 78.
25. See, for example, Hahn, 'Continuity and Change', p. 414; Gibson and Duch, 'Emerging Democratic Values', pp. 79–81.
26. *Argumenty i fakty*, 38 (1993), p. 1; see also *Sotsiologichiskie issledovaniya*, 2 (1991), p. 11; *Izvestiya*, 27 July 1992, p. 2 and 7 November 1992, p. 2.
27. See, for example, Nancy Bermeo, 'Redemocratization and Transition Elections: A Comparison of Spain and Portugal', *Comparative Politics*, 19 (1986–87), pp. 213–31.
28. Matthew Wyman, Stephen White, Bill Miller and Paul Heywood, 'Public Opinion, Parties and Voters in the December 1993 Russian Elections', *Europe-Asia Studies*, 47, 4 (1995) pp. 591–614.
29. The data are consistent with the findings of the New Soviet Citizen survey. See Arthur H. Miller, 'In Search of Regime Legitimacy', in Miller *et al.* (eds), *Public Opinion and Regime Change*, chapter 5.
30. Václav Havel, 'The Post-Communist Nightmare', *New York Review of Books*, 27 May 1993.

6 RUSSIANS AND NON-RUSSIANS ON THE COLLAPSE OF THE USSR

1. Robert Conquest, *The Nation Killers: The Soviet Deportation of Nationalities* (London: Sphere, 1972), and Robert Conquest, *The Harvest of Sorrow* (Oxford: Oxford University Press, 1986).
2. Victor Zaslavsky, 'Success and Collapse: Traditional Soviet Nationality Policy', in Ian Bremner and Ray Taras (eds), *Nations and Politics in the Soviet Successor States* (Cambridge: Cambridge University Press, 1993), chapter 2.
3. Hélène Carrère D'Encausse, *Decline of an Empire: The Soviet Socialist Republics in Revolt* (NY: Newsweek Publications, 1979).
4. Paul Goble, 'Imperial Endgame: Nationality Problems and the Soviet Future', in Harley D. Balzer (ed.), *Five Years That Shook The World: Gorbachev's Unfinished Revolution* (Boulder CO: Westview Press, 1991), pp. 91–104.
5. Isaiah Berlin, 'The Bent Twig: On the Rise of Nationalism', in *The Crooked Timber of Humanity* (London: Fontana, 1990), pp. 238–63.
6. See in particular Vicki L. Hesli and Joel D. Barkan, 'The Center–Periphery Debate: Pressures for Devolution Within the Republics', in Arthur H. Miller, William M. Reisinger and Vicki L. Hesli (eds), *Public Opinion and Regime Change: The New Politics of Post-Soviet Societies* (Boulder CO: Westview Press, 1993), pp. 124–52; also John Dunlop, 'Russia: Confronting the Loss of Empire', in Bremner and Taras (eds), *Nations and Politics*, pp. 43–72.
7. *Obshchestvennoe mnenie v tsifrakh*, 6 (1990), n = 2944.
8. *Obshchestvennoe mnenie v tsifrakh*, 14 (1990), n = 1476.
9. *Komsomolskaya pravda*, 18 January 1991, n = 962.
10. *Moskovskie novosti*, 27 January 1991, n = 1978.
11. *The Pulse of Europe: A Survey of Political and Social Values and Attitudes* (Washington DC: Times–Mirror Center for the People and the Press, 1991), pp. 45–7.
12. *Nezavisimaya gazeta*, 19 November 1991.
13. *Nezavisimaya gazeta*, 27 November 1991.
14. *Nezavisimaya gazeta*, 18 November 1991, n = 1005.
15. *Nezavisimaya gazeta*, 14 December 1991; *Izvestiya*, 12 December 1991.
16. *Mir mnenii i mneniya o mire*, 2 (1992), n = 1916.
17. *Izvestiya*, 27 April 1992.
18. *Nezavisimaya gazeta*, 30 May 1992, n = 1050.
19. *Nezavisimaya gazeta*, 12 June 1992.
20. Vladimir Rukavishnikov, 'Sotsial'no-politicheskaya situatsiya i obshchestvennoe mnenie', *Sotsiologicheskie issledovaniya*, 11 (1992), p. 56.
21. *Novoe vremya*, 3 (1992); *Nezavisimaya gazeta*, 6 November 1992.
22. See Lev Gudkov, 'The Disintegration of the USSR and Russians in the Republics', *Journal of Communist Studies*, 9, 1 (1993), pp. 75–87, which discusses the attitudes of Russians living in other former Soviet republics.
23. *Mir mnenii i mneniya o mire*, 11 (1992), n = 1590.
24. Alexander Solzhenitsyn, *Rebuilding Russia* (London: Harper Collins, 1991).

7 ATTITUDES TO THE MARKET ECONOMY

1. For a highly stimulating discussion of the systemic flaws of a planned economy, see Wlodzimierz Brus and Kazimierz Laski, *From Marx to the Market: Socialism in Search of an Economic System* (Oxford: Oxford University Press, 1989).
2. Robert Nozick, *Anarchy, State and Utopia* (Oxford: Blackwell, 1974).
3. V. Rutgaiser, L. Khakhulina, S. Shpil'ko, V. Kosmarskii and A. Grazhdankin, 'Otnoshenie naseleniya k radikal'noi ekonomischeskoi reforme', *Voprosy ekonomiki*, 10 (1989).
4. *Ekonomicheskie i sotsial'nye peremeny: monitoring obshchestvennogo mneniya*, 2 (1993), p. 53.
5. *The Pulse of Europe: A Survey of Political and Social Values and Attitudes* (Washington DC: Times-Mirror Center for the People and the Press, 1991); *Central and Eastern Eurobarometer*, 2 (1992) and 3 (1993) (n = 977 and n = 1000 respectively).
6. Page 258.
7. *Central and Eastern Eurobarometer*, 3 (1993), p. 13.
8. A number of other studies have found gloomy views of the state of the economy during transition. For detailed figures by republic see, for example, *Mnenie naseleniya o tsenakh na tovary i uslugi* (Moscow: Goskomstat SSSR, 1991), p. 19.
9. In particular, Anthony Jones and William Moskoff, *Ko-ops: The Rebirth of Entrepreneurship in the USSR* (Bloomington and Indianapolis: Indiana University Press, 1991), pp. 98–109.
10. *Kommersant*, 5 (1990), p. 10.
11. Reported BBC *Summary of Word Broadcasts*, SU/1105, 22 June 1991, B4.
12. *Mir mnenii i mneniya o mire*, 1 (1992).
13. *Radikal*, 4 (1990), n = 1492.
14. Aleksandr Komozin, 'Shokovaya ekonomika: tendentsii obshchestvennogo mneniya naseleniya Rossii', *Sotsiologicheskie issledovaniya*, 11 (1993), p. 16. For comparable VTsIOM data see *Ekonomicheskie i sotsial'nye peremeny: monitoring obshchestvennogo mneniya*, 2 (1993), questions 39–46.
15. I am grateful to Olga Kryshtanovskaya and to Stephen White for the data from which the table was calculated. The survey was of ten Russian cities, n = 1509. For data about support among different social groups prior to the onset of economic reform see *Voprosy ekonomiki*, 4 (1990).
16. David Butler and Donald Stokes, *Political Change in Britain* (London: Macmillan, 1969); Hilde T. Himmelweit, Patrick Humphreys and Marianne Jaeger, *How Voters Decide* (revised edition, Milton Keynes and Philadelphia: Open University Press, 1985).
17. 'Programma privatisatsiya – predvaritel'nye itogi v otsenkakh naseleniya', *Ekonomicheskie i sotsial'nye peremeny: monitoring obshchestvennogo mneniya*, 3 (1994), pp. 22–4.
18. *Ekonomicheskie i sotsial'nye peremeny: monitoring obshchestvennogo mneniya*, 2 (1994), p. 77.
19. *Ekonomicheskie i sotsial'nye peremeny: monitoring obshchestvennogo mneniya*, 6 (1994), p. 69.

20. This is one of the hypotheses of the literature on the social contract and corporatism. See for example the work of Valerie Bunce or Peter Hauslohner.
21. *Obshchestvennoe mnenie v tsifrakh*, 4 (1989), n = 1148. Poll carried out in the summer of 1989.
22. *Mnenie naseleniya o tsenakh na tovary i uslugi* (Moscow: Goskomstat SSSR, 1991).
23. *Obshchestvennoe mnenie v tsifrakh*, 10 (1991).
24. See, for example, *Pravitelstvenny vestnik*, 29 (1990); *VTsIOM informatsionnii byulleten*, 4 (1989), p. 13.
25. *The Pulse of Europe*, p. 90.
26. *Ekonomicheskie i sotsial'nye peremeny: monitoring obshchestvennogo mneniya*, 1 (1993), p. 22.
27. Vladimir Rukavishnikov, 'Sotsial'no-politicheskaya situatsiya i obshchestvennoe mnenie', *Sotsiologicheskie issledovaniya*, 11 (1992), p. 56.
28. See also the Times–Mirror survey, p. 90.
29. See, for example, Barry Bluestone, 'Deindustrialisation and Unemployment in America', in P.E. Straudohar and H.E. Brown (eds), *Deindustrialisation and Plant Closure* (Lexington: Lexington Books, 1987).
30. L. Zubova, N. Kovaleva, M. Krasil'nikova and L. Mityaeva, 'Otsenka naseleniem sistemy sotsial'nykh garantii i sotsial'noi zashchity', *Voprosy ekonomiki*, 7 (1992), pp. 97–8.
31. See David Lane, *The End of Social Inequality? Class, Status and Power under State Socialism* (London: Allen and Unwin, 1982).
32. David Mason, and Svetlana Sidorenko, 'Perestroika, Social Justice and Soviet Public Opinion', *Problems of Communism*, 40, 4 (1990), pp. 34–43; Hans Aage, 'Popular Attitudes and Perestroika', *Soviet Studies*, 43, 1 (1991), pp. 3–25.
33. *Obshchestvennoe mnenie v tsifrakh*, 4 (1989).
34. See Arkady Vaksberg, *The Soviet Mafia* (NY: St Martin's Press, 1992); Konstantin Simis, *The Corrupt Society* (NY: Simon and Shuster, 1982), and for an overview, David Remnick, 'Dons of the Don', *New York Review of Books*, 16 July 1992, pp. 45–51.
35. Boris Yeltsin, *Against the Grain* (NY: Simon and Schuster, 1990), esp. chapter 6.
36. *Obshchestvennoe mnenie v tsifrakh*, 13 (1990), n = 1345.
37. *Obshchestvennoe mnenie v tsifrakh*, 3 (1989).
38. Arthur H. Miller, William M. Reisinger and Vicki L. Hesli, 'Public Support for New Political Institutions in Russia, the Ukraine and Lithuania', *Journal of Soviet Nationalities*, 1, 4 (1990–91), p. 105.
39. Results for this question are in *Obshchestvennoe mnenie v tsifrakh*, 4 (1989) and 10 (1991).
40. *Mir mnenii i mneniya o mire*, 9 (1991), n = 2000.
41. Nugzar Betaneli in *Izvestiya*, 25 May 1992.
42. *Obshchestvennoe mnenie v tsifrakh*, 1 (1990).
43. *Obshchestvennoe mnenie v tsifrakh*, 10 (1991).
44. Page 118.
45. Roger Jowell, Sharon Witherspoon and Lindsay Brook (eds), *British Social Attitudes: The 1987 Report* (Aldershot: Gower, 1988).

46. Daniel Bell, *The Coming of Post-industrial Society* (London: Heinemann, 1974).
47. V.O. Key Jr., *Public Opinion and American Democracy* (NY: Knopf, 1961).
48. A similar argument is made, with characteristic clarity, in Zbigniew Brzezinski, *Out of Control: Global Turmoil, on the Eve of the 21st Century* (NY: Scribners, 1993), p. 179.

8 ONE NATION?

1. See in particular the volume edited by James R. Millar, *Politics, Work and Daily Life in the USSR: A Survey of Former Soviet Citizens* (Cambridge: Cambridge University Press, 1987), in particular the chapter by Donna Bahry, 'Politics, Generations and Change in the USSR'.
2. In particular Ada W. Finifter and Ellen Mickiewicz, 'Redefining the Political System of the USSR: Mass Support for Political Change', *American Political Science Review*, 86, 4 (1992), pp. 857–74.
3. For example, most of the contributors to Arthur H. Miller, William M. Reisinger and Vicki L. Hesli (eds), *Public Opinion and Regime Change: The New Politics of Post-Soviet Societies* (Boulder CO: Westview Press, 1993).
4. See, however, Vicki L. Hesli and Arthur H. Miller, 'The Gender Base of Institutional Support in Lithuania, Ukraine and Russia', *Europe–Asia Studies*, 45, 3 (1993), pp. 505–32. Of course the major exception to this is research into differences between the attitudes of the more important nationalities within the former USSR. Identifying such differences, however, is of limited help in understanding contemporary Russian politics.
5. See, for example, Finifter and Mickiewicz, 'Redefining the Political System', pp. 866–7; Miller *et al.* (eds), *Public Opinion and Regime Change*; Brian D. Silver, 'Political Beliefs of the Soviet Citizen: Sources of Support for Regime Norms', in Millar (ed.), *Politics, Work and Daily Life*.
6. James L. Gibson and Raymond M. Duch, 'Emerging Democratic Values in Soviet Political Culture', in Miller *et al.* (eds), *Public Opinion and Regime Change*, chapter 4.
7. For a useful breakdown of regional voting patterns see Aleksandr Sobyanin, Eduard Gel'man and Oleg Kayunov, 'Politicheskii klimat v Rossii v 1991–1993 gg.', *Mirovaya ekonomika i mezhdunarodnye otnosheniya*, 9 (1993), pp. 20–32.

9 PUBLIC OPINION AND POST-SOVIET POLITICS

1. Leo Bogart, *Silent Politics: Polls and the Awareness of Public Opinion* (NY: John Wiley, 1972), p. 75.
2. Based on empirical data, Jeffrey W. Hahn, 'Continuity and Change in Russian Political Culture', *British Journal of Political Science*, 21, 4 (1991), pp. 393–421. In a wider theoretical sense, Francis Fukuyama, *The End of History and the Last Man* (NY: Free Press, 1992); Dankwart Rustow,

'Democracy: A Global Revolution', *Foreign Affairs*, 69, 4 (1990), p. 75.
3. Bogart, *'Silent Politics*, p. 17.
4. See Vera Tolz, 'The New Role of the Media and Public Opinion Under Gorbachev', *Journal of Communist Studies*, 9, 1 (1993), esp. pp. 202–7.
5. Other versions of the scenario are found in Ralf Dahrendorf, *Reflections on the Revolution in Europe* (London: Chatto and Windus, 1990), pp. 104–8; Zbigniew Brzezinski, *Out of Control: Global Turmoil on the Eve of the Twenty-First Century* (NY: Scribners, 1993), in particular pp. 167–81. See also Hans Rogger, 'Afterthoughts', in Hans Rogger and Eugene Weber (eds), *The European Right: A Historical Profile* (Berkeley and Los Angeles: University of California Press, 1965), pp. 577–88.

Bibliography

PRIMARY SOURCES

Several of the newly established survey organisations publish regular bulletins of poll data. The most useful for the purposes of this study have been the All-Union Centre for Public Opinion Research (VTsIOM)'s *Obshchestvennoe mnenie v tsifrakh*; its successor the All-Russian Centre's *Ekonomicheskie i sotsial'nye peremeny: monitoring obshchestvennogo mneniya*; and the publication of the organisation Vox Populi, *Mir mnenii i mneniya o mire*. The most important newspaper sources have been *Izvestiya, Moskovskie novosti, Nezavisimaya gazeta, Argumenty i fakty, Komsomolskaya pravda* and *Kommersant*. Each of these has been consulted for the period 1988–93. Other newspapers cited include *Pravda, Kuranty, Poisk, Sankt-Peterburgskie vedomosti* and *Radikal*. The journal *Sotsiologicheskie issledovaniya* has also published a large number of relevant studies.

GENERAL BIBLIOGRAPHY

Aage, Hans, 'Popular Attitudes and *Perestroika*', *Soviet Studies*, 43, 1 (1991), pp. 3–25.
Adorno, T.W., E. Frenkel-Brunswick, D. Levinson and R. Sandford, *The Authoritarian Personality* (New York: Harper and Row, 1950).
Afsakhov, I.A., 'Otnoshenie cheloveka k zdrov'yu', *Sotsiologicheskie issledovaniya*, 6 (1992), pp. 102–3.
Almond, Gabriel A. and Sidney Verba, *The Civic Culture: Political Attitudes and Democracy in Five Nations* (Princeton NJ: Princeton University Press, 1963).
Almond, Gabriel A. and Sidney Verba, *The Civic Culture Revisited: An Analytic Study* (Boston: Little, Brown, 1980).
Alt, James, *The Politics of Economic Decline: Economic Management and Political Behaviour In Britain since 1964* (Cambridge: Cambridge University Press, 1979).
Amalrik, Andrei, *Will the Soviet Union Survive Until 1984?* (London: Allen Lane, 1970).
Avdeenko, T., A. Grazhdankin, V. Rutgaizer and S. Shpil'ko, 'Otnoshenie naseleniya k razvitiyu kooperatsii', *Voprosy ekonomiki*, 11 (1989), pp. 129–34.
Bahry, Donna, 'Politics, Generations and Change in the USSR', in James R. Millar (ed.), *Politics, Work and Daily Life in the USSR: A Survey of Former Soviet Citizens* (Cambridge: Cambridge University Press, 1987).
Bahry, Donna, 'Society Transformed? Rethinking the Social Roots of Perestroika', *Slavic Review*, 52, 3 (1993), pp. 512–54.
Bahry, Donna and Brian D. Silver, 'Soviet Citizen Participation on the Eve

of Democratization', *American Political Science Review*, 84, 3 (1990), pp. 821–47.
Bahry, Donna and Brian D. Silver, 'Public Perceptions and the Dilemmas of Party Reform in the USSR', *Comparative Political Studies*, 23, 2 (1990), pp. 171–209.
Barnes, Samuel H. and Max Kaase, *Political Action: Mass Participation in Five Western Democracies* (Beverley Hills: Sage, 1979).
Barry, Brian, *Sociologists, Economists and Democracy* (London: Macmillan, 1970).
Bashkirova, Elena I. and Vicki L. Hesli, 'Polling and *Perestroika*', in Arthur H. Miller, William M. Reisinger and Vicki L. Hesli (eds), *Public Opinion and Regime Change: The new politics of post-Soviet Societies* (Boulder CO: Westview Press, 1993), pp. 17–37.
Bell, Daniel, *The Coming of Post-Industrial Society* (London: Heinemann, 1974).
Bell, Daniel, *The Cultural Contradictions of Capitalism* (New York: Basic Books, 1976).
Berlin, Isaiah, 'The Bent Twig: On the Rise of Nationalism', in his *The Crooked Timber of Humanity* (London: Fontana, 1990), pp. 238–63.
Bermeo, Nancy, 'Redemocratization and Transition Elections: A Comparison of Spain and Portugal', *Comparative Politics*, 19 (1986–87), pp. 213–31.
Bialer, Serewyn, *The Soviet Paradox: External Expansion, Internal Decline* (London: I.B. Tauris, 1986).
Bluestone, Barry, 'Deindustrialisation and Unemployment in America', in P.E. Straudohar and H.E. Brown (eds), *Deindustrialisation and Plant Closure* (Lexington: Lexington Books, 1987).
Bluestone, Barry and Benjamin Harrison, *The Deindustrialisation of America* (New York: Basic Books, 1982).
Boeva, Irina and Viacheslav Shironin, 'Russians Between State and Market', *University of Strathclyde Studies in Public Policy*, 205 (1992).
Bogart, Leo, *Silent Politics: Polls and the Awareness of Public Opinion* (New York: John Wiley, 1972).
Bonner, Elena and Peter Reddaway, 'Yeltsin and Russia: Two Views', *New York Review of Books*, 22 April 1993, pp. 16–19.
Bradburn, Norman M. and Seymour Sudman, *Polls and Surveys: Understanding What They Tell Us* (San Francisco and London: Jossey-Bass Publishers, 1988).
Bremmer, Ian and Ray Taras (eds), *Nations and Politics in the Soviet Successor States* (Cambridge: Cambridge University Press, 1993).
Britvin, V.G., S.V. Kolobanov and E.G. Meshkova (eds), *Obshchestvennoe mnenie v usloviyakh perestroiki: problemy formirovaniya i funktsionirovaniya* (Moscow: Institut sotsiologii AN SSSR, 1990).
Brown, Archie, 'Ideology and Political Culture', in Seweryn Bialer (ed.), *Politics, Society and Nationality Inside Gorbachev's Russia* (Boulder CO: Westview Press, 1989).
Brown, Archie and Jack Grey (eds), *Political Culture and Political Change in Communist States* (London: Macmillan, 1977).
Brus, Wlodzimierz and Kazimierz Laski, *From Marx to the Market: Socialism in Search of an Economic System* (Oxford: Oxford University Press, 1989).

Bibliography 255

Bryman, Alan and Duncan Cramer, *Quantitative Data Analysis for Social Scientists* (London and New York: Routledge, 1990).
Brzezinski, Zbigniew, 'Soviet Politics: From the Future to the Past', in Paul Cocks, Robert V. Daniels, and Nancy Whittier Heer (eds), *The Dynamics of Soviet Politics* (Cambridge MA: Harvard University Press, 1976), pp. 337–51.
Brzezinski, Zbigniew, *The Grand Failure: The Birth and Death of Communism in the Twentieth Century* (London: Macdonald, 1989).
Brzezinski, Zbigniew, *Out of Control: Global Turmoil on the Eve of the 21st Century*, (New York: Scribners, 1993).
Butler, David and Donald Stokes, *Political Change in Britain* (London: Macmillan, 1969).
Campbell, Angus, Philip E. Converse, William E. Miller and Donald Stokes, *The American Voter* (New York: Wiley, 1960).
Carrère D'Encausse, Hélène, *Decline of an Empire: The Soviet Socialist Republics in Revolt* (New York: Newsweek Publications, 1979).
Cline, Mary, 'Attitude Towards Economic Reform in Russia', *Radio Free Europe / Radio Liberty Research Report*, 28 May 1993.
Connor, Walter D., 'Generations and Politics in the USSR', *Problems of Communism*, 24, 1 (1975), pp. 20–31.
Connor, Walter D. and Zvi Y. Gitelman (eds), *Public Opinion in European Socialist Systems* (New York: Praeger, 1977).
Conquest, Robert, *The Nation Killers: The Soviet Deportation of Nationalities* (London: Sphere, 1972).
Conquest, Robert, *The Harvest of Sorrow* (Oxford: Oxford University Press, 1986).
Converse, Philip, 'The Nature of Belief Systems in Mass Publics', in David E. Apter (ed.), *Ideology and Discontent* (New York: Free Press, 1964), pp. 206–61.
Corning, Amy, 'Critical Evaluations of the Russian Government', *Radio Free Europe / Radio Liberty Research Report*, 19 June 1992.
Corning, Amy, 'How Russians View Yeltsin and Rutskoi', *Radio Free Europe / Radio Liberty Research Report*, 19 March 1993.
Corning, Amy, 'The Russian Referendum: An Analysis of Exit Poll Results', *Radio Free Europe / Radio Liberty Research Report*, 7 May 1993, pp. 6–9.
Corning, Amy, 'Public Opinion and the Russian Parliamentary Elections', *Radio Free Europe / Radio Liberty Research Report*, 3 December 1993, pp. 16–23.
Crankshaw, Edward, *Russia and the Russians* (London: Macmillan, 1947).
Dahl, Robert, *Polyarchy* (New Haven: Yale University Press, 1971).
Dahl, Robert, *Democracy and Its Critics* (New Haven: Yale University Press, 1989).
Dahrendorf, Ralf, *Class and Class Conflict in Industrial Society* (London: Routledge, 1959).
Dahrendorf, Ralf, *Essays in the Theory of Society* (London: Routledge, 1968).
Dahrendorf, Ralf, *The Modern Social Conflict: An Essay in the Politics of Liberty* (London: Weidenfeld and Nicolson, 1988).
Dahrendorf, Ralf, *Reflections on the Revolution in Europe* (London: Chatto and Windus, 1990).

Demidov, A.M., 'Obshchestvennoe mnenie i sotsial'no politicheski voprosy perestroiki', in V.G. Britvin, S.V. Kolobanov and E.G. Meshkova, *Obschestvennoe mnenie v usloviyakh perestroiki: problemy formirovaniya i funktsionirovaniya* (Moscow: Institut Sotsiologii AN SSSR, 1990).

Dobson, Richard B. and Steven A. Grant, 'Public Opinion and the Transformation of the Soviet Union', *International Journal of Public Opinion Research*, 4, 4 (1992), pp. 302–20.

Downs, Anthony, 'Social Values and Democracy', in Kristen Renwick Moore (ed.), *The Economic Approach to Politics* (New York: Harper Collins, 1991), chapter 6.

Duch, Raymond M., 'Tolerating Economic Reform: Popular Support for Transition to a Free Market in the Former Soviet Union', *American Political Science Review*, 87, 3 (1993), pp. 590–609.

Dunlop, John, 'Russia: Confronting the Loss of Empire', in Ian Bremmer and Ray Taras (eds), *Nations and Politics in the Soviet Successor States* (Cambridge: Cambridge University Press, 1993), pp. 43–72.

'Fenomen propiski glazami moskvichei', *Obshchestvennye nauki*, 2 (1991), pp. 58 and 174.

Filatov, Sergei and Dmitrii Firman, 'Religiya i politika v massovom soznanii', *Sotsiologichiskie issledovaniya*, 7 (1992), pp. 3–12.

Finifter, Ada W., and Ellen Mickiewicz, 'Redefining the Political System of the USSR: Mass Support for Political Change', *American Political Science Review*, 86, 4 (1992), pp. 857–74.

Fukuyama, Francis, *The End of History and the Last Man* (New York: Free Press, 1992).

Gallup, George, *The Sophisticated Poll Watcher's Guide* (Princeton: Princeton University Press, 1976).

Gambrell, Jamey, 'The Front Page in Moscow', *New York Review of Books*, 8 October 1992, pp. 56–62.

Gibbins, John R. (ed.), *Contemporary Political Culture: Politics in a Post Modern Age* (London: Sage, 1989).

Gibson, James L., 'Perceived Political Freedom in the USSR', *The Journal of Politics*, 55, 4 (1993), pp. 936–75.

Gibson, James L., 'Political and Economic Markets: Connecting Attitudes Toward Political Democracy and a Market Economy Within the Mass Culture of the USSR', paper given at the 25th National Convention of the American Association for the Advancement of Slavic Studies, Honolulu, Hawaii, 19–22 November 1993.

Gibson, James L. and Raymond M. Duch, 'Attitudes Towards Jews and Soviet Political Culture', *Journal of Soviet Nationalities*, 2, 1 (1991), pp. 77–118.

Gibson, James L. and Raymond M. Duch, 'Emerging Democratic Values in Soviet Political Culture', in Arthur H. Miller, William M. Reisinger and Vicki L. Hesli (eds), *Public Opinion and Regime Change: The New Politics of Post-Soviet Societies* (Boulder CO: Westview Press, 1993), chapter 4.

Gibson, James L. and Raymond M. Duch, 'Political Intolerance in the USSR: The Distribution and Etiology of Mass Opinion', *Comparative Political Studies*, 26, 2 (1993), pp. 286–329.

Gibson, James L., Raymond M. Duch and Kent L. Tedin, 'Democratic Values and the Transformation of the Soviet Union', *Journal of Politics*, 54, 2 (1992), pp. 329–71.

Gimpel'son, V.E., 'Mezhdu sverkhzanyatost'yu i bezrabotitsei (sovetskie rabochie o situatsii v sfere truda', *Rabochii klass i sovremenyi mir*, 5 (1990), pp. 130–7.

Gitelman, Zvi Y., 'Public Opinion in Communist Political Systems', in Walter D. Connor and Zvi Y. Gitelman (eds), *Public Opinion in European Socialist Systems* (New York: Praeger, 1977).

Gitelman, Zvi Y., 'Soviet Political Culture: Insights from Jewish Émigrés', *Soviet Studies*, 29, 4 (1977), pp. 543–64.

Goble, Paul, 'Imperial Endgame: Nationality Problems and the Soviet Future', in Harley D. Balzer (ed.), *Five Years That Shook The World: Gorbachev's Unfinished Revolution* (Boulder CO: Westview Press, 1991), pp. 91–104.

Goldfarb, Jeffrey C., *Beyond Glasnost: The Post Totalitarian Mind* (Chicago: University of Chicago Press, 1991).

Goldfarb, Jeffrey C., *After the Fall: The Pursuit of Democracy in Central Europe* (New York: Basic Books, 1992).

Golovakha, E.I., N.V. Panina and N.N. Churilov, 'Obshchestvennoe mnenie o sovremennom sostoyanii i perspektive razvitiya atomnoi energetiki', *Sotsiologicheskie issledovaniya*, 8 (1991), pp. 51–5.

Golovakha, E.I., N.V. Panina, Yu. N. Pakhomov, N.N. Churilov and I.V. Burov, *Politicheskaya kul'tura naseleniya Ukrainy* (Kiev: Naukova dumka, 1993).

Gorbachev, Mikhail, *Perestroika: New Thinking for our Country and the World* (London: Collins, 1987).

Gradnitsyn, A.A., 'Obshchestvennoe mnenie o vozrozhdenii donskogo kazachestva', *Sotsiologicheskie issledovaniya*, 12 (1991), pp. 78–84.

Granick, David, *Job Rights in the Soviet Union: Their Consequences* (Cambridge: Cambridge University Press, 1987).

Grey, Robert D., Lauri A. Jennisch and Alanna S. Tyler, 'Soviet Public Opinion and the Gorbachev Reforms', *Slavic Review*, 49, 2 (1990), pp. 261–71.

Grushin, B. and L. Onikov (eds), *Massovaya informatsiya v sovetskom promyshlennom gorode* (Moscow: Politizdat, 1980).

Grushin, Boris 'Pochemu nel'zya verit' bol'shinstvu oprosov, provodimykh v byvshem SSSR', *Nezavisimaya gazeta*, 28 October 1992.

Grushin, Boris, 'Fiasko sotsial'noi mysli, ili razmyshleniya o tom, pochemu glavnoi formoi znaniya o nyneshnei Rossii yavlyaetsya neznanie o nei', *Mir mnenii i mneniya o mire*, 6 (1994), pp. 9–12.

Gudkov, Lev, 'The Disintegration of the USSR and Russians in the Republics', *Journal of Communist Studies*, 9, 1 (1993), pp. 75–87.

Hahn, Jeffrey W., 'Continuity and Change in Russian Political Culture', *British Journal of Political Science*, 21, 4 (1991), pp. 393–421.

Hahn, Jeffrey W., 'Public Opinion Research in the Soviet Union: Problems and Possibilities', in Arthur H. Miller, William M. Reisinger and Vicki L. Hesli (eds), *Public Opinion and Regime Change: The New Politics of Post-Soviet Societies* (Boulder CO: Westview Press, 1993), pp. 37–50.

Hahn, Jeffrey W., 'Changes in Contemporary Russian Political Culture', paper given at the 25th National Convention of the American Association for the Advancement of Slavic Studies, Honolulu, Hawaii, 19–22 November 1993.

Hauslohner, Peter, 'Gorbachev's Social Contract', *Soviet Economy*, 3, 1 (1987), pp. 54–89.

Havel, Václav, 'The Post-Communist Nightmare', *New York Review of Books*, 27 May 1993, pp. 8–10.

Heleniak, Timothy, 'Glasnost and the Publication of Soviet Census Results', *Journal of Soviet Nationalities*, 2, 1 (1991), pp. 139–60.
Hesli, Vicki L. and Joel D. Barkan, 'The Center–Periphery Debate: Pressures for Devolution Within the Republics', in Arthur H. Miller, William M. Reisinger and Vicki L. Hesli (eds), *Public Opinion and Regime Change: The New Politics of Post-Soviet Societies* (Boulder CO: Westview Press, 1993), pp. 124–52.
Hesli, Vicki L. and Arthur H. Miller, 'The Gender Base of Institutional Support in Lithuania, Ukraine and Russia', *Europe–Asia Studies*, 45, 3 (1993), pp. 505–32.
Hill, Ronald J., *Soviet Political Elites* (London: Martin Robertson, 1977).
Himmelweit, Hilde T., Patrick Humphreys and Marianne Jaeger, *How Voters Decide* (revised edition, Milton Keynes and Philadelphia: Open University Press, 1985).
Hingley, Ronald, *The Russian Mind* (London: The Bodley Head, 1977).
Hosking, Geoffrey, *The Awakening of the Soviet Union* (enlarged edition, Cambridge MA: Harvard University Press, 1991).
Hosking, Geoffrey, 'Yeltsin's Long Revolution', *The Independent*, 5 October 1993.
Huntington, Samuel P., *Political Order in Changing Societies* (New Haven and London: Yale University Press, 1968).
Huntington, Samuel P., 'How Countries Democratize', *Political Science Quarterly*, 106, 4 (1991-2), pp. 579–616.
Inkeles, Alex and Raymond Bauer, *The Soviet Citizen: Daily Life in a Totalitarian Society* (Cambridge MA: Harvard University Press, 1959).
Ivanov, Vilen, 'Mezhnatsional'nie otnosheniya', *Dialog*, 18 (1990), pp. 3 and 26.
Jacobs, Eric and Robert Worcester, *Typically British?* (London: Bloomsbury, 1991).
Jones, Anthony and William Moskoff, *Ko-ops: The Rebirth of Entrepreneurship in the USSR* (Bloomington and Indianapolis: Indiana University Press, 1991).
Jowell, Roger *et al.* (eds), *British Social Attitudes: The 1987 Report* (Aldershot: Gower, 1988).
Kaplan, Cynthia S., 'New Forms of Political Participation', in Arthur H. Miller, William M. Reisinger and Vicki L. Hesli (eds), *Public Opinion and Regime Change: The New Politics of Post-Soviet Societies*, (Boulder CO: Westview Press, 1993), chapter 7.
Kavanagh, Dennis, *Political Science and Political Behaviour* (London: Allen and Unwin, 1983).
Key Jr., V.O., *Public Opinion and American Democracy* (New York: Alfred A. Knopf, 1965).
Khaikin, S.P. and E.P. Pavlov, 'Kak pomoch' interv'yueru', *Sotsiologicheskie issledovaniya*, 4 (1991), pp. 58–65.
Khasbulatov, Ruslan, *The Struggle for Russia: Power and Change in the Democratic Revolution* (London: Routledge, 1993).
King, Anthony, 'Nation's Morale Approaching a Crisis', *The Daily Telegraph*, 22 February 1993, p. 4.
Kol'tsov, V.B. and V.A. Mansurov, 'Politicheskie ideologii perioda perestroiki', *Sotsiologicheskie issledovaniya*, 10 (1991), pp. 22–35.

Komarovskii, Vladimir, 'Politicheskii vybor izbiratelya', *Sotsiologicheskie issledovaniya*, 3 (1992), pp. 23–34.
Kosmarskii, Vladimir, V. Rutgaiser, L. Khakhulina and S. Shpil'ko, 'Otnoshenie naseleniya k perspektive perekhoda k rynku', *Voprosy ekonomiki*, 7 (1990).
Kosmarskii, Vladimir, 'Public Attitudes to the Transition', unpublished paper given to international conference on the Soviet economy in crisis and transition, Stockholm, June 1991.
Kosmarskii, Vladimir, 'Aktsii: sobiraetsya li pokupat' naselenie?' *Voprosy ekonomiki*, 7 (1991).
Kotkin, Stephen, *Steeltown, USSR: Soviet Society in the Gorbachev Era* (London: Weidenfeld and Nicolson, 1991).
Krasil'novka, M. and T. Avdeenko, 'Potrebitel'skoe povedenie naseleniya v krizisnykh situatsiyakh', *Voprosy ekonomiki*, 1 (1992), pp. 74–82.
Ladygina, I.E., 'Mnenie naseleniya ob usloviyakh udovletvoreniya potrebnostei', in V.G. Britvin, S.V. Kolobanov and E.G. Meshkova (eds), *Obshchestvennoe mnenie v usloviyakh perestroiki: problemy formirovaniya i funktsionirovaniya* (Moscow: Institut sotsiologii AN SSSR, 1990, pp. 81–93).
Lane, David, *The End of Social Inequality? Class, Status and Power under State Socialism* (London: Allen and Unwin, 1982).
Levada, Yuri, 'Dinamika sotsial'nogo pereloma: vozmozhnosti analiza', *Kommunist*, 2 (1989), pp. 34–43.
Levada, Yuri (ed.), *Est' mnenie! itogi sotsiologicheskogo oprosa* (Moscow: Progress, 1990).
Levada, Yuri, Leonid Sedov and Lev Timofeev, 'Is a New Revolution in the Making?', *Uncaptive Minds*, 4, 1 (1991), pp. 86–96.
Levada, Yuri et al. (eds), *Sovetskii prostoi chelovek: opyt sotsial' nogo portreta na rubezhe 90-kh* (Moscow: Nauka, 1993).
Lewin, Moshe, *The Gorbachev Phenomenon: A Historical Interpretation* (London: Hutchinson Radius, 1988).
Lippmann, Walter, *The Phantom Public* (New York: Harcourt Brace, 1925).
Lippmann, Walter, *Public Opinion* (London: Macmillan, 1922).
Lipset, Seymour Martin, *Political Man: The Social Bases of Politics* (Baltimore: Johns Hopkins University Press, 1981).
Lloyd, John, 'Democracy in Russia', *The Political Quarterly*, 64, 2 (1993), pp. 147–56.
Lubrano, Linda, Wesley Fisher, Janet Schwartz and Kate Tomlinson, 'The Soviet Union', in William A. Welsh (ed.), *Survey Research and Public Attitudes in Eastern Europe and the Soviet Union* (New York: Pergamon, 1981).
McAuley, Mary, 'Political Culture and Communist Politics: One Step Forward, Two Steps Back', in Archie Brown (ed.), *Political Culture and Communist Studies* (London: Macmillan, 1984).
McCloskey, Herbert and Alida Brill, *Dimensions of Tolerance: What Americans Think About Civil Liberties* (New York: Sage, 1983).
Makogon, Yu.V. and A.I. Butko, 'Kakaya armiya nam nuzhna?', *Sotsiologicheskie issledovaniya*, 6 (1992), pp. 92–4.
Mason, David S., Daniel N. Nelson and Bohdan M. Sklarski, 'Apathy and the Birth of Democracy: The Polish Struggle', *East European Politics and Societies*, 5, 2 (1991), pp. 205–33.

Mason, David S. and Svetlana Sidorenko, 'Perestroika, Social Justice and Soviet Public Opinion', *Problems of Communism* (1990), pp. 34–43.
Mel'vil', A. and A. Nikitin, 'Rostki novoi grazhdanskoi kultury?', *Politicheskie issledovaniya*, 2 (1991), pp. 50–5.
Mickiewicz, Ellen, 'Ethnicity and Support: Findings from a Soviet–American Public Opinion Poll', *Journal of Soviet Nationalities*, 1, 2 (1990), pp. 140–7.
Millar, James R. (ed.), *Politics, Work and Daily Life in the USSR* (Cambridge: Cambridge University Press, 1987).
Miller, Arthur H., 'In Search of Regime Legitimacy', in Arthur H. Miller, William M. Reisinger and Vicki L. Hesli (eds), *Public Opinion and Regime Change: The New Politics of Post-Soviet Societies* (Boulder CO: Westview Press, 1993), chapter 5.
Miller, Arthur H., William M. Reisinger and Vicki L. Hesli, 'Public Support for New Political Instititions in Russia, the Ukraine and Lithuania', *Journal of Soviet Nationalities*, 1, 4 (1990–91), pp. 82–107.
Miller, Arthur H., William M. Reisinger and Vicki L. Hesli (eds), *Public Opinion and Regime Change: The New Politics of Post-Soviet societies* (Boulder CO: Westview Press, 1993).
Miller, William L., *The Survey Method in Social and Political Science* (London: Pinter, 1983).
Milosz, Czeslaw, *The Captive Mind* (London: Penguin, 1980).
'Mnenie naseleniya o tsenakh na tovary i uslugy v usloviyakh perekhoda ekonomiki strany na rynochnye otnosheniya', *Staticheskii press–byulleten*, 1 (1991), pp. 16–19.
'Mnenie naseleniya o razlichnikh formakh khozyaistvovaniya i sobstvennosti', *Statiticheskii press-byulleten*', 5 (1991), pp. 17–19.
Mnenie naseleniya o tsenakh na tovary i uslugi (Moscow: Goskomstat SSSR, 1991).
'Mnenie o proekte platformy TsK KPSS', *Partiinaya zhizn*', 7 (1990), p. 26.
Moore, Barrington Jr., *Social Origins of Dictatorship and Democracy: Lord and Peasant in the Making of the Modern World* (Harmondsworth: Penguin, 1966).
Moore, Barrington Jr., 'Liberal Prospects Under Soviet Socialism: A Comparative Historical Perspective', the First Annual W. Averell Harriman Lecture, delivered at Columbia University, 15 November 1989.
Morrison, John, *Boris Yeltsin: From Bolshevik to Democrat* (Harmondsworth: Penguin, 1991).
Motivans, Albert and Elizabeth Teague, 'Capital Punishment in the Former USSR', *Radio Free Europe / Radio Liberty Research Report*, 26 June 1992, pp. 67–73.
Moy, Patricia, 'Roundup: Life in Russia', *Radio Free Europe / Radio Liberty Research Report*, 8 May 1992, pp. 57–8.
Nazarov, Mikhail, 'Tipy politicheskogo soznaniya', *Sotsiologicheskie issledovaniya*, 6 (1992), pp. 64–71.
Nazarov, Mikhail, 'Ob osobennostyakh politicheskogo soznaniya v postperestroechnyi period', *Sotsiologicheskie issledovaniya*, 8 (1993), pp. 37–46.
Nelson, Lynn D., Lilia V. Babaeva and Rufat O. Babaev, 'Perspectives on Entrepreneurship and Privatisation in Russia: Policy and Public Opinion', *Slavic Review*, 51, 2 (1992), pp. 271–86.
'Nicheinaya vlast', *Dialog*, 1 (1991), pp. 10–11.

Noelle-Neumann, Elisabeth, *The Spiral of Silence: Public Opinion – Our Social Skin* (Chicago and London: Chicago University Press, 1980).
Oates, Sarah, 'Elected Officials, Political Groups and Voting in Russia', *Radio Free Europe / Radio Liberty Research Report*, 20 August 1993, pp. 62–4.
Odom, William E., 'Soviet Politics and After: Old and New Concepts', *World Politics*, 45, 1 (1992), pp. 66–98.
'Otnoshenie naseleniya k armii', *Narodnyi deputat*, 3 (1991), p. 87.
Ovsyannikov, Vasilii, 'O nauchnosti oprosov obshchestvennogo mneniya', *Sotsiologicheskie issledovaniya*, 9 (1991), pp. 18–21.
Parker, Tony, *Russian Voices* (London: Picador, 1992).
Petrenko, Elena, 'Kul'turnyi sdvig ili religiosnii bum', *Moskovskie novosti*, 11 August 1991.
Pipes, Richard, *Russia Under the Old Regime* (London: Peregrine, 1976).
Pishchulin, Nikolai and Sergei Sokol, 'Za-Protiv', *Dialog*, 16 (1990), p. 3.
Popov, Nikolai P., 'Political Views of the Russian People', *International Journal of Public Opinion Research*, 4, 4 (1992), pp. 321–34.
'Pravo na trud – pravo na zabastovku', *Obshchestvennye nauki*, 3 (1990), pp. 11, 22, 36 and 128.
'Pravo na trud – pravo na zabastovku', *Obshchestvennye nauki*, 6 (1990), pp. 234–6.
'Pravo na trud – pravo na zabastovku', *Obshchestvennye nauki*, 1 (1991), pp. 47, 55, 190–1.
Przeworski, Adam, *Democracy and the Market: Political and Economic Reforms in Eastern Europe and Latin America* (Cambridge: Cambridge University Press, 1991).
The Pulse of Europe: A Survey of Political and Social Values and Attitudes (Washington, DC: Times–Mirror Center for the People and the Press, 1991).
Reddaway, Peter, 'The End of Empire', *New York Review of Books*, 7 November 1991, pp. 53–9.
Reddaway, Peter, 'Russia on the Brink?', *New York Review of Books*, 28 January 1993, pp. 30–4.
Reddaway, Peter, 'On the Eve', *New York Review of Books*, 2 December 1993, pp. 16–21.
Reisinger, William M., 'Conclusions: Mass Public Opinion and the Study of Post-Soviet Societies', in Arthur H. Miller, William M. Reisinger and Vicki L. Hesli (eds), *Public Opinion and Regime Change: The new politics of post-Soviet societies* (Boulder CO: Westview Press, 1993), pp. 271–7.
Reisinger, William M., Arthur H. Miller, Vicki L. Hesli and Kristen Hill Maher, 'Political Values in Russia, Ukraine and Lithuania: Sources and Implications for Democracy', unpublished manuscript, April 1993.
Remnick, David, 'Dons of the Don', *New York Review of Books*, 16 July 1992, pp. 45–51.
Rhodes, Mark, 'The Coup in Retrospect: Views from the Russian Heartland', *Radio Free Europe / Radio Liberty Research Report*, 17 July 1992, pp. 66–7.
Rhodes, Mark, 'Roundup: How Russians View Their Media', *Radio Free Europe / Radio Liberty Research Report*, 31 July 1992, pp. 70–1.
Rhodes, Mark, 'Political Attitudes in Russia', *Radio Free Europe / Radio Liberty Research Report*, 15 January 1993, pp. 43–5.

Richards, Susan, *Epics of Everyday Life: Encounters in a Changing Russia* (Harmondsworth: Penguin, 1990).
Rogger, Hans, 'Afterthoughts', in Hans Rogger and Eugene Weber (eds), *The European Right: A Historical Profile* (Berkeley and Los Angeles: University of California Press, 1965), pp. 577–88.
Rose, Richard, 'Contradictions Between Micro- and Macro-Economic Goals in Post-Communist Societies', *Europe–Asia Studies*, 45, 3 (1993), pp. 419–44.
Rose, Richard, Irina Boeva and Viacheslav Shironin, 'How Russians Are Coping With Transition', *University of Strathclyde Studies in Public Policy*, 216 (1993).
Rose, Richard and Christian Haerpfer, 'Adapting to Transformation in Eastern Europe', *University of Strathclyde Studies in Public Policy*, 212 (1992).
Rukavishnikov, Vladimir, 'Pik napryazhennosti pod znakom belogo konya', *Sotsiologicheskie issledovaniya*, 10 (1990), pp. 12–25.
Rukavishnikov, Vladimir, 'Sotsial' no-politicheskaya situatsiya i obshchestvennoe mnenie', *Sotsiologicheskie issledovaniya*, 11 (1992), pp. 47–57.
Rukavishnikov, Vladimir, 'Sotsial'naya dinamika i politicheskii konflikt v Rossii: vesna 1993 goda – adaptatsiya k krizisu', *Sotsiologicheskie issledovaniya*, 9 (1993), pp. 28–42.
Rukavishnikov, Vladimir, Vilen Ivanov, Vladimir Kozlov, Anatolii Kotov, Irina Ladoda, Eduard Petrov, Vil'yam Smirnov and Nikolai Shchipanov, 'Sotsial'naya napryazhennost': diagnoz i prognoz', *Sotsiologicheskie issledovaniya*, 3 (1992), pp. 3–23.
Rustow, Dankwart, 'Democracy: A Global Revolution', *Foreign Affairs*, 69, 4 (1990), pp. 75–91.
Rutgaiser, V., A. Grazhdankin, V. Kosmarskii, L. Khakhulina and S. Shpil'ko, 'Ekonomicheskaya reforma v glazakh obshchestvennogo mneniya', *Rabochii klass i sovremennii mir*, 3 (1990), pp. 35–48.
Rutgaiser, V., A. Grazhdankin, V. Kosmarskii, L. Khakhulina and S. Shpil'ko, 'Otnoshenie naseleniya k ekonomicheskoi reforme', *Voprosy ekonomiki*, 4 (1990), pp. 37–46.
Rutgaiser, V., L. Khakhulina, S. Shpil'ko, V. Kosmarskii and A. Grazhdankin, 'Otnoshenie naseleniya k radikal'noi ekonomicheskoi reforme', *Voprosy ekonomiki*, 10 (1989), pp. 129–34.
Rutkevich, M.N. 'Sotsiologiya, vlast', obshchestvennoe mnenie', *Sotsiologicheskie issledovaniya*, 7 (1993), pp. 3–14.
Sakwa, Richard, *Gorbachev and His Reforms: 1985–1990* (Hemel Hempstead: Philip Allan, 1990).
Sakwa, Richard, 'The Revolution of 1991: Interpretations of the Moscow Coup', *Coexistence*, 29, 4 (1992), pp. 335–77.
Sakwa, Richard, *Russian Politics and Society* (London and New York: Routledge, 1993).
Schlozman, Kay and Sidney Verba, *Insult to Injury: Unemployment, Class and Political Response* (Cambridge MA: Harvard University Press, 1979).
Sedov, Leonid, 'Soprotivlenie materiala, ili reformy v zhertskom zerkale sotsiologii', *Golos*, 26 (1993), p. 4.
Shiller, Robert J., Maxim Boycko and Vladimir Korobov, 'Hunting for Homo Sovieticus: Situational versus Attitudinal Factors in Economic Behaviour', *Brookings Papers on Economic Activity*, 1 (1992), pp. 127–94.

Shlapentokh, Vladimir, *The Politics of Sociology in the Soviet Union* (Boulder CO: Westview Press, 1987).
Shlapentokh, Vladimir, *The Public and Private Lives of Soviet Citizens: Changing Values in Post-Stalin Russia* (New York and Oxford: Oxford University Press, 1989).
Shpil'ko, S., 'Otnoshenie naseleniya k privitisatsii sobstvennosti', *Voprosy ekonomiki*, 4 (1991), pp. 108–16.
Shpil'ko, S., 'Sobstvennost' na perekrestke mnenie', *Vestnik Akademii Nauk SSSR*, 9 (1991), pp. 3–13.
Silver, Brian D., 'Political Beliefs of the Soviet Citizen: Sources of Support for Regime Norms', in James R. Millar (ed.), *Politics, Work and Daily Life in the USSR* (Cambridge: Cambridge University Press, 1987), chapter 4.
Simis, Konstantin, *The Corrupt Society* (New York: Simon and Shuster, 1982).
Slater, Wendy, 'The Russian Orthodox Church', *Radio Free Europe / Radio Liberty Research Report*, 14 May 1993, pp. 92–5.
Slider, Darell, 'Soviet Public Opinion on the Eve of Elections', *Journal of Soviet Nationalities*, 1, 2 (1990), pp. 155–62.
Slider, Darrell, 'Public Opinion and the Political Process', in Stephen White, Graeme Gill and Darrell Slider (eds), *The Politics of Transition: Shaping a Post-Soviet Future* (Cambridge: Cambridge University Press, 1993).
Slider, Darrell, Vladimir Magun and Vladimir Gimpel'son, 'Public Opinion on Privatisation: Republic Differences', *Soviet Economy*, 7, 3 (1991), pp. 256–75.
Smirnov, G., 'Otnoshenie k Leninu (itogy sotsiologicheskogo issledovaniya)', *Izvestiya TsK KPSS*, 2 (1991), pp. 50–1.
Smith, Hedrick, *The New Russians* (updated edition, London: Vintage, 1991).
Sobyanin, Aleksandr, Eduard Gel'man and Oleg Kayunov, 'Politicheskii klimat v Rossii v 1991–1993 gg.', *Mirovaya ekonomika i mezhdunarodnye otnosheniya*, 9 (1993), pp. 20–32.
Sogomonov, A. and A. Tolstykh, 'O nashikh zabotakh', *Kommunist*, 9 (1989), pp. 74–6.
Solzhenitsyn, Alexander, *Rebuilding Russia* (London: Harper Collins, 1991).
'Soyuznyi dogovor', *Dialog*, 1 (1991), p. 47.
Street, John, 'Review Article: Political Culture – from Civic Culture to Mass Culture', *British Journal of Political Science*, 24, 1 (1994), pp. 95–114.
Swafford, Michael, 'Sociological Aspects of Survey Research in the Commonwealth of Independent States', *International Journal of Public Opinion Research*, 4, 4 (1992), pp. 346–59.
Sycheva, V.S., 'Perekhodnyi period po otsenkam naseleniya (obzor sotsiologicheskikh issledovanii', *Sotsiologicheskie issledovaniya*, 3 (1993), pp. 12–20.
Taubman, William, *Governing Soviet Cities* (New York: Praeger, 1973).
Tocqueville, Alexis de, *Democracy in America* (New York: Harper, 1966).
Tolz, Vera, 'The New Role of the Media and Public Opinion Under Mikhail Gorbachev', *Journal of Communist Studies*, 9, 1 (1993), pp. 192–212.
Tolz, Vera, 'The Burden of the Imperial Legacy', *Radio Free Europe / Radio Liberty Research Report*, 14 May 1993.
Toshchenko, Zh., 'Zemlya', *Dialog*, 10 (1991), p. 3.
Toshchenko, Zh., V. Boikov and E. Levanov, 'Kak obnovlyaetsya KPSS',

Voprosy istorii KPSS, 8 (1990), pp. 3-14.
Trubina, L. V., A.A. Neshchadin and V.K. Kashin, 'Sinusoidy obshchestvennogo mneniya', *Sotsiologicheskie issledovaniya*, 7 (1993), pp. 14-25.
Ulam, Adam, *The Communists: The Story of Power and Lost Illusions: 1948-1991* (New York: Scribners, 1992).
Urnov, M., 'Naskol'ko my gotovy k demokratii?', *Rabochii klass i sovremennii mir*, 4 (1989), pp. 75-91.
Vainshtein, Grigorii, 'The Socio-Psychological Aspect of Reform of the Soviet Economy', *Communist Economies and Economic Transformation*, 4, 3 (1992), pp. 361-72.
Vaksberg, Arkady, *The Soviet Mafia* (New York: St Martin's Press, 1992).
'Vashi otnosheniya k istorii', *Informatsionnii byulleten', tsentr sotsiologicheskikh issledovanii akademii obshchestvennykh nauk pri TsK KPSS*, 1 (1991), pp. 90-113.
Vaus, D.A. de, *Surveys in Social Research* (third edition, London: Allen and Unwin, 1991).
Verba, Sidney and Norman H. Nie, *Participation in America: Political Democracy and Social Equality* (New York: Harper and Row, 1972).
Verba, Sidney, Norman H. Nie and Jae-on Kim, *Participation and Political Equality: A Seven Nation Comparison* (Chicago: University of Chicago Press, 1978).
Vil'chek, Vsevolod, 'Killery s anketoi v rukakh', *Moskovskie novosti*, 24 November 1993, p. 7.
'Vo chto verim, chego zhdem?', *Dialog*, 9 (1991), p. 58.
Voikov, Vladimir, 'Partiya', *Dialog*, 15 (1990), p. 3.
Voikov, Vladimir, 'Rynok: bolshinstvo - "za"', *Dialog*, 8 (1991), p. 3.
Wegren, Stephen K. 'Market Reform and Public Opinion', *Radio Free Europe / Radio Liberty Report on the USSR*, 30 November 1990, pp. 4-8.
Wegren, Stephen K., 'Dilemmas of Agrarian Reform in the Soviet Union', *Soviet Studies*, 44, 1 (1992), pp. 3-36.
Welch, Stephen, 'Issues in the Study of Political Culture - the Example of Communist Party States', *British Journal of Political Science*, 19, 2 (1987), pp. 479-500.
Welch, Stephen, *The Concept of Political Culture* (London: Macmillan, 1993).
Welsh, William A. (ed.), *Survey Research and Public Attitudes in Eastern Europe and the Soviet Union* (New York: Pergamon, 1981).
White, Stephen, *Political Culture and Soviet Politics* (London: Macmillan, 1979).
White, Stephen, 'The USSR: Patterns of Autocracy and Industrialisation', in Archie Brown and Jack Grey (eds), *Political Culture and Political Change in Communist Societies* (second edition, London: Macmillan, 1979).
White, Stephen, 'Soviet Political Culture Reassessed', in Archie Brown (ed.), *Political Culture and Communist Studies* (London: Macmillan, 1984).
White, Stephen, 'Post-Communist Politics: Towards Democratic Pluralism', *Journal of Communist Studies*, 9, 1 (1993), pp. 18-32.
White, Stephen and Ian McAllister, 'Political Participation in Postcommunist Russia: Voting, Activism and the Potential For Mass Protest', unpublished manuscript, July 1993.
White, Stephen, Ian McAllister and Olga Kryshtanovskaya, 'El'tsin and His

Voters: Popular Support in the 1991 Russian Presidential Elections and After', *Europe-Asia Studies*, 46, 2 (1993), pp. 285-303.
Willerton, John P. and Lee Sigelman, 'Public Opinion Research in the USSR: Opportunities and Pitfalls', *Journal of Communist Studies*, 7, 2 (1991), pp. 217-34.
Wishnevsky, Julia, 'Media Still Far From Free', *Radio Free Europe / Radio Liberty Research Report*, 14 May 1993, pp. 86-91.
Wyman, Matthew, 'The Economic Functions of the Intermediate Level Party Apparatus', unpublished thesis presented for the degree of M. Soc. Sci., Birmingham University, December 1989.
Yadov, V.A. *et al.*, 'The Sociopolitical Situation in Russia in Mid-February 1992', *Soviet Sociology*, 32, 2, (1992) pp. 6-32.
Yeltsin, Boris, *Against the Grain* (New York: Simon and Schuster, 1990).
Yeric, Jerry L. and John R. Todd, *Public Opinion: The Visible Politics* (Itasca, IL: F.E. Peacock, 1989).
Zaslavskaya, Tatyana, 'Perestroika i sotsiologiya', *Pravda*, 1 February 1987.
Zaslavskaya, Tatyana, 'Zhit' s otkrytymi glazami', *Kommunist*, 8 (1989), pp. 45-54.
Zaslavskaya, Tatyana, 'Ekonomika v zerkale obshchestvennogo mneniya', *Voprosy ekonomiki*, 11 (1989), pp. 127-8.
Zaslavskaya, Tatyana, *The Second Socialist Revolution* (Bloomington: Indiana University Press, 1990).
Zaslavskaya, Tatyana, 'Sotsialism, perestroika i obshchestvennoe mnenie', *Sotsiologichiskie issledovaniya*, 8 (1991), pp. 3-21.
Zaslavskaya, Tatyana, 'V peregonki so vremmenem', *Obshchestvennye nauki i sovremennost'*, 3 (1993), pp. 5-16.
Zaslavsky, Victor, *The Neo-Stalinist State: Class, Ethnicity and Consensus in Soviet Society* (Armonk: M.E. Sharpe, 1982).
Zaslavsky, Victor, 'Success and Collapse: Traditional Soviet Nationality Policy', in Ian Bremmer and Ray Taras (eds), *Nations and Politics in the Soviet Successor States* (Cambridge: Cambridge University Press, 1993), chapter 2.
Zdravomyslov, Andrei G., 'Konfrontatsiya ili soglasie', *Dialog*, 17 (1990), p. 3.
Zdravomyslov, Andrei G., 'Changes in Mass Consciousness and Outlines of Parliamentary Activity', *Journal of Communist Studies*, 7, 2 (1991), pp. 235-56.
Zubova, L., N. Kovaleva and L. Khakhulina, 'Bednost'' v SSSR: tochka zreniya naseleniya', *Voprosy ekonomiki*, 6 (1991), pp. 60-7.
Zubova, L., N. Kovaleva, M. Krasil'nikova and L. Mityaeva, 'Otsenka naseleniem sistemy sotsial'nykh garantii i sotsial'noi zashchity', *Voprosy ekonomiki*, 7 (1992), pp. 91-100.

Index

Academy of Sciences 5, 20–1
Academy of Social Science 5, 6
Age, influence of 23, 27, 44, 47, 48–50, 64, 69, 81–2, 91, 94–5, 104–5, 117, 125–6, 131, 159, 178–81, 206–7, 213–21
Agriculture, reform of 29, 78, 188, 190–1
All-Union Centre for Public Opinion Research (VTsIOM) 6, 9
Anti-Semitism *see* Jews
Armed Forces, attitudes to 66–71, 109–13, 231
Armenia and Armenians 72, 152–4
Article Six 61–2, 143
Authoritarianism *see* Dictatorship

Bell, Daniel 211
Belorussia (Belarus) and Belorussians 70
Belovezhskaya Woods agreement 165
Black market *see* Corruption
Black Sea Fleet 97
Bogart, Leo 122
Brezhnev, Leonid 53–4, 59, 197, 202–4
Broadcasting *see* Mass media
Brzezinski, Zbigniew 123
Buddhism 80, 149

Capitalism *see* Economy
Chechnya 98, 149, 169–71
Chernomyrdin, Viktor 92, 102
Civil society 100
Class, influence of 63, 95, 221–4
Collectivisation, attitudes to 63
Command economy 174–84, 221–6
Commonwealth of Independent States (CIS) 43, 163, 165–8
Communism, attitudes to 53–4, 59–64, 89–91
Communist Party
attitudes to 56–64, 87–8, 215–17, 226, 230–1

banning of (1991) 64
Central Committee 56–7, 65
role of in USSR 55–7
Congress of People's Deputies
of Russia 87–8, 92, 95, 101–5, 119
of the USSR 56–9, 65–6, 84, 87–8
Constitution 103, 159
Constitutional Court 112
Co-operatives, attitudes to 34–5, 78, 177, 185–8
Corruption 2, 39–44, 55, 76–7, 214, 231
Coup attempt, of 1991 64, 76, 161, 165
Courts, attitudes to 66–71, 109–13
Crime 23, 39–44, 68, 111–12, 138, 200, 230
Crimea 169–71
Currency reform 86

De-imperialisation 152, 172–3, 232–3
Declarations of sovereignty 154–60
Democracy, attitudes to 89–91, 131–3, 218–21, 225–6, 231–2
Democratic Platform 60
Democratic Russia 101, 144
Demonstrations, attitudes to 138–41
Deported peoples 149
Deviance, attitudes to 135–7
Dictatorship, attitudes to 131–3
Diet 23, 29–31, 38–9
Disability, attitudes to 135–7

Economic sector, influence of 27, 39
Economy, reform of 21, 25–7, 94, 100–1, 174–212
Education, influence of 23, 44, 47, 69, 91, 94, 104–5, 131, 159, 178–81, 206–7, 213, 216–17, 219–21
Efficacy 128–9

266

Index 267

Elections, in Russia
  attitudes to 130-1
  of 1989 59-60
  of 1990 154-5
  of 1991 12, 168, 237
  of 1993 91-6, 119, 130,
    237-8
Émigrés 3-4
Empire, attitudes to 149-73
Environment 23, 39-44
Estonia and Estonians 70, 72, 152,
  164
Expectations 44-8, 50-2, 182-4,
  230

Fears 47-8
Federal Counterintelligence Service
  (FKS) see KGB
Federalism, attitudes to 71-6
500-day plan 45
Foreign ownership 191-3

Gaidar, Yegor 27, 92, 94, 178-81
Gender, influence of 23, 42-4,
  48-50, 64, 81-2, 91, 94, 117,
  126, 131, 158, 178-81, 214-19
Georgia and Georgians 70, 72, 80,
  102
Glasnost 21, 34-5, 54, 69, 78-80
Gor'kii 76-7
Gorbachev, Mikhail
  and economic reform 175-8,
    184-212
  and political reform 5-6, 20,
    54-88, 235-8
  and public opinion 5-7
  and nationality policy 150-1
  attitudes towards 1-2, 54, 84-6,
    92-3, 231
Government
  of Russia 66, 75, 97-101
  of USSR 65-6, 87
Great Patriotic War 70, 149, 214
Great Terror 63
Grushin, Boris 3, 6, 9, 10-11

Happiness 20-5
Harvard project 3-4
Harvest of Sorrow 149

Havel, Václav 20, 147
Health and health care 23, 34, 97
Homosexuality, attitudes to 136-7
Housing 39-44
Human rights 123, 138-41

Income distribution see Inequality
Income, influence of 47, 91, 104-5,
  131, 180-1
Individual rights see Human rights
Industrialisation 63, 150
Inequality 39-44, 97, 202-11, 226,
  233-4
Inflation 39-44, 97, 202-11,
  233-4
Informal groups 56-8
Inter-personal trust 146
Islam 149

Jews and Judaism 80, 114, 149
Judges 57

Kazakhstan and Kazakhs 151, 164
Key, V.O. 212
KGB, attitudes to 66-71, 109-13
Khaltura 11
Khasbulatov, Ruslan 102, 104, 106
Khrushchev, Nikita 53, 72, 197,
  202, 215
Komsomol 53, 58
Kryuchkov, Vladimir 69

Land reform see Agriculture,
  reform of
Latvia and Latvians 69, 72, 152
Law on Associations (1990) 62
Lenin, Vladimir 54, 56, 78
Levada, Yuri 6
Liberal Democratic Party 142
Lithuania and Lithuanians 56,
  69-75, 79-80, 152, 160-3, 204
Local government, attitudes to 56-7,
  76-8

Mafia see crime
Makashov, Albert 125
Mandelstam, Nadezhda 3
Markets, attitudes to 2, 174-212,
  221-6, 233-4

Mass media 34–5, 58, 78–80, 105–9, 138–9
Military see Armed Forces
Militsia, attitudes to 34, 66–71, 109–13
Millionaires 205–6
Milosz, Czeslaw 4
Miners' strike (1989) 60
Minorities, attitudes to 134–7
Moldova and Moldovans 72, 102, 110, 152, 169

Nationality policy 72–6, 100–1, 149–51
NEP 63
New rich 204–9
Nomenklatura 29, 55
Nutrition see Diet

October events, of 1993 92–4, 96–8
October revolution (1917) 62–3
Odessa 76–7
Opinion polls, attitudes to 7–10
Orthodox church 80–4, 114–16, 226–8, 231
Ownership changes 184–97

Participation, political 126–8
Parties and party system 142–5, 229
Party identification 144–5
Pavlov, Valentin 65, 98
Planning see Command economy
Police see Militsia
Political interest 124–6, 215–17
Popular Fronts 57
positivity bias 8
Poverty 27, 209–11
Press see Mass media
Price control 42–3
Price reform see Inflation
Privatisation, attitudes to 188–97, 218, 220, 237
Privileges, attitudes to 2, 59, 60, 72, 202–3
Prostitution, attitudes to 136–7
Public opinion
  development of 3–19
  impact of 235–8

main features of 230–8
nature of 1–2, 122–3

Question wording 12–15

Red Terror 78
Referendum of March 1993 92, 130
Region, influence of 23, 131, 228–9
Religion, influence of 80–4, 98, 114–16, 226–8
Republican governments, attitudes to 57, 71–6
Republics and regions 155–7, 167–73
Response effects 7–10
Response rates 8
Rights consciousness see Human rights
Rights see Human rights
Rule of law 68–9, 111–12
Rurality, influence of 9, 27, 64, 95, 131, 168, 178–81, 224–6
Russia's Choice 2
Rutskoi, Aleksandr 18, 95, 106
Ryzhkov, Nikolai 65–6, 125, 169, 193–4

Sajudis 56, 153
Sakharov, Andrei 59, 61
Sampling 15–18
Secession 153–73
Shevardnadze, Eduard 92
Shortages 39–44, 48
Silaev, Ivan 66, 75
Social welfare 42–3, 174, 210
Socialism, attitudes to 62, 89–91
Spare time 38, 48–50
Stalin era, attitudes to 53
Stalin, Josef 3, 7, 20, 53, 59, 214–16
Standard of living xiii, 25–39, 176
Strikes, attitudes to 13
Superpower status 53, 61, 68, 160, 214
Supreme Soviet 65–6
Swafford, Michael 11, 15

Taganrog 3

Tatars and Tatarstan 149, 156, 169–71, 228
Tblisi massacre 110
Television see Mass media
Tocqueville, Alexis de 1, 2, 45
Tolerance 7, 134–7
Trade unions, attitudes to 56–7, 116–19
Translation 10, 12
Turnout 130

Ukraine and Ukrainians 70, 73–5, 79–80, 104, 152–4, 164–6, 204
Ukrainian Catholic (Uniate) church 80
Unemployment 39–44, 94, 97, 176, 182–4, 199–202, 218, 230, 233
Union of Soviet Socialist Republics, dissolution of 43, 92, 97, 151–73, 232–3

Union treaty, draft (1991) 76, 161–2
Uzbekistan and Uzbeks 70, 76–7

Vilnius 45, 71, 78, 80, 110, 160–1, 172
Vox Populi 9–11
VTsIOM see All-Union Centre for Public Opinion Research

Yeltsin, Boris
 and Gorbachev 2, 203
 and public opinion 236–8
 and Russian Parliament 101–5
 attitudes towards 18, 84–8, 92–6, 231
 reform programme of 178–81

Zaslavskaya, Tatyana 6
Zhirinovsky, Vladimir 42, 125, 142, 172, 237

The manufacturer's authorised representative in the EU is Springer Nature Customer Service Centre GmbH, Europaplatz 3, 69115 Heidelberg, Germany. If you have any concerns regarding our products, please contact ProductSafety@springernature.com

Printed and bound by CPI Group (UK) Ltd, Croydon, CR0 4YY
23/03/2026
02076673-0007